Sports and the Physically Challenged

Sports and the Physically Challenged

An Encyclopedia of People, Events, and Organizations

Linda Mastandrea and Donna Czubernat

Foreword by Ann Cody

GREENWOOD PRESS

Westport, Connecticut • London

Library of Congress Cataloging-in-Publication Data

Mastandrea, Linda.
   Sports and the physically challenged : an encyclopedia of people,
events, and organizations / Linda Mastandrea and Donna Czubernat ;
foreword by Ann Cody.
     p. cm.
  Includes bibliographical references and index.
  ISBN 0–313–32453–0
  1. Sports for people with disabilities—United States—Encyclopedias.
2. Athletes with disabilities—United States—Encyclopedias. I.
Czubernat, Donna. II. Title.
  GV709.3.M37   2006
  796'.019603—dc22   2006021460

British Library Cataloguing in Publication Data is available.

Library of Congress Catalog Card Number: 2006021460

ISBN: 0–313–32453–0

First published in 2006

Greenwood Press, 88 Post Road West, Westport, CT 06881
An imprint of Greenwood Publishing Group, Inc.
www.greenwood.com

Printed in the United States of America

The paper used in this book complies with the
Permanent Paper Standard issued by the National
Information Standards Organization (Z39.48–1984).

10 9 8 7 6 5 4 3 2 1

Contents

Alphabetical List of Entries

ALPHABETICAL LIST OF ENTRIES

Topical List of Entries

EQUIPMENT

All Terrain Ski Terminal
  Device
Amputee Golf Grip
Aquatic Wheelchair
ARGO Off-Road Vehicle
Arm Ergometer
Beachmaster Wheelchair
Bi-Ski
Boccia Ramp
Bowling Ramp
Bowling Stick
Crossbow
Ergometer
Freedom Independence
Mono-Ski
Off-Road Wheelchair
Prosthesis
Pulk
Rugby Wheelchairs
Seattle Foot
Sip and Puff
Ski-Bra
Tennis Wheelchair
Tether
Wrist Support (Cuff)

LEGISLATION

Amateur Sports Act of 1978
Americans with Disabilities
  Act (ADA)

ORGANIZATIONS

Achilles Track Club International
American Amputee Soccer
  Association (AASA)
American Association of Adapted
  Sports Programs (AAASP)
American Hearing Impaired Hockey
  Association (AHIHA)
American Wheelchair Bowling
  Association (AWBA)
American Wheelchair Table Tennis
  Association (AWTTA)
Blaze Sports
Blind Sailing International
Boy Scouts of America (Scouts with
  Disabilities and Special Needs)
Breckenridge Outdoor Education
  Center (BOEC)
Buckmasters Quadriplegic Hunters
  Association (BQHA)
Cerebral Palsy International Sports and
  Recreation Association (CP-ISRA)
Committee on Sports for the
  Disabled (COSD)
Courage Center
Dancing Wheels
Disabled Hunters of North
  America, Inc. (DHNA)
Disabled Sports USA
Dwarf Athletic Association of
  America (DAAA)

TOPICAL LIST OF ENTRIES

Oehler, Dennis
Parks, Brad
Popovich, Erin
Rebollo, Antonio
Shirley, Marlon
Snow, Randy
Szott, Kevin
Szyman, Bob
Thiboutot, Tip
Volpentest, Tony
Waddell, Camille
Waddell, Chris
Wellman, Mark
Whittaker, Tom
Willis, Tim
Wyeth, Duncan
Yilla, Abu
Zorn, Trischa

SPORTS AND EVENTS

Amputee Soccer
Archery
Bankshot Basketball
Beep Baseball
Bi-Skiing
Blind Golf
Blister Bowl
Blowdarts
Boccia
Crutch Racing
Cycling
Deaflympics
Equestrian
Field Events

Floor Hockey
Four Track Skiing
Goalball
Handcycling
Lawn Bowls
Murderball
Paralympic Games
Poly Hockey
Power Hockey
Powerlifting
Power Soccer
Quad Rugby (wheelchair rugby,
  murderball)
Road Racing
Sailing for People with
  Disabilities
Shooting
Sitting Volleyball
Skiing
Slalom
Sled Hockey
Table Tennis
Tandem Cycling
Three-Tracking
Wheelchair Basketball
Wheelchair Dance Sport
Wheelchair Fencing
Wheelchair Football
Wheelchair Racquetball
Wheelchair Rollers
Wheelchair Softball
Wheelchair Tennis
Wheelchair Track and Field
Wrestling

Acknowledgments

This book is dedicated first and foremost to my parents, Robert and Dorothy Mastandrea. Without their unconditional love and support, I would not be who I am today. It is also dedicated to my twin sister, Laura, for being my biggest fan and always my best friend. To my sister and co-author Donna, I am so glad you joined me in this endeavor to share the importance of disability sport with the world. Your support and love has meant the world to me. This book is also dedicated to the rest of our family—Bobby, Tony, Larry, Mark, Chris, John, Dan, Connor, Brian, Brennan and Griffin, we love you all!

Finally, this book goes to all those who encouraged me along the way, from teachers, to coaches, to friends. To my coach and dear friend Norm, I couldn't have done it without you. You knew exactly how to get me out of bed and to the track in the morning (Starbucks mocha), and you also always knew how to get out of me what I didn't even know I had.

To Ann Cody, your friendship, love, and commitment to disability sport and disability advocacy are a constant source of encouragement to me. To Brad and Marty and Sharon, I can't imagine my life if I hadn't met you back when I was a naïve freshman at the University of Illinois away from home for the first time. To Jeff, and Jerry, and Phil and Kim, and everyone affiliated with the National Disability Sports Alliance (NDSA), my life is so much better for having known you. It is because of the work that you do, that I am able to be who I am.

To everyone at the Rehabilitation Institute of Chicago Center for Health and Fitness—you have my eternal gratitude for all that you have done and continue to do. Finally, to all the athletes with disabilities past, present, and future—this is for you.

Foreword

At the outset, I want to salute each individual and organization featured in this encyclopedia for your unyielding commitment to improving opportunities and access to sports and physical activity for all people with disabilities. I am indebted to you for the opportunities that your actions opened up for my life.

Since I was five, sport has played an integral role in defining who I am. Whether it was learning to swim, ride a bike, or ice skate, or playing a game of kick ball on the playground, I was always active. I was and am an athlete at heart. At 16 years of age, I acquired a disability, and it was disability sports that gave me the confidence to pursue the life I knew was possible.

It is widely understood in health and sports science circles that regular physical activity is an essential part of a healthy lifestyle. We also know that sport is important to the physical, psychological, and sociological well-being of human beings and that sports participation develops skills like teamwork, goal-setting, the pursuit of excellence in performance, and other achievement-oriented behaviors that serve us well in life. For me, disability sports provided access to independence, self-expression, mobility, self-confidence, role models, and a thriving social network.

Unfortunately, for many people with disabilities, access to these fundamental life activities is limited by attitudinal, architectural, and programmatic barriers. So, it should not surprise us that there are pervasive health disparities between people with disabilities and those without. The U.S. Centers for Disease Control and Prevention (CDC) reports that the prevalence of chronic health conditions such as arthritis, diabetes, and high blood pressure is three to four times higher in people with disabilities (U.S. Centers for Disease Control and Prevention, Healthy People 2010 Data on Disability Health Disparities).

I attribute the quality of my life, health, and career to my early exposure to and participation in sports as a young girl and subsequently as a young woman with a disability. All people with disabilities can benefit from participation in sports and physical activity in the same ways as our nondisabled peers. In fact, due to the substantially greater risk of developing secondary conditions such as heart disease and diabetes, participation in sports and physical activity is of even greater benefit to people with disabilities.

As an adult, my commitment is to live a healthy, active lifestyle and maintain the quality of life to which I have become accustomed while ensuring that others have access to sports

FOREWORD

and physical activity and all of the benefits that come with being active. I invite you to find an activity, sport, organization, or piece of equipment that calls to you from the pages of this book and get started on the road to life-long fitness. It could just change your life!

Ann Cody

Preface

Sports and the Physically Challenged: An Encyclopedia of People, Events, and Organizations was written to be a resource for people with disabilities, their families and friends, rehabilitation professionals, and students in rehabilitation, recreation, and physical education programs.

There are only a handful of books on disability sport that are aimed at the general public. The bulk of disability sport literature is contained in the scientific journals. While these journals are without a doubt useful and beneficial, their utility is limited to a specific population. For the young girl with cerebral palsy looking for information on a sport to try, or the new amputee wanting to find out about prosthetics they can use to play golf, however, there just isn't that much print information available.

Disability sport has a rich history and is an ever evolving field, thus it was important to try and capture some of that in one place, in one volume, to make it simpler for anyone to find, including athletes with disabilities, therapists, and all other interested people.

This book cannot be a complete chronicle of all of disability sport. Each country has its own history, athletes, and moments of significance. Therefore, we tried to create a volume that was as useful as possible to those most likely to read it here in the United States.

Once we realized that we couldn't keep to the size constraints of the book and include organizations from all over the world, we decided the first limitation we would impose would be to include primarily U.S.-based individuals and organizations. There are, of necessity, some foreign-born individuals and some international organizations featured, since they are of major significance to the movement as a whole. However, the bulk of the selections are people, places, and organizations found here in the United States.

We thought it was important to feature a cross-section of men and women, as well as individuals representing various disability groups to make it truly representative of the disability sport movement as a whole. Since the entirety of the disability sport world encompasses tens of thousands of individuals at a minimum, we were necessarily constrained. Selecting those who would be featured, then, came down to personal knowledge of the authors, Paralympic and other world team membership, award recognition, and media attention. There were some athletes who we knew were significant, yet we could find literally no internet hits, print articles, or other media on them; therefore, they were excluded.

Thus, this book does not encompass every individual, event, or organization significant to the disability sport movement and its history. Instead, it focuses on those significant to the U.S. disability sport movement based on the selection criteria outlined above.

Introduction

Sports and the Physically Challenged: An Encyclopedia of People, Events, and Organizations features athletes with disabilities and people important to the disability sport movement, some key pieces of the history of the movement, and many of the organizations and events that have been a part of it.

While there were certainly people with disabilities participating in sports long before there were any organized opportunities for them to participate and compete, disability sport has been undergoing both an evolution and a revolution over the past 50 plus years. Many of the early efforts focused on providing opportunities to men injured in military service who often were housed in Veterans Administration hospitals. There were few, if any, opportunities for women and those more significantly disabled.

Early events also were premised on the goal of sport as therapy, not solely for recreation or competition and not as an end in itself. Sport was used as a vehicle to get disabled veterans active again, presumably leading them back to jobs and self-sufficiency.

Because there are many disability groups and many disability sport organizations all with their own unique histories, people, and places, it is virtually impossible to chronicle the entire "history of disability sport" within the confines of one volume. There are, however, many widely recognized moments of significance to the broader disability sport movement. For example, one such moment is the first Stoke Mandeville Games in Aylesbury, England, which were the precursor to today's Paralympic Games. While it seems unlikely that Sir Ludwig von Guttmann envisioned games on the scale of today's Paralympic Games, what is abundantly clear is that he had a vision of what life could be like for someone who found themselves living it from a wheelchair, and that vision included a life filled with many facets, including sport and recreation.

Another such moment is the first Special Olympics World Games held in Chicago, Illinois, at Soldier Field in the 1960s. It was there that Eunice Kennedy Shriver showed the world that people like her sister could participate in and benefit from sports competition.

The movement is filled with such firsts—the first Silent Games, the first wheelchair basketball game, the first amputee soccer match, the first goal ball game, the first team handball game for athletes with cerebral palsy, and the list goes on.

Even now, over 100 years since sport for athletes who are deaf and hearing impaired began, and 60 years since the first wheelchair sports competition, advances in technology enable athletes with disabilities to exceed all expectation. Amputees can run the 100m on prosthetic legs nearly as fast as those without disabilities. Wheelchair marathoners complete the 26.2 mile distance nearly an hour faster than their nondisabled counterparts.

Legislation and litigation has also allowed athletes with disabilities to go where none have gone before. Casey Martin, thanks to a U.S. Supreme Court decision in his favor, was able to compete in PGA golf tournament events using a golf cart. Legislative initiatives created a statewide disability sports program in Georgia and led to the creation of the first high school level wheelchair basketball league in the state of Illinois.

Forty or fifty years ago, it was unimaginable for a woman wheelchair user to compete in events longer than the 60 meter track event. Today, such women not only compete, they excel. Jean Driscoll is a prime example. She is the winningest Boston Marathon athlete ever … man, woman, disabled or not. No one bothered to tell her she couldn't do it. She just did.

Similarly, it was widely believed that athletes who were visually impaired couldn't compete against sighted swimmers. No one told Trischa Zorn, she became the first visually impaired swimmer to earn a college scholarship for her swimming ability.

Barriers continue to be broken. Milestones continue to be set. In the scheme of things, disability sport is still in its infancy, or at most, in its young adolescence. Every day new sports are created and old ones adapted for people with disabilities.

This book is a useful tool for learning about the history of the disability sport movement and providing information on programs and resources available. By increasing public awareness of the people, organizations, and events in the disability sport movement, we hope that there will soon come a day when no one with a disability has to sit on the sidelines.

Disability Sport Timeline

1870s	Schools for the deaf participate in sporting events, including baseball.
1885	Football is introduced at schools for the deaf.
1906	Basketball is introduced at the Wisconsin School for the Deaf.
1907	A track meet takes place between Overbrook and Baltimore Schools for the Blind.
1924	The first International Silent Games are held in Paris, France, for deaf athletes. Athletes from Belgium, Czechoslovakia, France, Great Britain, the Netherlands, Poland, Hungary, Italy, and Romania compete. The 133 competitors compete in athletics, cycling, shooting, football, and swimming.
	The International Committee of Silent Sports (CISS) is formed to govern elite deaf competition.
1928	The International Silent Games are held in Amsterdam.
1931	The International Silent Games are held in Nuremberg, West Germany.
1935	The International Silent Games are held in London, England.
1939	The International Silent Games are held in Stockholm, Sweden.
1945	The USA Deaf Sports Federation (USADSF) is formed in Akron, Ohio.
	The first wheelchair basketball game is played by WWII veterans at Corona Naval Station in California.
1946	The Flying Wheels wheelchair basketball team tours the United States.
1947–1948	The Pioneers wheelchair basketball team in Kansas City, Missouri, is formed; The Whirlaways in Brooklyn; the Gophers in Minneapolis; the Bulova Watchmakers in Woodside, New York; the Chairioteers in Queens; and the New York Spokesmen in Manhattan.
1948	The first Stoke Mandeville Games are held in Aylesbury, England. Fourteen male and two female athletes compete in archery.
1949	Tim Nugent organizes the first wheelchair basketball tournament at the University of Illinois in Galesburg. The National Wheelchair Basketball Association (NWBA) is born after this tournament.
	The International Silent Summer Games are held in Copenhagen, Denmark.
	The first International Silent Winter Games are held in Seefeld, Austria. Thirty-three competitors from five nations attend.

DISABILITY SPORT TIMELINE

1952	The first International Stoke Mandeville Games are held in Aylesbury, England, when 130 Dutch ex-servicemen join their English competitors at the games to contest snooker, darts, archery, and table tennis.
	Liz Hartell, who had polio as a child, wins the silver medal for Grand Prix Dressage in the Helsinki Olympics.
1953	The International Silent Games are held in Brussels, Belgium (summer), and Oslo, Norway (winter).
	The International Stoke Mandeville Games adds Canada, Finland, France, and Israel to the roster of competitors.
1955	The IOC unanimously recognizes CISS as an "International Federation with Olympic standing."
	The International Silent Winter Games are held in Oberammergau, West Germany.
1956	The IOC awards the Fearnley Cup to the International Stoke Mandeville Games organization for their outstanding achievement in the service of Olympic ideals.
1957	The International Silent Summer Games are held in Milan, Italy.
	Ben Lipton together with the Paralyzed Veteran's Association of America and Adelphi College in New York organized the first national wheelchair games, including the 60-, 100-, and 200-yard dashes as well as the 220- and 400-yard shuttle relays.
	The National Wheelchair Athletic Association is formed by Ben Lipton and his committee (now Wheelchair Sports USA).
1959	The International Silent Winter Games are held in Montana, Switzerland.
1960	The International Stoke Mandeville Games are held in Rome, the first time the Games are held outside of England since their inception. The United States enters a team for the first time. This is also the first time the event is held in the same host city as the Olympics.
	The International Stoke Mandeville Games Committee is formed by Sir Ludwig Guttman to promote and sanction international sport for wheelchair athletes.
	The International Working Group on Sports for the Disabled is formed to study the problems in sport for people with disabilities.
1961	The International Silent Summer Games are held in Helsinki, Finland.
1963	The International Silent Winter Games are held in Are, Sweden.
1964	The International Sport Organization for the Disabled is formed to offer sports opportunities to athletes who are blind, amputees, or have cerebral palsy.
	The Summer Paralympics are held in Tokyo, Japan.
1965	The International Silent Summer Games are held in Washington, D.C.
1966	The IOC awards CISS the Olympic, or Coubertin, Cup in recognition of its "strict adherence to the Olympic ideal and its service to international sport."

1967	The International Silent Games officially changes its name to the World Silent Games.
	The World Silent Games are held in Berchtesgaden, West Germany.
	The National Handicapped Sports and Recreation Association is formed by amputee Vietnam veterans, primarily to govern winter sports for people with disabilities (now Disabled Sports USA).
	The Pan American Games for the Disabled is held for the first time.
1968	The first Special Olympic Games are held in Chicago, Illinois.
	The International Cerebral Palsy Society holds the first international sports competition for athletes with cerebral palsy in France.
	The Summer Paralympics are held in Tel Aviv, Israel.
1969	The World Silent Games are held in Belgrade, Yugoslavia.
1970	Floor Hockey is introduced at the Special Olympics World Winter Games.
1971	The World Silent Games are held in Abelboden, Switzerland.
1972	The International Stoke Mandeville Games Committee changes its name to the International Stoke Mandeville Games Federation.
	The Summer Paralympics are held in Heidelburg, Germany.
1973	The World Silent Games are held in Malmo, Sweden.
	Sports 'n' Spokes magazine is founded.
	Tim Nugent is elected into the NWBA Hall of Fame on the 25th anniversary of the founding of the organization.
1974	The first women's national wheelchair basketball tournament is held between the University of Illinois Ms. Kids and the Southern Illinois University Squidettes.
	The Handicapped Scuba Association is formed.
	The First World Festival of Sport is held at Stoke Mandeville for amputee, blind, and cerebral palsy athletes.
	Stan Mikita launches the American Hearing Impaired Hockey Association.
1975	The World Silent Games are held in Lake Placid, New York.
	Bob Hall is the first wheelchair racer ever to compete in the Boston Marathon. He finishes in 2:58 and is the first wheelchair athlete to receive a finisher's certificate.
	The World Silent Games changes its name again to the World Games for the Deaf.
1976	The National Foundation for Wheelchair Tennis is formed.
	North American Riding for the Handicapped (NARHA) is formed.
	The Olympiad for the Disabled (now Paralympic Games) is held in Toronto. Blind and amputee athletes are included for the first time.
	The National Wheelchair Softball Association (NWSA) is formed.
	The U.S. Association for Blind Athletes is formed.
	The first Paralympic Winter Games are held in Ornskoldvik, Sweden.
1977	The World Games for the Deaf are held in Bucharest, Romania.
	The First Winter Special Olympic Games are held in Steamboat, Colorado.

	Bob Hall (2:40.10) and Sharon Rahn (Hedrick) (3:48.51) win the first official wheelchair race of the Boston Marathon.
1978	The National Association of Sports for Cerebral Palsy is formed by Commander Archie Cameron.
	The Amateur Sports Act of 1978, PL 95–606 is passed. This act charges the U.S. Olympic Committee with, among other things, encouraging and promoting amateur athletic activity for people with disabilities.
1979	The World Games for the Deaf are held in Meribel, France.
	The U.S. Olympic Committee establishes the Committee on Sports for the Disabled (COSD).
	The International Multi-Disabled Games of the International Sports Organization for the Disabled (ISOD) are held in England. These games serve to establish qualification standards for athletes with cerebral palsy, in addition to hosting competitors who are amputees or visually impaired.
1980	The Summer Paralympics are held in Arnhem, Holland. Athletes compete in the following categories: wheelchair, cerebral palsy, amputee, visually impaired. This is the first Paralympics in which athletes with cerebral palsy compete.
	The Winter Paralympics are held in Geilo, Norway.
	Brad Parks forms the National Foundation of Wheelchair Tennis.
1981	The World Games for the Deaf are held in Cologne, West Germany.
	The first world wheelchair marathon is won by George Murray (2:12.31).
	Candace Cable-Brookes wins her first Boston Marathon in the women's wheelchair division. She will go on to win five more times between 1982–1988, a string of victories that will remain unbroken until 1996 when Jean Driscoll wins her seventh title.
	The U.S. Amputee Athletic Association is formed.
	The National Veteran's Wheelchair Games are held for the first time.
	The International Blind Sports Association (IBSA) is formed by Dr. Helmut Pielasch.
1982	The International Coordinating Committee for the World Organization of Sports for the Disabled (ICC) is formed with each of the four international sports organizations (the International Stoke Mandeville Games Federation, the Cerebral Palsy International Sports and Recreation Association [CP-ISRA], the IBSA, and the ISOD), having three representatives on the committee.
1983	The World Games for the Deaf are held in Madonna di Campiglio, Italy.
1984	The Winter Paralympics are held in Innsbruck, Austria.
	Randy Snow and Sharon Hedrick compete in the first U.S. Olympic exhibition events for athletes with disabilities at the Los Angeles Olympic Games. Snow takes silver in the men's 1500m wheelchair event; Hedrick wins gold and sets a new world record in the women's 800m wheelchair event.
	The Summer Paralympics are held in two locations—Stoke Mandeville, England, for wheelchair athletes and New York for blind, amputee, and cerebral palsy athletes.

1985	George Murray becomes the first male wheelchair athlete to break the 4-minute mile in wheelchair racing. He is then the first athlete with a disability to appear on a Wheaties box.
	Juan Antonio Samaranch, then president of the IOC, requests CISS join the ICC.
	The first National Cerebral Palsy/Les Autres Games is held. Athletes with cerebral palsy, dwarfism, and *les autres* (those with disabilities that don't fit into any existing disability sport category) compete in these games.
	The Dwarf Athletic Association is formed.
	The U.S. Les Autres Sports Association is formed.
	The World Games for the Deaf are held in Los Angeles, California.
1986	The National Association of Sport for Cerebral Palsy (NASCP) is reorganized as the U.S. Cerebral Palsy Athletic Association (now National Disability Sports Alliance).
	CISS and the International Sports Federation for Persons with Mental Handicaps (INAS-FMH) join the ICC.
	Doug Heir becomes the second Paralympic athlete to grace the cover of a Wheaties Box.
1987	The World Games for the Deaf are held in Oslo, Norway.
1988	Special Olympics International is formally recognized by the IOC.
	Diana Golden is named the U.S. Ski and Snowboard Association Skier of the Year, the first time an athlete with a disability earned that distinction.
	The Winter Paralympics are held in Innsbruck, Austria.
	Sharon Hedrick wins gold at the 800m women's wheelchair exhibition event at the Seoul Olympics, setting a new world record. University of Illinois teammate Ann Cody places sixth. Three-wheeled racing chairs make their international debut at this event.
	The Summer Paralympics is held in Seoul, Korea, the first time the Paralympics are held in the same host city and venues as the Olympic Games. They have been held in the same city and same venues in every Paralympic Games since.
	Disabled alpine skiing becomes a full medal sport in the 1988 Pan American Winter Games in Argentina.
1989	The Victory Games for the Disabled is held for the first time.
	International Sports Federation for Persons with an Intellectual Disability (INAS-FID) World Championships in athletics and swimming are held in Harnosand, Sweden.
	The U.S. Amputee Athletic Association dissolves.
	The ICC is replaced by the International Paralympic Committee (IPC) as the governing body of elite disability sport. The CP-ISRA, International Stoke Mandeville Games Federation (ISMGF), ISOD, IBSA, and INAS-FID are members.
	The World Games for the Deaf are held in Christchurch, New Zealand.
	The Robin Hood Games, world games for athletes with cerebral palsy, are held in England for the first time.
	Mark Wellman climbs El Capitan.

DISABILITY SPORT TIMELINE

1990 Jean Driscoll wins what will be her first of seven consecutive Boston Marathon victories in the women's wheelchair division.

Craig Blanchett, wheelchair racer, is the first disabled athlete to appear in a television ad for Nike. That same year, Blanchette sets the world wheelchair record in the mile (3:51) at the Prefontaine Classic.

The International Stoke Mandeville Games Federation changes its name to the International Stoke Mandeville Wheelchair Sports Federation (ISMWSF).

National Handicapped Sports (now Disabled Sports USA [DSUSA]) receives approval from the Committee on Sports for the Disabled to conduct summer sports for amputee athletes.

Mustapha Badid breaks the 1:30 barrier with 1:29.53 win at the Boston Marathon.

1991 The World Games for the Deaf are held in Banff, Canada.

Jean Driscoll is named Amateur Athlete of the Year by the Women's Sports Foundation after winning her second straight title at the Boston Marathon.

1992 The Winter Paralympics is held in Tignes-Albertville, France.

Jean Driscoll wins her third championship in the women's wheelchair division of the Boston Marathon.

The Summer Paralympics are held in Barcelona, Spain.

INAS-FID Paralympic Games are held in Madrid, Spain. Athletics, swimming, indoor soccer, table tennis, and basketball are contested.

Antonio Rebollo, a Spanish archer with a disability, lights the torch at the Barcelona Olympic and Paralympic opening ceremonies.

At the Barcelona Paralympic Games, Ross Davis, David Larson, and Chris Ridgway of the United States sweep the 200m, 400m, and 800m men's T34 track events for athletes with cerebral palsy, a feat that hadn't been accomplished before or since.

1993 The World Games for the Deaf are held in Sofia, Bulgaria.

Jean Driscoll continues her streak of wins in the women's wheelchair division of the Boston Marathon.

1994 The IPC World Athletics Championships in Berlin, a cross-disability event, offers events for athletes with intellectual disabilities for the first time.

Linda Mastandrea wins three gold medals setting two world records at the IPC World Athletics Championships in the T34 events for women with cerebral palsy, the first time a U.S. athlete held these records.

Sled Hockey attains full medal status at the Paralympic games in Albertville, France.

Jean Driscoll and Heinz Frei both set world marks en route to victories in the Boston Marathon wheelchair division. Driscoll's mark remains unbeaten.

The IPC World Swimming Championships in Malta, a cross-disability event, offers events for athletes with intellectual disabilities for the first time.

The Winter Paralympics are held in Lillehammer, Norway.

INAS-FID athletes have two demonstration events at the Winter Paralympics in Lillehammer for the first time.

Sailing for blind athletes is contested for the first time.

1995 CISS withdraws from the IPC. The IOC announces it will continue to recognize CISS and its games.

The World Games for the Deaf are held in Ylass, Finland.

Jean Driscoll wins her sixth consecutive title at the Boston Marathon.

1996 Mark Wellman, disabled climber, lights the Paralympic flame by climbing it with the lit torch between his legs to open the Atlanta Paralympic Games.

Jean Driscoll wins her seventh consecutive title at the Boston Marathon, tying the record for the most wins ever.

Cheri Beccera becomes the first Native American woman and wheelchair racer to compete in the Olympics, winning bronze in the women's 800m exhibition event. She also earns two silver and two bronze in Paralympic competition this same year.

The Summer Paralympics are held in Atlanta, Georgia.

INAS-FID athletes with intellectual disabilities participate in the Summer Paralympics with full medal status for their events for the first time.

1997 CISS games are renamed the Deaf World Games.

The Deaf World Games are held in Copenhagen, Denmark.

1998 The Winter Paralympics are held in Nagano, Japan.

INAS-FID holds World Championships in basketball in Brazil and soccer in the United Kingdom.

Chris Waddell is named one of People magazine's 50 most beautiful people.

1999 The Deaf World Games are held in Davos, Switzerland.

INAS-FID World Championships are held in athletics in Spain, swimming in the Czech Republic, and table tennis in Portugal.

The ParaPanamerican Games are held in Mexico City.

2000 Jean Driscoll wins the women's wheelchair division of the Boston Marathon for an unprecedented eighth time, becoming the only athlete in any division to post as many wins, besting the record held by men's runner Clarence DeMar (seven victories).

The Summer Paralympics are held in Sydney, Australia.

2001 Deaf World Games are renamed Deaflympics with IOC approval.

INAS-FID World Championships are held in cross country in Portugal and athletics in Tunisia.

Deaflympics are held in Rome, Italy.

Casey Martin wins the right to play golf in PGA Tour events from a golf cart in the case of PGA Tour v. Martin, 532 US 661.

2002 Cheri Blauwett is named in USA Today's 2002 Academic All American 1st woman team.

The Winter Paralympics are held in Salt Lake City, Utah.

INAS-FID World Championships are held in rhythmic gymnastics in Belgium, cross country in Poland, tennis in the Czech Republic, basketball in Portugal, and football in Japan.

2003   Deaflympics are held in Sundsvall, Sweden.

Marlon Shirley wins the ESPY Award for the best athlete with a disability.

2004   Ernst Van Dyk, South African wheelchair racer, becomes the first to break the 1:20 barrier in the wheelchair marathon en route to his fourth Boston Marathon victory.

The Summer Paralympics is held in Athens, Greece.

Randy Snow is the first Paralympic athlete to be inducted into the U.S. Olympic Hall of Fame.

2005   Heinz Frei, one of the world's most prolific wheelchair marathoners, wins his 100th marathon in Berlin.

Deaflympics are held in Melbourne, Australia.

Erin Popovich, swimmer of short stature, becomes the second disabled athlete to win the Women's Sports Foundation Amateur Athlete of the Year (Jean Driscoll was first in 1991); Popovich also wins the ESPY for Best Disabled Athlete after winning five gold medals in swimming at the 2004 Paralympics in Athens.

2006   Diana Golden is the first female Paralympian to be inducted into the U.S. Olympic Hall of Fame.

The Winter Paralympics are held in Turin, Italy.

2007   Deaflympics are scheduled for Salt Lake City, Utah.

2008   The Summer Paralympics are scheduled for Beijing, China.

ACHILLES TRACK CLUB INTERNATIONAL The Achilles Track Club International was founded in 1983 by Dick Traum, an amputee marathoner. An avid runner and competitor, Traum knew of the barriers people with disabilities like himself encountered when trying to integrate into the mainstream of sport. He thought that providing opportunities for joint training and competition might be the way to eradicate those barriers.

Achilles Track Club International became the vehicle for providing these joint training and competition opportunities, with the first chapter in New York City formed in 1983. Today there are 40 chapters in the United States and over 110 chapters worldwide including chapters in Norway, New Zealand, Mongolia, the Dominican Republic, Russia, South Africa, Vietnam, and Japan.

Traum created goals for each Achilles chapter to follow, including creating training programs for both ambulatory and wheelchair racers, access to coaching, team workouts, races, and events for children and adults of all ages. Thanks to Traum's background as a marathoner, Achilles is active in promoting competition in the New York City Marathon both for people who want to compete in the next year, and for children who would like to run a marathon when they turn 18, through a program called Achilles Kids.

In addition to activities that promote the sport of track and running, Achilles has taken an active role in providing prosthetics, wheelchairs, and medical assistance to individuals who have acquired disabilities due to war-related activities and still-buried landmines in countries such as Vietnam, Bosnia, and South Africa.

BIBLIOGRAPHY. Achilles Track Club International, http://achillestrackclub.org; Paciorek, Michael J., and Jeffery A. Jones. *Sports and Recreation for the Disabled,* 2nd ed. Carmel, IN: Cooper Publishing Group, 1994.

ALL TERRAIN SKI TERMINAL DEVICE The All Terrain Ski Terminal (also known as the Ski-2d) was designed by Bob Radocy, an upper limb amputee who lost his left hand below the elbow in a 1971 auto accident. While he was in graduate school in 1977, he designed the first prehensor which allowed him to grip and perform two-handed activities; three years later, the GRIP prehensile hand came on the market.

AMATEUR SPORTS ACT OF 1978

The All Terrain Ski Terminal was devised for upper limb amputees like Radocy. The prosthetic terminal device, used for skiing, fits standard prosthetic wrists, and allows the wearer to use poles while either downhill or cross-country skiing. It allows upper limb amputees to hold ski poles whether or not they have hands, and includes a safety quick release system to help the user avoid injury in case of falls.

BIBLIOGRAPHY. Radocy, Bob. "Upper Extremity Prosthetics: Considerations and Designs for Sports and Recreation." *Clinical Prosthetics and Orthotics* 11, no. 3 (1987): 131–153.

AMATEUR SPORTS ACT OF 1978 The Amateur Sports Act of 1978 ("ASA") (Public Law 95–606) governs the provision of Olympic and Paralympic sport in the United States. It contains many important provisions, but some of the most significant are those that prohibit discrimination in amateur sports based on gender, race, national origin, and disability.

The Amateur Sports Act of 1978 set up the governance structure for amateur sports in this country. Under the Act, the U.S. Olympic Committee (USOC) is charged with governing amateur sports. The USOC can designate that authority to a national governing body (NGB), which is usually a sport-specific body created specifically to run one sport. The NGB then develops the sport from grassroots through Olympic and Paralympic level, makes the rules, chooses teams for international competitions, certifies officials, and runs national and other championships.

In the first incarnation of the ASA, language was included that provided for assistance to amateur athletic programs and competitions for athletes with disabilities, specifically "to encourage and provide assistance to amateur athletic programs and competition for handicapped individuals, including, where feasible, the expansion of meaningful participation by handicapped individuals in programs of athletic competition for able-bodied individuals" (Amateur Sports Act, PL 95-606). No specific mention was made about the Paralympic Games or the preparation for and participation in those games.

The USOC, as part of its responsibility under the first version of the ASA, provided support in the form of grants to disability sports organizations such as the Dwarf Athletic Association of America, Disabled Sports USA, the National Disability Sports Alliance, Special Olympics International, USA Deaf Sports Federation, U.S. Association of Blind Athletes, and Wheelchair Sports, USA. These disability sport organizations then used those grants to not only develop athletes with disabilities at the grassroots level, but also to select and train Paralympic team athletes. Under the original version of the ASA, the USOC had no real responsibility in either the day to day governance of sport for people with disabilities in the United States, or in the selection and funding of Paralympic teams.

The USOC acquired a greater role with the amendments to the ASA, however. The Act was amended in 1998, becoming the Ted Stevens Olympic and Amateur Sports Act, in honor of the Alaska senator who drafted the language. It was originally created as a charter for the creation of the USOC, but was expanded to accomplish several important goals.

First, it strengthened protections for U.S. athletes so they couldn't be unfairly denied the opportunity to compete. This is a critical provision that is often invoked around selection or lack thereof to an Olympic or Paralympic team. The amendments also firmly established the

USOC as the coordinating body for U.S. amateur athletic competition directly related to international competition. And, most significantly to the community of athletes with disabilities, Paralympic and disabled sport received greater prominence with the revisions to the Act.

The USOC assumed greater responsibility for athletes with disabilities under the 1998 Amendments. First and foremost, the amendments mandated that the USOC would be the National Paralympic Committee for the United States in all its dealings with the International Paralympic Committee. They also conferred exclusive jurisdiction on the USOC for all matters pertaining to U.S. participation in the Paralympic Games. Additionally, the amendments transferred responsibility for selecting Paralympic teams to the USOC instead of on the disabled sports organizations (DSOs). As part of the new governance system, the amendments also created a new category of organization called Paralympic Sports Organizations (PSOs) which would function much like an NGB in governing a sport. Another significant change included a mechanism for Paralympic athletes to be part of the USOC governance structure through membership on the Athletes Advisory Committee. Finally, the amendments included reporting requirements that the USOC must fulfill every four years, which are to include data on the participation of disabled individuals in amateur athletic activities and a description of the steps taken by the USOC to encourage the participation of athletes with disabilities in those activities.

BIBLIOGRAPHY. MSU Disability Sports Web Site, Law-Olympic and Amateur Sports Act, http://edweb6.educ.msu.edu/kin866/lawoasa.htm; Steadward, Robert Daniel, E. J. Watkinson, and Garry David Wheeler. *Adapted Physical Activity.* Edmonton: University of Alberta Press, 2003; United States Olympic Committee, Ted Stevens Olympic and Amateur Sports Act, http://www.usoc.org/12699_12720.htm; Woman's Sports Foundation Know Your Rights, http://www.womenssportsfoundation.org/cgi-bin/iowa/issues/rights/article.html?record=996.

AMERICAN AMPUTEE SOCCER ASSOCIATION (AASA) Soccer is a sport that transcends national origin, gender, and even disability; a lesson soccer coach Bill Barry learned early on. With a background in coaching U.S. and Canadian professional soccer, he had an opportunity to coach a team at the Seattle Handicapped Sports and Recreation Association in the early 1990s, which ultimately led to a large-scale amputee soccer workshop in Philadelphia.

The high level of interest shown in that workshop led to the creation of both a competitive and a recreational team in Philadelphia. Once the sport began to develop, Barry was involved in the formation of the American Amputee Soccer Association (AASA), created to further promote the sport of amputee soccer.

Through the combined efforts of Barry and his Seattle group, amputee soccer has blossomed in many other countries, establishing a truly international sport. In many other countries, amputee soccer has developed into a program ranging from local recreational offerings to highly competitive international squads. For example, member nations of the former Soviet Union now field more than 20 teams, with European Championships contested there each year.

AMERICAN ASSOCIATION OF ADAPTED SPORTS PROGRAMS

In the United States, however, amputee soccer has not developed very well on the local or regional level. It has remained primarily a national level competitive sport, with teams selected from across the country participating in a number of international events. AASA is responsible for identifying, developing, and training the athletes who represent the United States in these elite international soccer competitions. AASA's efforts to get amputee soccer added to the Paralympic sports program have, to date, been unsuccessful; as a result, AASA is expanding its focus to developing recreational programs in the United States for young adult amputees.

Amputee soccer follows the same basic rules as nondisabled soccer with a few modifications. For example, amputee soccer allows seven players, including the goalie, on the field as well as unlimited substitution, with a game consisting of two 25-minute periods. Players who have a leg amputation can use crutches on the field but cannot use them to contact the ball. In order to equalize the competition between athletes with and without leg amputations, athletes who have both legs are required to wear a red sock on one leg, and cannot use that leg to contact the ball. Finally, unlike many other sports for people with disabilities, amputee soccer is co-ed, so girls and women are also able to participate.

BIBLIOGRAPHY. American Amputee Soccer Association, http://www.ampsoccer.org; Paciorek, Michael J., and Jeffery A. Jones. *Sports and Recreation for the Disabled,* 2nd ed. Carmel, IN: Cooper Publishing Group, 1994.

AMERICAN ASSOCIATION OF ADAPTED SPORTS PROGRAMS (AAASP) Bev Vaughn, a recreation professional working with kids with disabilities in Georgia, saw a problem. There were children with disabilities who had no opportunity to participate in sports and recreation in their communities, missing out on the critical physical and psychological benefits that maintaining a healthy, active lifestyle can bring. Vaughn began offering a program modeled after youth sports programs for children without disabilities, grouping the children according to age. Her approach was revolutionary, since most disability sports grouped participants according to their disability, not their age.

Vaughn offered a variety of after-school sports to students with physical disabilities in DeKalb County, Georgia, adapting them so that children with a range of disabilities, such as cerebral palsy, spinal cord injury, and visual impairment could participate in the same game or event.

After a decade of great success, Vaughn, together with partner Tommie Storm, formed the American Association of Adapted Sports Programs (AAASP) to serve children with disabilities from kindergarten through high school throughout the state.

Vaughn and Storm, capitalizing on the momentum and awareness created by the 1996 Atlanta Paralympic Games, expanded the DeKalb County program into Gwinnett, Cobb, and Clayton counties in Georgia. By the fall of that year, AAASP was providing interscholastic sports for children with disabilities throughout the four counties, including wheelchair basketball, indoor wheelchair soccer, and track and field. Building on the success of the programs in those four counties, AAASP was instrumental in getting the Georgia Senate to pass Resolution 262, which called on all school systems within the state to develop similar programs to serve children with disabilities.

BIBLIOGRAPHY. American Association of Adapted Sports Programs, http://www.aaasp.org.

AMERICAN BLIND SKIING FOUNDATION (ABSF). *See* Skiing

AMERICAN DEAF VOLLEYBALL ASSOCIATION. *See* USA Deaf Sports Federation (USADSF)

AMERICAN HEARING IMPAIRED HOCKEY ASSOCIATION (AHIHA) Stan Mikita, former Chicago Blackhawks standout, knew what it was like to have communication problems. He was born in the Republic of Slovakia, so when he began to play hockey in the United States, he couldn't always understand what coaches, teammates, or other players were saying to him.

It was a natural fit, then, when his good friend Irv Tiahnybik came to him with an idea. Irv had a son, Lex, who was hearing impaired. Irv, however, wanted his son to experience the joys of hockey without the frustration of communication barriers.

In the early 1970s, Irv and Stan got together and launched a school—the Stan Mikita Hockey School for the Hearing Impaired. They offered a program for the first time in 1974 in Mount Prospect, Illinois, and had over 30 boys from all over the nation come to Chicago to play. Those numbers continue to grow every year; since 1973, the American Hearing Impaired Hockey Association (AHIHA) has served over 2,000 hearing impaired children.

The AHIHA was formed side by side with Mikita's hockey school, and together they have helped field many successful U.S. Deaflympics Hockey Teams. Team USA skated to the silver at the XII World Winter Games for the Deaf in 1991, and followed that up with a Gold medal performance at the XIII Games in Finland in 1995. In 1999 and 2003, Team USA added silver and bronze to its tally.

In addition to Deaflympic competitors, the AHIHA has helped foster many deaf hockey players who have played on high school and collegiate teams alongside hearing hockey players. Jeff Mansfield is just one example. Jeff played on AHIHA hockey teams for 11 years before attending college at Princeton, where he now plays on their hockey team.

In spite of the focus on teaching hearing impaired youngsters how to win on the ice, AHIHA isn't all about hockey. They offer scholarships to students and provide assistance to youngsters so they can obtain hearing aids and therapies.

BIBLIOGRAPHY. American Hearing Impaired Hockey Association, http://www.ahiha. org/index.html; Chicago Blackhawks in the Community, http://www.chicagoblackhawks. com/community/; "Deaf and Hard of Hearing Children Participate in Hockey Program," http://http://abclocal.go.com/wls/story?section=community&id=3361917; "Hearing Loss Can't Silence These Skills." *Hearing Loss News and Reviews,* http://www.4hearingloss.com/ archives/2005/02/hearing_loss_ca.html; "Mansfield Announced Recipient of USA Hockey's Disabled Athlete of the Year." *Deaf Today,* http://www.deaftoday.com/v3/archives/2005/05/ mansfield_annou.html; United Cerebral Palsy Association, http://www.ucp.org/ucp_ channeldoc.cfm/1/15/61/61–61/3564.

AMERICANS WITH DISABILITIES ACT (ADA) The Americans with Disabilities Act (ADA) was widely hailed as one of the most important civil rights laws by many in the disability community. It traces its origins to The Rehabilitation Act of 1973 and, in particular, Section 504 of that Act. Section 504 of the Rehabilitation Act prohibited discrimination on the basis of disability by recipients of federal funds and was initially a piece of legislation used to prohibit discrimination against people with disabilities by federal entities like the U.S. Postal Service and federally funded colleges and universities.

In recognition of the fact that preventing discrimination by federally funded entities didn't go far enough to provide access to employment, transportation, places of public accommodation, state and local government entities (who may not receive federal funding, and thus be beyond the reach of 504), disability advocates began organizing in the early 1980s to create what would become the Americans with Disabilities Act. After years of drafting, redrafting, and lobbying, the final text of the bill was signed into law in 1990 by then President George Bush.

The protections offered under the Americans with Disabilities Act mirror much of what is found in the Rehabilitation Act; however, the reach of the ADA is far more expansive than its predecessor. The definitions of disability found in the two statutes are identical, the antidiscrimination provisions the same. Where the Rehabilitation Act solely focused on discrimination by federally funded entities, however, the ADA expanded into previously uncharted territory and prohibited discrimination against people with disabilities in employment, public accommodations and services, public transportation, and telecommunications.

Titles II and III of the ADA have the most interaction with the world of disability sport. Title II covers activities of state and local governments, and Title III covers public accommodations. Title II may cover a university program, or a park district sports and recreation program. Title III covers a wide variety of facilities which may include private recreation facilities, health clubs, golf courses, and the like.

Under the Americans with Disabilities Act, an entity covered under Title II must be accessible when viewed in its entirety. This means, for example, that not every swimming pool offered by a park district has to be accessible. The program when viewed as a whole has to provide access to persons with disabilities, and barriers must be removed which are readily achievable to remove. If a town had one swimming pool in its park district program, that one pool would have to be accessible. In the case of a large city that has dozens of pools, all the pools would not have to be accessible. This is a very fact specific inquiry that often requires the involvement of the legal system to sort out.

Title III provides that places of public accommodation must be accessible to persons with disabilities unless to do so would either pose an undue hardship or cause a fundamental alteration to the program. An undue hardship is defined as significant difficulty or expense and must truly be a significant burden. For example, if a private health club needed an elevator to become accessible, and it would cost a major portion of that club's revenues to provide the elevator, that may be an undue hardship. On the other hand, if a health club that was part of a nationwide chain needed an elevator to become accessible, it is likely that would not be an undue hardship, and they would have to provide the elevator.

Fundamental alteration simply means that a program doesn't have to offer some special service or change what it does to accommodate a person with a disability. For example, it would be a fundamental alteration for a wheelchair basketball player to want to play in a league with individuals who did not use wheelchairs; therefore, this type of accommodation would not be required.

The overarching purpose of the ADA is to provide individuals with disabilities with an equal opportunity to participate in and benefit from programs and facilities in the most integrated setting possible, and to prohibit decision-making based on stereotypes, fears, myths, and misconceptions about disability. Both the Rehabilitation Act and the ADA define an individual with a disability as an individual with a physical or mental impairment that substantially limits a major life activity. Major life activities include walking, seeing, hearing, breathing, talking, eating, and caring for oneself, among others.

The ADA's limits with regard to accommodating a person with a disability in a sports and recreation setting have been tested in various courts. The most significant decision to date, however, came from the U.S. Supreme Court in *PGA Tour Inc. v. Martin.* In that case, the Supreme Court was asked to decide whether Casey Martin, an individual with a disability that affected his ability to walk, should be allowed to use a golf cart in PGA Tour events. The PGA argued that allowing Martin to use a cart fundamentally altered the game of golf, giving him an unfair advantage. Many other organizations supported the PGA's side of the argument, fearing that a decision in Martin's favor would lead to wheelchair basketball players trying out for the NBA and blind individuals wanting to play pro baseball. Ultimately, the Court disagreed and sided with Martin, finding that the PGA should accommodate Martin by allowing the use of a golf cart. The PGA's fears of an unfair advantage didn't come to light; in fact, the next year, Martin didn't even make the cut.

BIBLIOGRAPHY. ADA Portal, http://adaportal.org; Karp, Gary. *Life on Wheels for the Active Wheelchair User.* Sebastopol, CA: O'Reilly and Associates, 1999; *PGA Tour Inc. v. Martin.* No. 532 U.S. 661. United States Supreme Court. 2001; U.S. Department of Justice ADA Home Page, http://www.usdoj.gov/crt/ada/adahom1.htm; Winnick, Joseph P. *Adapted Physical Education and Sport,* 4th ed. Champaign, IL: Human Kinetics, 2005.

AMERICAN WHEELCHAIR BOWLING ASSOCIATION (AWBA) Wheelchair bowling was developed in the early years of wheelchair sport, during and immediately after World War II, when large numbers of veterans returned home with disabilities but wanted to find some way to return to active life. Wheelchair basketball and wheelchair racing were popular choices, but for those who wanted an activity they could enjoy with their friends or family without disabilities, bowling provided a great avenue.

Veterans groups were instrumental in getting bowling for people with disabilities off the ground. In 1942, the Bowler's Victory Legion (now known as the BVL Fund), was formed to provide recreational supplies, activities, and visits by star bowlers to veterans hospitals. A few years later in 1945, Veterans' Civilian volunteers organized fund-raising drives to provide a bowling and billiard clubroom for the Birmingham Veteran's Hospital in Van Nuys, California. Two short years later, in 1947, 21 hospitals were conducting bowling programs, and the Bowler's Victory Legion held the first national tournament for paralyzed veterans with seven hospitals participating. That same year, three winners of the BVL tourney were guests of President Harry S. Truman, having the distinct privilege of bowling on the two lanes at the White House that were placed into service three months earlier at the request of Truman, an avid bowler. Today, more than 100 hospitals and medical centers offer bowling as a basic form of recreation and therapy for people with a wide range of disabilities.

Most wheelchair bowlers found they were the only bowler with a disability in their leagues. That changed in the spring of 1962, when Richard Carlson of Huntsville, Alabama, the sole wheelchair participant in the Annual Southern Bowling Congress Tourney in Louisville, Kentucky, decided to conduct a tournament solely for wheelchair users. Later that same year, 30 bowlers from 13 states participated in Carlson's tournament, which marked the founding of the American Wheelchair Bowling Association.

With the help of organizations like AWBA, bowling centers are learning that some of the accommodations needed by bowlers who use wheelchairs actually make the experience friendlier to those without disabilities as well. Many newer facilities have removed the step at the lip of the approach, which, in addition to aiding bowlers with disabilities in accessing the lane, has helped those without disabilities by reducing the number of slip and fall accidents in the lanes.

Though there are now wheelchair bowling leagues throughout the country, it is important to remember that a wheelchair bowler is not restricted from bowling in ANY league. Many AWBA members are still the only wheelchair bowler in their sanctioned American Bowling Congress (ABC) or Women's International Bowling Congress (WIBC) league.

Some AWBA members bowl in "Up and Down" leagues where a wheelchair bowler is paired with a nondisabled partner. Still others use adaptive devices that have been league approved, such as a snap handle ball or a bowling stick. The bowling stick, a pole with four prongs that conform to the shape of the bowling ball, is used to push the ball down the lane. The snap handle ball, used by those with gripping difficulties, is a gripper that fits into the three finger holes of the ball which then releases the ball when the bowler puts the ball down to roll it.

A bowling ramp is used by bowlers who can't throw the ball independently, which can enable bowlers to achieve scores of 200 or better. The ramp is metal or wood with a level surface on the top. The bowler points the ramp in the direction they wish the ball to go and pushes the ball down the ramp. Ramp bowlers compete in their own division in the league.

Averages of 170 and higher are common for the best wheelchair bowlers, dispelling the notion that bowling from a wheelchair is not competitive. Records include the highest league average of 200, held by Walt Roy, with runner up Al Utrecht at 196. The record for high game is held by Walt Roy with a score of 299, with runner up Roger Dixon at 297.

Wheelchair bowling is one of the sports that are easy to integrate between people with and without disabilities, allowing families, friends and colleagues the opportunity to socialize and be active together.

See also Bowling Ramp; Bowling Stick

BIBLIOGRAPHY. American Wheelchair Bowling Association, http://www.awba.com; Apple, Jr., David F. *Physical Fitness: A Guide for Individuals with Spinal Cord Injury.* Washington, DC: Department of Veteran's Affairs, Rehabilitation Research and Development Service, 1995; Karp, Gary. *Life on Wheels for the Active Wheelchair User.* Sebastopol, CA: O'Reilly and Associates, 1999; Kelley, Jerry D., and Lex Frieden. *Go For It! A Book on*

Sport and Recreation for Persons with Disabilities. Orlando, FL: Harcourt Brace Jovanovich, 1989; Sullivan, James. "Hot Lanes in Florida." *Sports 'n' Spokes* (September 1991): 26.

AMERICAN WHEELCHAIR TABLE TENNIS ASSOCIATION (AWTTA) The American Wheelchair Table Tennis Association (AWTTA) was founded in March of 1986 and became recognized as the national governing body (NGB) for wheelchair table tennis the next year. AWTTA's mission is "to promote, initiate, and stimulate the growth and development of wheelchair and stand-up table tennis for the disabled in the United States of America." To attain this objective, the AWTTA leads fund-raisers, conducts clinics, promotes a juniors program, and selects athletes for world competitions such as the World Championships, the Paralympic Games, and the Pan-American Games.

The rules for wheelchair table tennis are easily adapted to meet individual ability levels, making it increasingly popular. At the Paralympic Games, two classes of competition exist–wheelchair and standing. A player's class takes into account functional mobility and rank.

While standing athletes are subject to the same rules as nondisabled players, there are a few modifications for wheelchair players: (1) wheelchairs must have at least two large wheels and one small wheel; (2) wheelchair athletes may grip the table to maintain balance as long as the table is not moved, and the service must clear the end of the table; (3) footrests may be fitted if required, but neither footrests nor feet shall touch the floor during play; (4) no part of the body above the knees may be attached to the chair, as this could improve balance. If a player requires strapping or binding for medical reasons, it will be taken into account when assessing the players playing class; (5) there are no restrictions on size, number, or shape of cushions.

Wheelchair table tennis is one of the few Paralympic or disabled sports that have had some successful integration with its able-bodied counterpart. U.S. Table Tennis has incorporated disability championships into its able-bodied events so that athletes with and without disabilities, while not competing against each other, are competing side by side. This integration has led to better visibility, access to competition, and funding and sponsorship access for this sport.

See also Table Tennis

BIBLIOGRAPHY. American Wheelchair Table Tennis Association, http://www.atta.org; Paciorek, Michael J., and Jeffery A. Jones. *Sports and Recreation for the Disabled,* 2nd ed. Carmel, IN: Cooper Publishing Group, 1994; "Sporting Events: Table Tennis." *ICan Online,* http://www.icanonline.net/news/fullpage.cfm?articleid=8476B92D-692D-48AF-B3738E3 D76FA8449&cx=sports.get_active; "Table Tennis: Sports and Team Games." *United Cerebral Palsy,* http://www.ucp.org/ucp_channeldoc.cfm/1/15/61/61–61/3585.

AMPUTEE GOLF GRIP The Amputee Golf Grip and Golf Pro are adaptive devices designed by and for amputees who want to play competitive golf. The Amputee Golf Grip is designed for those missing their left hand, and uses the gripping pressure of the right hand to lock the grip in place anywhere the golfer chooses to place it on their club. The Golf Pro is a similar device, used for people missing their right hand. It slips over the club shaft and sets in place when the golfer pulls it up. Sizing rings are adjustable to fit the individual golfer's clubs.

AQUATIC WHEELCHAIR

Both the Golf Grip and the Golf Pro duplicate the wrist action needed for a controlled swing, allowing golfers with one hand to continue to golf on a recreational or competitive basis. These are the only commercially manufactured devices for amputees missing either hand.

BIBLIOGRAPHY. O & P Digital Technologies, http://www.oandp.com/products/trs/sports-recreation/golf.asp; O & P Digital Technologies, http://www.oandp.com/products/trs/assets/product_pdfs/Golf_grip.pdf; The War Amps: Recreation—Golf for Arm Amputees, http://www.waramps.ca/nac/golf2.htm.

AMPUTEE SOCCER. *See* American Amputee Soccer Association (AASA)

AQUATIC WHEELCHAIR Summer days at the beach don't have to be given up just because of a disability. In recent years, several companies have developed aquatic wheelchairs, which allow people with mobility impairments to gain access to swimming pools, lakes, and beaches in addition to forest trails, snow, and other terrain not usually accessible to people using wheelchairs. There are a few varieties on the market, with features to appeal to everyone.

Some allow the individual to propel themselves for the greatest independence, like some of the Landeez models. Others, like the Tiralo, require someone else to push. One model has inflatable, buggy-like, rubberized wheels and a polyvinyl, lightweight and anticorrosive frame. Yet another has a stainless steel frame, plastic mag wheels, security straps, and wheel locks.

The Landeez, in addition to being an aquatic wheelchair, can serve as an all-terrain chair, rolling easily over sand, gravel, soft soils, rocks, pebbles, and forest trails. The Landeez wheelchair weighs only 37 pounds and can be easily disassembled for storage or portability. The chair's rugged, noncorroding frame is made of welded stainless steel with a lightweight aluminum axle. Both the length and angle of the footrest are also adjustable, and the omni-directional front wheels can rotate 360 degrees for easier maneuverability. The DeBug is similar to the Landeez, but it doesn't work as an all-terrain chair.

The Tiralo, while it doesn't allow for independent mobility, can be used to access the beach or pool, and even to float in the water. It also has a foldable frame which allows for easy transport in the trunk of a car.

The Polymedic pool wheelchair is a rust-proof chair that aides people with disabilities in accessing pools. It can be fully immersed or used to allow someone access to the edge of the pool. Unlike the Tiralo, the Polymedic doesn't float. Whatever a person's level of ability or mobility, there is an aquatic chair on the market that can help them enjoy the pool, the lake, or the ocean.

BIBLIOGRAPHY. Paciorek, Michael J., and Jeffery A. Jones. *Sports and Recreation for the Disabled,* 3rd ed. Carmel, IN: Cooper Publishing Group, 2001.

ARCHERY The bow and arrow have been used for over 70 centuries for hunting and war. In modern society, while archery may still be used as one method of hunting, it is primarily considered a sport for recreation and competition.

In archery competition, rounds have a fixed number of arrows shot from specified distances. There have been many instances of archers with disabilities competing alongside those without (*see* Rebollo, Antonio). There are some classifications specific to wheelchair users, providing adaptations so that people with particular disabilities can compete in archery.

For example, archers who are quadriplegic may wear a cuff with a hook that allows them to grasp and release the bow. They may also use a compound bow which reduces the amount of force required to pull back.

People with and without disabilities can compete alongside each other in archery. FITA, the Federation Internationale de Tir a l'Arc, is the international governing body of archery. Founded in 1931, FITA governs all archery competition including that for disabled archers.

There are three classifications for wheelchair archers: Class AR 1 are quadriplegic athletes with no functional finger movement. They may use a release, compound, or recurved bow, as well as strapping and other stabilizing support. If the athlete uses a mechanical release, they are allowed to receive assistance loading arrows into the bow. Class AR 2 is the class for all other wheelchair archers. No support strapping is allowed for athletes in this classification, and FITA rules govern the equipment used. Class AR 3 is the division for ambulatory athletes with disabilities.

In wheelchair archery competition, men and women shoot separately, and compound bow is a separate division as well. Some important considerations for archers with disabilities involve careful selection of equipment. The weight of the bow and the weight necessary to draw it are key factors that go into choosing the best equipment for the archer. Heavier bows shoot longer distances; however beginning archers generally shoot a lighter bow to practice form and technique. Equipment needed includes straight or recurve bows, arrows, arm guards, visual aides such as field glasses, and a bow sling, belt, or ground quiver. Cuffs to allow athletes in class AR 1 to pull and release the bow may also be required.

In novice competition, archers shoot 36 arrows from both 50 and 30 meters at a 122 cm target. The short metric round is 36 arrows from 50 and 30 meters at an 80 cm target. The advanced metric is different for men and women. Men's are 70-, 50-, and 30-meter distances and women's are 60, 50, and 30, shooting 36 arrows at each distance. The final or FITA round is the Olympic medal round. For the men, it is 36 arrows at 90, 70, 50, and 30 meters. The women's round is 36 arrows at 70, 60, 50, and 30 meters.

Archers have created various modifications to be able to compete, such as an archer without arms using his teeth. Visually impaired archers may use an electronic sensing device. Hearing impaired archers may use photoelectric devices and lights to signal them. Adaptations make it possible for virtually anyone to compete in archery, allowing athletes with disabilities to compete successfully alongside nondisabled competitors.

Worldwide, there have been many archers with disabilities who have achieved outstanding success. Antonio Rebollo of Spain is one, who lit the torch for both the Barcelona Olympic and Paralympic Games. Bodil Elgh and Patrik Norstrom, disabled archers from Sweden, were some of the best archers in their country, disabled or not. Similarly, Susan Hagel of the United States, also renowned for her talent on the wheelchair basketball court, has won several state tournaments in her home state of Minnesota and holds records against nondisabled archers.

ARGO OFF-ROAD VEHICLE

BIBLIOGRAPHY. Apple, Jr., David F. *Physical Fitness: A Guide for Individuals with Spinal Cord Injury.* Washington, DC: Department of Veteran's Affairs, Rehabilitation Research and Development Service, 1995; Karp, Gary. *Life on Wheels for the Active Wheelchair User.* Sebastopol, CA: O'Reilly and Associates, 1999; Kelley, Jerry D., and Lex Frieden. *Go for It! A Book on Sport and Recreation for Persons with Disabilities.* Orlando, FL: Harcourt Brace Jovanovich, 1989.

ARGO OFF-ROAD VEHICLE The ARGO off-road vehicle is an example of technology created for nondisabled people that has proven to be an effective tool for individuals with disabilities. The ARGO, originally developed as an off-road vehicle to be used in some of the most remote regions of the world, has proven to be a safe and reliable transportation mode for people with disabilities. The ARGO and vehicles like it allow people with mobility impairments to access the outdoors, providing a means to enjoy hunting, fishing, and other outdoor activities.

BIBLIOGRAPHY. Argo, http://argoatv.com/.

ARM ERGOMETER. *See* Ergometer

B

BALL, MARTY Marty Ball has made a career out of making other wheelchair users lives better. He had polio as a child, and grew up using crutches to get around. As a teen, he learned about wheelchair sports, and found himself able to leave the crutches behind for the first time in his life. In the wheelchair, Ball found a natural affinity for speed, excelling in track and road racing. For the past three decades, Ball has held many world and national records on the track and road.

In addition to winning races and setting records, Ball used his time as a competitor to learn about wheelchair design. Since retiring from active competition, he has used that knowledge to make a name for himself in the wheelchair industry working with various wheelchair companies to improve upon the current designs. He has been instrumental in helping the industry to give wheelchair users better, lighter, and more functional wheelchairs.

Ball, a Wheelchair Sports Hall of Fame inductee, has devoted himself not only to improving wheelchair design, but to providing equipment to those who don't have the means to obtain it. Over the years, he has donated countless wheelchairs, parts and sport specific chairs to programs and teams, as well as to individuals with disabilities who don't have insurance or the other means to get a needed wheelchair.

Ball is always willing to share his thoughts and expertise, and is a frequent lecturer at events nationwide on everything from sports and recreation to wheelchair technology to motivation. He is also a well-known contributor to many disability related publications like *Sports 'n' Spokes*, *Paraplegia News*, and *New Mobility*, writing about issues relating to wheelchair technology, selection, and fit.

BIBLIOGRAPHY. "Buddhism Plus Disability: One Step Closer to Nirvana." *New Mobility* (November 1999); Fields, Cheryl D. "Casters." *Team Rehab Report* (April–May 1992). http://www.wheelchairnet.org/WCN_ProdServ/Docs/TeamRehab/RR_92/9203art2. PDF; Lilac Bloomsday Association Bloomsday 12K Run 1986 Wheelchair Results, http://www.bloomsdayrun.org/1986WheelchairOpenStats.htm; Lilac Bloomsday Association Bloomsday 12K Run 1985 Wheelchair Results, http://www.bloomsdayrun. org/1985WheelchairOpenStats.htm; "Performance: How About a Boost?" *Sports 'n' Spokes* (May 2001). http://www.pvamagazines.com/sns/magazine/article.php?art=502; Vogel, Bob. "Shouldering the Load." *New Mobility* (September 2005). http://newmobility.com/review_article.cfm?id=1055&action=browse.

BANKSHOT BASKETBALL

BANKSHOT BASKETBALL Bankshot basketball is described as miniature golf with a basketball. The game was created by Rabbi Reeve Brenner of Rockville, Maryland in 1981 for people with and without disabilities to play together, inspired by a cousin who was a wheelchair user.

Brenner grew up playing basketball as a child learning to bank shots off the ceiling of his high school gymnasium. This is one of the premises of bankshot basketball—banking shots off different types of backboards.

The game may remind players of the playground basketball game known as "HORSE" where a player takes a shot and the rest of the players must replicate it. In Bankshot, however, the shots are determined not so much by the previous player as by the angled, curved, and unconventionally configured brightly colored backboards.

Bankshot courses have a different number of stations depending on the size of the course, with shots becoming increasingly more difficult as the player progresses through the course. Scorecards are used to track points, and the player with the highest number of points at the end wins.

BIBLIOGRAPHY. *Bankshot Basketball,* http://www.Bankshot.com.

BEACHMASTER AQUATIC WHEELCHAIR. *See* Aquatic Wheelchair

BEEP BASEBALL Springtime and baseball go together for many Americans. Until a few decades ago, however, people with visual impairments weren't able to play. In 1964, Charley Banks, an engineer with the Telephone Pioneers, changed that when he put a small electronic module in a ball so it would beep, and he and his coworkers created some cone shaped rubber bases that would emit high pitched whistles. Beep baseball was born.

In the early years, the sport wasn't perceived as competitive, so there wasn't much interest. Within the decade, however, after equipment problems were straightened out and rules were modified to make it more competitive, beep baseball's popularity surged.

Beep baseball is played with standard softball bats, a 16-inch ball modified to emit an audible beep tone, and two bases (48-inch pylons) which emit an audible buzz. A beep baseball team has six players, along with two sighted spotters for defense, a sighted pitcher and catcher. All the visually impaired players are blindfolded to eradicate any advantage a player with more vision might have.

The game consists of six innings with three outs per inning. To begin, the umpire activates a base when the ball is hit; the batter doesn't know which base it will be. Audible signals from the pitcher alert the batter that a pitch is coming. Runs are scored when a batter hits a fair ball and reaches base prior to the ball being fielded.

On defense, sighted spotters aid the players in determining the direction of the ball, calling out numbers to indicate the general direction in which the ball is traveling. Defensive play only requires that the ball be picked up or fielded; it does not have to be thrown to another player. Spotters can also call out safety warnings.

The dimensions of a beep baseball field are established by the National Beep Baseball Association (NBBA) and are standard throughout the country. First and third base are positioned 100 feet from home plate. The pitcher's mound is 21 feet, 6 inches from home plate.

The umpires play a different role in beep baseball than in the traditional version of the game. First, one or more field umpires yell "caught" when a fielder gains control of a batted ball, when the ball is held off the ground and away from the fielder's body. Second, the base umpire's job is to watch the batter and call out "there" when any part of the batter's body contacts the base. The home plate umpire makes the final determination on whether a batter is safe or out. The team with the most runs at the end wins.

BIBLIOGRAPHY. Kelley, Jerry D., and Lex Frieden. *Go For It! A Book on Sport and Recreation for Persons with Disabilities.* Orlando, FL: Harcourt Brace Jovanovich, 1989; Paciorek, Michael J., and Jeffery A. Jones. *Sports and Recreation for the Disabled,* 2nd ed. Carmel, IN: Cooper Publishing Group, 1994.

BI-SKI; BI-SKIING A bi-ski is one of several adaptations to downhill skis that allow people with disabilities the opportunity to experience getting on the slopes. The bi-ski, like the sit-ski and mono-ski, is an adapted ski that allows individuals with a variety of orthopedic and mobility impairments to ski from a sitting position.

Because of its stability and maneuverability, the bi-ski is appropriate for individuals with cerebral palsy, multiple sclerosis, spinal cord injury, and other disabilities that cause a lack of trunk stability and balance. A bi-ski doesn't require the balance and trunk strength that are needed to use a mono-ski, making it an attractive choice for beginners with any type of disability as well.

A bi-ski is a molded fiberglass shell mounted to an articulating undercarriage above two specially designed skis. The seat is usually rigid, sitting low to the ground, and has many straps to ensure a ski-boot snug fit. The skis, unlike stand-up skis, are short and wide, and the foot tray has a cover to keep snow off the skier's feet and legs. For beginners, fixed outriggers and handlebars can be added, and a tether or strap for the instructor to control the ski is available. For more experienced skiers, outrigger ski poles which aid in balance and turning can be used.

Bi-skis allow for skiers to self-load onto ski lifts with the use of hydraulic jacks, and they usually have roll bars, shoulder harnesses, and tether hooks for safety and support.

BIBLIOGRAPHY. Discover Ability, http://coloradodiscoverability.com/programs_biskiing.cfm; Mono and Bi-Ski Manufacturer's Page, http://www.sitski.com/manufac.html; Sit-Ski.com, http://www.sitski.com/whatisit.htm; Spokes 'n Motion, http://www.spokesnmotion.com/products_shop/product_detail.asp?product_id=1029.

BLANCHETTE, CRAIG Craig Blanchette has made a career out of being first. Blanchette, a congenital double amputee, was introduced to wheelchair sports when he saw Kevin Hansen, the man who would become his coach, passing by his house in a racing wheelchair. Blanchette dominated throughout the better part of the next decade in wheelchair track and road racing holding records at many long distance road races including the Lilac Bloomsday 12K in Spokane, Washington and the Peachtree 10K in Atlanta.

Blanchette was also one of the first athletes with a disability to compete in the Olympic Games, where he won a bronze for the United States in the 1,500 m wheelchair race in

Seoul, Korea in 1988. The next first came when Blanchette was featured in *Sports Illustrated* in July, 1989, in a five-page, full-color spread detailing his racing accomplishments. But Blanchette wasn't done yet.

In the early 1990s, Blanchette was the first athlete with a disability to appear in a major television ad. Appearing in a Nike commercial, only the top half of his body was shown while he was lifting weights, playing basketball, and playing tennis. At the end of the commercial the camera shows his wheelchair and he races down the track, saying, "So I never quit."

Blanchette didn't quit. He set and met goal after goal, including getting the wheelchair mile record from George Murray. Murray, a racing legend himself, was the first to run a sub-4 minute wheelchair mile, going the distance in 3:59.4.

Four years later, at the Steve Prefontaine Classic in Eugene, Oregon, Blanchette made his way into the history books, beating Murray's time by nearly eight seconds to clock a 3:51. Blanchette wasn't alone, though; five competitors in the race finished the mile in less than 4 minutes—Tony Noguiera, Rafael Ibarra, Doug Kennedy, and Tom Foran.

Blanchette, though retired from racing, now competes in handcycling events nationally and worldwide, once again proving he is the man to beat.

BIBLIOGRAPHY. Bauman, J. "How Changing Ads in Health and Fitness can Change Attitudes," http://www.ncpad.org; Challenged Athlete's Foundation, http://challengedathletes. org; Craig Blanchette. "Highlights," http://craigblanchette.com; Crase, Cliff. "Cliff's Corner." *Sports 'n' Spokes* (September–October 1989): 5; Lipman, J. "Disabled People Featured in More Ads." *Wall Street Journal* (28 February 1990): B6.

BLAUWET, CHERI Blauwet is one of the fastest rising stars on the disability sport scene today. Born in Larchwood, Iowa, she became disabled in a farm accident at the age of 15 months. She was as active as any other youngster, participating in wheelchair sports early on. By the eighth grade, she started competing in track events.

In high school, she joined the track team, because Iowa had started sanctioning wheelchair events as part of the state track finals. Within her first couple of years of competition, she had set state and national records in her events. She was also a standout academically and was named a National Merit Scholar and one of Iowa's "All-Academic Team."

Blauwet attended college at the University of Arizona, where they had started a wheelchair sports program. There, she continued her successes on both the academic and athletic fronts, maintaining a perfect 4.0 GPA in molecular biology and being named to *USA Today*'s 2002 Academic All-America Team. She represented the United States at the 2000 Paralympic Games in Sydney, winning a silver and three bronze for her efforts. After that she switched her focus to roadracing.

She did a half marathon in Taegu, Korea in 2001, and she debuted in the marathon distance in Japan the next year. She has since raced in New York City, Los Angeles, and Boston, winning the marathon in each city. In New York in 2003, she became the first woman to break the two-hour barrier in the wheelchair division, going the distance in 1:59.30. In Boston, she ran a personal best of 1:39.53 in 2004. She made her second Paralympic appearance in Athens in 2004, winning Gold in the 800 m and bronze in both the 5000 m and the marathon.

Blauwet has received numerous accolades in her young life. She received a Paul G. Hearne Leadership Award from the American Association of People with Disabilities which carried a $10,000 prize along with it. She received the Vince Lombardi Champion Award in 2003. That same year, she was a finalist for the Women's Sports Foundation Sportswoman of the Year. She was nominated for an ESPY Award in 2004 and 2005. She was named 2005 Sportsperson with a Disability at the Laureus World Sports Awards held in Portugal.

Blauwet is currently in medical school and planning a career in developmental pediatrics.

BIBLIOGRAPHY. AbroadView, http://www.abroadviewmagazine.com/fall_04/blauwet. html; Boston.com, Boston Marathon Runner Bios, http://www.boston.com/marathon/ runners/2005_runners/blauwet.htm; Eule, Brian. "On to Athens," *Stanford Magazine* (July/August 2004), http://www.stanfordalumni.org/news/magazine/2004/julaug/features/ olympians.html; Gambaccini, Peter. "Blauwet: Hell on Wheels," http://www.villagevoice.com/ news/0344,jockbeat,48214,3.html; The Heartford Group Benefits Division U.S. Paralympics Athletes, http://groupbenefits.thehartford.com/usp/athletes/blauwet.html; Underwood, Brian. "A Day in the Life of Work: No Brakes," (September 2004), http://www.fastcompany. com/magazine/86/lifeofwork.html.

BLAZE SPORTS. *See* United States Disabled Athletes Fund

BLIND GOLF Golf for individuals who are blind and visually impaired has been played at least since 1938. That's when Clint Russell of Duluth, Minnesota and Dr. Beach Oxenham of London, England played against each other at the Ridgeview Country Club in Duluth.

Both golfers were featured in "Ripley's Believe it or Not" as the world's first blind golfer. They found out about each other, and challenged each other to a tournament, which Russell won.

The number of golfers with visual impairments grew after WWII, when the Veteran's Administration advocated the sport as a form of rehabilitation for those injured in the war. As the number of visually impaired golfers grew, Bob Allman, a visually impaired attorney and a golfer himself, formed the U.S. Blind Golfers Association (USBGA) in 1953.

Since that time, national championships have been contested annually in partnership with the Lions Club. The invitational Ken Venturi Guiding Eyes Classic, the Masters Tournament of blind golf, has been held in Mt. Kisco, New York since 1978.

Golf for people with visual impairments, or "blind golf," is played with the assistance of a coach. The coach functions somewhat like a caddy, only providing more in-depth assistance. The coach describes the shot and distance, helps the golfer select the club, and line up to hit the ball. The coach also describes the ball's flight and where it lands. Good communication between the player and coach is crucial.

There are some rules for visually impaired golfers that are different from the traditional game. For example, a coach can be a caddie and vice versa, but it is not required that one individual serve both functions; therefore, a blind golfer can have a coach *and* a caddy if they choose. If a player has both, however, the coach isn't allowed to handle the clubs except to help the player take a stance or line up to take a stroke.

Another modification of the rules for blind golfers is that the golfer can ask for assistance from a partner, caddie, or coach. Additionally, a modification that allows the coach to position themselves on or close to an extension of the line of putt behind the ball during a stroke played from the putting green, provides that the coach can be located there as long as they don't assist the player during the stroke.

Similar to other disability sports, there are classifications or categories in blind golf that are recognized by the International Blind Golf Association. A B-1 golfer is totally blind with no light perception, or light perception that is not functional, central, or peripheral, with or without light projection, up to, but not including hand motion. This includes the inability to recognize the shape of a hand at any distance or in any direction. The B-2 golfer has the ability to recognize the shape of a hand up to visual acuity of 20/600, and the B-3 golfer has visual acuity above 20/600 and less than 20/200. While classifications aren't relevant to recreational play, in national and international competitions they ensure fairness to the competitors.

BIBLIOGRAPHY. United States Blind Golf Association, History, http://www.blindgolf.com/history; United States Blind Golf Association, Rules, http://www.blindgolf.com/usga_blind_golf_rules.htm.

BLIND SAILING INTERNATIONAL (BSI) In 1992 the New Zealand Council for Vision Impaired Persons organized the first international regatta for the blind and visually impaired. As a result of this success, Blind Sailing International (BSI) was formed in 1994. In the last decade, 5 worldwide regattas for blind sailors have been held with as many as 14 countries participating.

One of the benefits of sailing for people who are blind is that no specialized equipment is needed. The main accommodation required is an orientation to the particular boat being used.

BSI, which is affiliated with the International Blind Sports Association (IBSA) and the International Foundation of Disabled Sailing (IFDS), follows international rules with a few modifications. One modification provides that there are sighted guides on the boat at all times. In BSI regattas, the sighted guide is there solely to provide verbal guidance and safety assistance, not to help with the physical sailing of the boat. Sailing teams consist of four individuals; two IBSA classified blind sailors and two sighted guides.

BSI sailors are classified into one of three vision classifications, adopted from IBSA rules, B1, B2, and B3. B1 is a total absence of light perception or the inability to recognize the form of a hand to a visual acuity of 2/600 or a visual field of less than 5 degrees. B2 is the ability to recognize the shape of a hand up to a visual acuity of 2/600. B3 is a visual acuity of above 2/600 to 2/200 or a field of more than 5 degrees but less than 20 degrees. It is conceivable that as the sport grows, countries could field three teams, one for each classification.

BIBLIOGRAPHY. International Association for Disabled Sailing (ISAF), http://sailing.org/disabled; International Blind Sports Federation. http://www.ibsa.org.

BLISTER BOWL. *See* Wheelchair Football

BLOWDARTS The motto "once an athlete, always an athlete" held true for Andrew Batavia, a successful high school distance runner who saw his dreams of great athletic feats shattered when a 1977 car accident left him with a C2–3 spinal cord injury. Batavia couldn't fathom a life without activity, but he didn't know what he would be able to do anymore. As a result, Batavia became interested in researching activities that could be adapted for athletes such as himself, who had sustained high level spinal cord injuries.

Batavia used his years as a researcher for the National Rehabilitation Hospital in Washington, D.C., to investigate different activities he could participate in. One of the most popular was blowdarts.

Blowdarts is a sport that consists of target shooting with a blowgun, allowing people who have limited or no hand function to participate. In addition to providing a physical outlet for individuals with a high-level injury, blowdarts offers important health benefits. Since the sport requires using the respiratory muscles, participating in blowdarts helps individuals with spinal injuries and other disabilities increase their respiratory capacity and lung function.

Blowdarts requires only a minimal investment in equipment, because velcro darts and a blow gun are all that are needed to participate.

BIBLIOGRAPHY. Paciorek, Michael J., and Jeffery A. Jones. *Sports and Recreation for the Disabled,* 2nd ed. Carmel, IN: Cooper Publishing Group, 1994.

BOCCIA Boccia is more than just a lawn game played by Italian families. It is a game of precision, skill, and accuracy, originating from the French game of boule. Boccia is played primarily by athletes with cerebral palsy. Introduced to the Paralympic stage in 1984, it has grown in popularity ever since.

Boccia is played in singles, pairs, or teams; and while the rules are similar to the lawn version of the game, Paralympic boccia is played indoors on a solid court. The game begins when one of the players throws a white "jack" onto the playing court. Then, players take turns throwing either red or blue leather boccia balls toward the jack. Teams or individuals alternate throws. When all the balls are thrown, the referee scores the match, awarding one point for the closest ball to the jack and another point for each ball from that same individual or team that is closer to the jack than any of the opponent's balls.

Boccia is one of the Paralympic and disabled sports that is co-ed, with men and women playing against each other or as members of the same team. Boccia is played in four different classifications based on level of disability—BC1–BC4. To compete in pairs, the individual must be classified a BC3, and teams are for players in classes BC1 and BC2. The use of chutes and ramps allow players who don't have the ability to manually release the ball the ability to play.

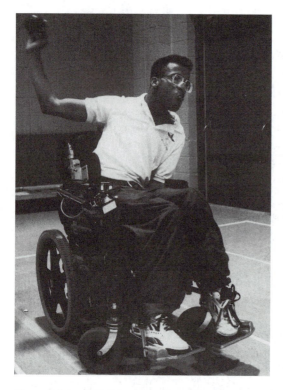

Kenny Johnson, U. S. boccia athlete. *Photo courtesy of Rehabilitation Institute of Chicago Wirtz Sports Program.*

The regulation boccia court is made up of two areas: the individual player box and the common playing area. The player makes all throws from the box and must remain within his or her box during the match.

In the United States, the National Disability Sport Alliance governs boccia competition. Internationally, boccia is governed by the International Boccia Commission (IBC), a Sports Commission of the Cerebral Palsy International Sport and Recreation Association (CP-ISRA) and a member of the International Paralympic Committee (IPC) Sports Council.

BIBLIOGRAPHY. Kelley, Jerry D., and Lex Frieden. *Go For It! A Book on Sport and Recreation for Persons with Disabilities.* Orlando, FL: Harcourt Brace Jovanovich, 1989; Paciorek, Michael J., and Jeffery A. Jones. *Sports and Recreation for the Disabled,* 2nd ed. Carmel, IN: Cooper Publishing Group, 1994; "Sports and Leisure: Boccia." *United Cerebral Palsy Association,* http://www.ucpa.org/ucp_channeldoc.cfm/1/15/11383/11383–11383/2819; "Sports: Boccia." *International Paralympic Committee,* http://www.paralympic.org/sports/sections/bo.asp.

BOCCIA RAMP Ramps and chutes are adaptations to the game of boccia that allow individuals with more significant disability the opportunity to play, and are used only by class BC3 players. The ramp or chute allows a player who can't manually release the ball to put the ball in play during a match.

When using a ramp, the athlete is allowed to use an assistant to help position the ball. The assistant sits facing the athlete so they can't view the playing field and they follow the athlete's directions.

Rules regarding the materials used and dimension of ramps and chutes can be found in the International Paralympic Committee (IPC) boccia rules. They are often made of plastic or aluminum pipe, and some have a swivel base to allow players to adjust the direction of the ramp independently.

See also Boccia

BIBLIOGRAPHY. "Sports and Leisure: Boccia." *United Cerebral Palsy Association,* http://www.ucpa.org/ucp_channeldoc.cfm/1/15/11383/11383–11383/2819; "Sports: Boccia." *International Paralympic Committee,* http://www.paralympic.org/sports/sections/bo.asp.

BOWLING RAMP Bowling is a sport that almost anyone can play thanks to assistive devices available on the market. Wheelchair users and others with limited upper body strength or mobility can bowl using an assistive device called a bowling ramp. A bowling ramp can be made of wood or metal and is commercially available or can be homemade. It allows bowlers who can't physically lift or propel a bowling ball the opportunity to bowl alongside anyone else.

Bowlers who use a ramp can propel the ball down the ramp a few ways. Some bowlers push the ball down the ramp themselves once it is placed there by an assistant. Others with limited hand function or arm strength can use a headstick, a remote control device, or even their feet to propel the ball down the ramp.

If a bowler wants to build their own ramp, some considerations are its portability and whether it will be easy to transport and set up. In addition, cost may be a factor for the bowler who wants to buy a commercially available ramp.

There are recreational opportunities for bowlers nationwide. Or, they can participate at a higher level in competitions held by the National Disability Sports Alliance, Special Olympics, or the ramp/chute division of the American Wheelchair Bowling Association.

BIBLIOGRAPHY. National Disability Sports Alliance, http://www.ndsaonline.org; Paciorek, Michael J., and Jeffery A. Jones. *Sports and Recreation for the Disabled,* 2nd ed. Carmel, IN: Cooper Publishing Group, 1994; Special Olympics International, http://www.specialolympics.org.

BOWLING STICK Bowling sticks are another example of an assistive device available to aid bowlers with limited strength, balance, or hand function. Bowling sticks are similar in design to shuffleboard sticks, and the bowler uses them to push the ball forward down the lane after it is placed on the ground by an assistant. In order to use a bowling stick, the bowler has to be able to independently grasp the stick, though this can be accomplished with the use of a cuff or other grip assistance if the individual doesn't have sufficient hand function.

See also American Wheelchair Bowling Association (AWBA)

BIBLIOGRAPHY. Crase, Nancy. "Wheelchair Specialized Bowling Equipment." *Sports 'n' Spokes* 1, no. 3 (1975): 16–17; Nunnekamp, B. "Bowling from a Wheelchair." *Sports 'n' Spokes* (February–March 1976): 17–19.

BOWMAN, DANA Dana Bowman is the first amputee member of the U.S. Army's elite skydiving team, the Golden Knights. During a career that has spanned more than 1,500 jumps, Bowman was injured in a midair collision in 1994 when he and his partner, Jose Aguillon, collided during a routine training exercise in Yuma, Arizona. They were practicing the Diamond Track, a maneuver they had done hundreds of times before, but this time, instead of crossing each other midair, they ended up slamming into each other. Aguillon died instantly, and Bowman's legs were sheared off, one above and one below the knee.

While undergoing rehabilitation for the injury, Bowman petitioned for and was granted permission to re-enlist in the Army and rejoin the Golden Knights. Bowman then retired from the Army in 1996, the same year he parachuted into the opening ceremonies of the Atlanta Paralympic Games.

Bowman continued his education after retiring from the Army, receiving a Bachelor's degree in commercial aviation from the University of North Dakota. Along with furthering his education, Bowman continues to jump, adding a delivery of the game ball into a Monday Night Football game between Houston and New York in 2002 to his long list of credits.

Bowman spends much of his time flying and teaching others how to fly. When he's not in the air, Bowman and fellow amputee athlete John Siciliano, work with their foundation, the Bowman Siciliano Limb Bank Foundation. Through the Foundation, they provide prosthetics and orthotics to individuals who need them, both in the United States and in developing nations worldwide.

BIBLIOGRAPHY. Dana Bowman, http://www.danabowman.com.

BOY SCOUTS OF AMERICA (SCOUTS WITH

DISABILITIES AND SPECIAL NEEDS) Since it's founding in 1910, the Boy Scouts of America (BSA) has involved scouts having physical, mental, and emotional disabilities—not too surprising, since Dr. James E. West, the first Chief Scout Executive, had a disability himself. Boy Scouts with visual impairments can access the Boy Scout Handbook in Braille, and merit badge pamphlets on audiotape. Recently, closed-captioned training videos were developed for hearing impaired Scouts as well.

The program for Scouts with Disabilities and Special Needs helps unit leaders develop an awareness and understanding of disability and integrates those with and without disabilities into the same activities. While there are some packs and troops made up of all visually impaired or all hearing impaired individuals, those groups are encouraged to participate in scouting activities at all levels from district to national.

Additionally, BSA created a disability awareness trail at the Scout Jamboree in 1977 to help other Scouts learn about issues faced by Scouts and others with disabilities. It was so successful it is used by local troops and still continues to be featured at the Scout Jamboree. To encourage learning, BSA has created an interpreter strip for Signing for the Deaf as well as a Disabilities Awareness Merit Badge.

BIBLIOGRAPHY. Boy Scouts of America, "Scouts with Disabilities and Special Needs Fact Sheet," http://www.scouting.org/nav/enter.jsp?s=mc&c=fs.

BRECKENRIDGE OUTDOOR EDUCATION CENTER (BOEC) The Breckenridge Outdoor Education Center (BOEC) began in 1976, and in the last 30 years it has grown to be one of the most respected outdoor education programs for people with disabilities. The BOEC got its start when Olav Pedersen together with colleague Erling Stordahl, both well-known as instructors of visually impaired skiers in Norway, created a U.S. version of Norway's own "Knight's Race," a Nordic skiing event for people who were blind or visually impaired. Pedersen and Stordahl brought a group of visually impaired skiers from Norway to the United States in 1975 for the event, and the first Ski for Light was held, ultimately leading to the formation of the BOEC.

The volunteers from that first Ski for Light stayed loosely organized over the next months and decided to offer outdoor activities for people with disabilities that next summer. A few years later, the BOEC incorporated as a nonprofit, but still relied solely on volunteers to run the programs. Gene Dayton and Bob Burwick, two volunteers from the first Ski for Light program became the first official Course Directors for the BOEC, coordinating activities such as cross-country skiing and sledding in the winter, and backpacking, camping, and canoeing in the summer.

In the early 1980s the BOEC offered only cross-country skiing for people with disabilities, as alpine skis for people with disabilities had yet to be developed. The adaptive ski instructors, however, started offering a version of Alpine skiing to participants, towing skiers with disabilities up ski runs on sleds, which they would then ski down a few hundred yards at a time. Within a couple of years, the Arroya sled for Alpine skiing was produced and made commercially available. The BOEC staff and volunteers worked on chair lift procedure and adaptive ski techniques, creating a program to bring the ski resorts.

The Breckenridge Ski Area was the first to offer the adapted ski program, leading to a period of explosive growth in Alpine skiing for people with disabilities. In the mid-1980s, the BOEC began organizing and hosting disabled ski competitions. The most notable of these early competitions was the 1985 National Handicap Ski Championship where the first prototype mono-ski was tested.

Today, the Breckenridge Outdoor Education Center (BOEC) offers adaptive skiing, snowboarding, and wilderness courses. The wilderness courses include activities such as rock climbing, canoeing, backpacking and hiking, whitewater rafting, high ropes courses, camping, skiing, sea kayaking, orienteering, and fishing.

BIBLIOGRAPHY. Breckenridge Outdoor Education Center, http://www.boec.org/.

BUCKMASTERS QUADRIPLEGIC HUNTERS ASSOCIATION (BQHA) The Buckmasters Quadriplegic Hunters Association (BQHA) helps disabled hunters return to or experience for the first time, an active outdoor lifestyle. A branch of the Buckmasters American Deer Foundation, the BQHA has provided assistance to people with a wide array of disabilities, including cancer survivors, amputees, and people with spinal cord injuries, among others.

Whether a hunter wants to hunt deer, bear, moose, or wild boar, the BQHA has the resources to help. They developed a video titled "Solutions for Adaptive Shooting," which helps the disabled shooter learn about available technologies. They also pair experienced hunters with disabilities with those who are newly disabled through the program Special Partners, which helps the new hunter determine which adaptive equipment and hunting techniques best meet their needs.

The BQHA also works with outfitters to help them modify their lodges, campsites, and hunting areas to make them accessible to hunters with disabilities.

BIBLIOGRAPHY. Buckmasters American Deer Foundation, http://www.badf.org/.

CABLE, CANDACE Candace Cable is one of the pioneers for women in disabled sport, with numerous medals and records to her credit from a career spanning nearly 30 years. Cable was born on July 15, 1954, in Glendale, California. As a child, she participated in many sports, including track and field, surfing, and skiing. She graduated high school in 1972 and moved to Lake Tahoe to pursue competitive downhill skiing, but her plans were derailed when Cable sustained a spinal cord injury in a car accident three years later.

Cable underwent rehabilitation at the Rancho Los Amigos Hospital in California, and then attended Cal State University, majoring in Physical Education. She knew she wanted to be active again, and she wanted to help others with disabilities learn about sports and recreation possibilities open to them.

Cable competed in swimming at her first disabled sports competition, the National Wheelchair Games in New York in 1979. The next year, wheelchair track and road racing became her passion, and Cable, along with others such as Sharon Hedrick, paved the way for generations of wheelchair athletes to come.

Cable has not only won more than 50 marathons during her career, but she has held world records at multiple distances, including the 4 × 100 relay which she won alongside teammates Ann Cody, Carol Hetherington, and Sharon Hedrick at the Barcelona Paralympics in 1992. Cable was one of the first women with a disability to compete in the Olympic Games, and she received bronze medals in the Olympic 800 meter wheelchair races in Los Angeles in 1984 and Seoul in 1988.

Cable returned to skiing in 1988. Two years later, in her first world competition, she was fourth in giant slalom and sixth in slalom. At the Paralympics in Albertville, France in 1992, she medaled in three events winning one silver and two bronze medals for the United States. In 1993, Cable switched to cross-country skiing, representing the United States in every Paralympics since.

BIBLIOGRAPHY. Against the Wind: Candace Cable, http://www.will.uiuc.edu; *Candace Cable.* http://www.candacecable.com; The Deak Group—Candace Cable, http://www.deakgroup.com/candacecable.html.

CAMBER Camber refers to the inward or outward tilt of a tire or wheel assembly on a wheelchair. The angle is measured from a vertical line; therefore, a wheel that is exactly perpendicular to the ground is said to have zero camber. If it is tilted outward at the top, it is said to have positive camber, and if it is tilted inward at the top, it has negative camber.

Camber is a term that refers to all wheels, not just wheelchair wheels. For purposes of wheelchairs, however, the degree of camber in the wheels helps determine the stability, handling, turning, and cornering ability of the chair.

For an everyday chair, a small degree of camber might be appropriate. This is because for everyday purposes, the individual wheelchair user probably isn't going to be going very fast or turning quickly. Additionally, a wheelchair with a smaller degree of camber will more easily fit through narrow doorways and in tight spaces. In a sport specific chair, however, a high degree of camber may be appropriate, such as the high degree of camber in most tennis wheelchairs, which assists the user to turn smoothly and swiftly without tipping over.

Some wheelchairs have adjustable camber bars, which enable the user to quickly interchange between 0 and 12 degrees or somewhere in between. Wheelchairs with fixed camber don't allow for adjustment; therefore, the angle desired must be specified when the chair is being built. Though a larger degree of camber is more common in sports wheelchairs than in everyday wheelchairs, there are benefits to having more camber in an everyday chair.

For example, a wider camber angle may increase the lateral stability of the chair for people with limited trunk balance. It will also put the pushrims in a more ergonomically sound position and protect the hands from crashing into walls and doors. The degree of camber in the wheelchair is determined by personal preference and trial and error over time. For the novice wheelchair user, a good seating and positioning expert can help set up the best position.

BIBLIOGRAPHY. Smith, Mark E. "Get it Straight: A Wheelchair Junkie's Guide to Sports Chair Alignment," http://www.wheelchairjunkie.com/alignment.html.

CEREBRAL PALSY Cerebral palsy is one of the many disability categories that athletes who compete in disability sport and recreation may have. Cerebral palsy is loosely defined as disordered movement or posture caused by damage to certain areas of the brain. Cerebral palsy, or CP as it is called, is a nonprogressive, nonfatal disability caused generally by damage to the motor control areas of the brain. It is commonly thought that this damage can occur before, during, or soon after birth, though some cerebral palsy has been caused by high fevers and similar conditions.

Cerebral palsy comes in three forms: spastic, athetoid, and ataxic. Spastic cerebral palsy means damage has occurred in the cerebrum, causing stiff muscles and restricted movement. Muscles are hypertonic, or spastic. Athetoid cerebral palsy occurs when there is damage to the basal ganglia, resulting in uncontrollable movement. Ataxic cerebral palsy occurs with damage to the cerebellum, causing unbalanced movement with fluctuating muscle tone.

Athletes with cerebral palsy compete in a wide variety of sports, many without any special adaptation. However, technology has assisted many other individuals with cerebral palsy to participate in sports and recreation through the creation of adaptive devices such as bowling ramps, head sticks, and starter pistols with a visual signal.

BIBLIOGRAPHY. Steadward, Robert Daniel, E. J. Watkinson, and Garry David Wheeler. *Adapted Physical Activity.* Edmonton: University of Alberta Press, 2003.

CEREBRAL PALSY INTERNATIONAL SPORTS AND RECREATION ASSOCIA-TION (CP-ISRA) CP-ISRA, the Cerebral Palsy International Sport and Recreation Association, is widely recognized as the world leader on sports and recreation for people with cerebral palsy. It began as the International Cerebral Palsy Society, which was first responsible for organizing sports and recreation activities for people with cerebral palsy. The Society put together the first organized competition for athletes with cerebral palsy in France in 1968.

Athletes with cerebral palsy were then served under the International Sports Organization for the Disabled (ISOD) in combination with athletes who were visually impaired or amputees. As the movement grew, each disability group formed its own organization to govern sports and recreation for its particular members. CP-ISRA was founded during this movement by Archibald Cameron in 1978. Today there are 60 member nations representing thousands of athletes with cerebral palsy worldwide who compete in athletics, boccia, bowls, cycling, powerlifting, race runner, soccer, swimming, table tennis, and winter sports.

CP-ISRA was one of the founding members of the International Coordinating Council (ICC). CP-ISRA was also a founding member of the International Paralympic Committee (IPC), now the international body which oversees all Paralympic sport competition around the globe. CP-ISRA was behind athletes with cerebral palsy in their first appearance at the Paralympic Games, which took place at the 1980 Games in Arnhem, Holland. They have been involved in developing athletes with cerebral palsy to compete in every Paralympic Games and other regional and world competitions since.

Athletes with cerebral palsy compete in track at the Paralympic Games. *Copyright Chris Hamilton Photography.*

CHAFEE, ELLA

CP-ISRA, like the other disability specific organizations, has held its own world championships for athletes with cerebral palsy in addition to those put forth by the IPC. The Robinhood Games, as they were known, were usually staged in England. They have grown exponentially over time, from a primarily European regional game to a truly international championship, which most recently saw 1,000 athletes from 33 nations converge on New London, Connecticut to contest 10 sports—bowls, boccia, cycling, soccer, athletics, pentathlon, powerlifting, table tennis, swimming, and slalom. In those championships, 32 world records were set, 20 on the track, 7 in swimming, and 5 in powerlifting.

BIBLIOGRAPHY. Cerebral Palsy International Sports and Recreation Association, http://www.cpisra.org/; Steadward, Robert Daniel, E. J. Watkinson, and Garry David Wheeler. *Adapted Physical Activity.* Edmonton: University of Alberta Press, 2003.

CHAFEE, ELLA Ella Chafee is one of the pioneers in women's wheelchair sport. She has been competing in sports for people with disabilities for nearly 40 years, with over 20 of those years spent playing for the Rehabilitation Institute of Chicago Express women's wheelchair basketball team.

Chafee's sporting career began with her days at college at the University of Illinois in Urbana-Champaign where she was one of the first members of the Ms. Kids (now the Fightin' Illini) women's wheelchair basketball team.

Ella Chafee (center) at the Opening Ceremonies of the 1996 Paralympic Games. *Photo courtesy of Rehabilitation Institute of Chicago Wirtz Sports Program.*

Chafee was also one of only five women who qualified to race in the wheelchair division of the 1979 Boston Marathon, finishing 20th overall. Chafee didn't have one of the new, ultra light racing wheelchairs back then, either. Instead, she and the other racers competed in their everyday wheelchairs, which weighed upwards of 50 pounds. Chafee has qualified for and competed in 25 National Wheelchair Games, the only female athlete to achieve this distinction.

Chafee's long list of sporting achievements includes over 100 Gold, silver, and bronze medals in international competition in swimming, track and field, archery, basketball, and fencing. Most recently, Chafee had the distinction of being the oldest female athlete to qualify for the 1996 U.S. Paralympic team in fencing, where she competed in women's foil and epee, finishing 8th in foil.

Chafee cofounded many different women's wheelchair basketball teams in the Chicago area, including the Windy City Spitfires, the Chicago Charmers, and the RIC Express. Chafee's many years of dedication to the RIC Express paid off in 2005, when for the first time in the team's history, they won the National Women's Wheelchair Basketball Tournament.

Off the field, Chafee has been involved as a guest lecturer for Project C.H.A.N.G.E., a federally sponsored program to eliminate stereotypes concerning people with disabilities.

BIBLIOGRAPHY. Center for Health and Fitness—Sports Talk, http://www.richealthfit.org/paralympic%20history/paralympichistorymain.htm; *Sports 'n' Spokes* (January–February 1991): 23.

CLASSIFICATION SYSTEMS Classification is a way of grouping athletes together to ensure a fair and equitable competition. In sports such as powerlifting, judo, and wrestling classification by weight is routine. The athlete makes weight, or they don't. In road races, participants are grouped by age. The runner either fits the age group, or they don't. Classification in disability sport is different and much less exact.

The first role of classification systems in disability sport is to screen out those who are not eligible, such as those who do not have a disability or those who do not meet the criteria for the particular disability. For example, a person with some visual impairment that doesn't meet the definition of legal blindness will not be eligible to compete in sport for blind individuals.

Once a person is determined eligible, classification is used to slot the athlete into the particular grouping in which they will compete. Classification systems in disability sport may be based on one or all of the following: the nature and severity of the athlete's disability, their functional ability to perform sport specific skills, and their prior performances.

There are three major systems used to classify athletes with disabilities: (1) disability specific, (2) functional, and (3) performance based. The disability-specific classification system was the disability sport movement's first attempt at classifying. In this system, athletes are categorized solely based on their disability category, taking into account the nature and severity of the disability and classified accordingly. For example, an athlete with cerebral palsy who uses a wheelchair is classified differently than an athlete who walks with crutches. And, an athlete with a spinal cord injury at the C5 level is classified differently than an athlete with a T10 level injury. This system is based on the premise that competition is most equitable among those with similar disabilities and similar levels of function within that disability category. Thus, the information obtained from a medical doctor regarding the particular disability diagnosis the individual has is given great weight in this system.

Classification based on functional ability to perform sport specific skills, on the other hand, gives less weight to a particular disability category and more weight to the functional limitations imposed by the disability. Functional classification was first developed and tested for wheelchair basketball by Dr. Horst Strohkendl, a professor in Germany, who tested it on athletes at the 1983 Wheelchair Basketball Gold Cup in Halifax, Nova Scotia.

Functional classification systems are created by observing sports and analyzing them to determine what muscle groups are used to perform an activity, and the differences in function between athletes who have that muscle and those who don't. Additionally, the functional system is now being expanded to consider sensory disabilities and the functional limitations imposed by particular levels of vision loss.

Classifying an athlete in the functional system involves a muscle test, measuring the strength of the affected muscles, and a coordination test, analyzing the effect of the disability on coordination. The athlete may then be asked to demonstrate techniques used during the sport, such as pushing a racing wheelchair, dribbling a basketball, or performing a swimming stroke. The athlete may also be observed on the field of play during an actual competition.

The third category of classification systems, performance-based systems, are primarily used in Special Olympics competition. There, athletes are grouped according to recent past performance times or measures. An important point to remember is that these systems are not mutually exclusive, and classification systems may contain some elements of all three.

No matter which system is used, meaningful classification must be conducted by trained and qualified classifiers. In the disability-specific system, classifiers must have relevant medical experience, education, and training in order to assess such criteria as vision loss, level of spinal injury, residual limb length, or neurological deficit. In functional classification, classifiers must have some medical or disability-specific knowledge, but they must also be expert in the particular sport in question.

Each system of classification has its own challenges and considerations. For example, proponents of the disability specific classification system argue that it is the most fair, because athletes with similar disabilities compete against each other. Proponents of the functional classification system, on the other hand, argue that considering only a medical diagnosis without taking into account the specific skills needed to perform a sport results in unfair classification.

No matter which system is used, several considerations need to be addressed. Does the classification system measure the factors that are associated with performance in the particular sport? Do the tests accurately measure the factors they are supposed to measure? What effect does training and conditioning have on the athlete's classification? Do available accommodations or the lack of accommodations affect the classification? Are the tests applied in settings that allow the results to be extrapolated to the competitive setting? Are the criteria objective enough so that a trained classifier can understand and implement them?

Classification is an inexact science, to be sure. While no system has yet proven perfect, disability sport professionals, researchers, and medical personnel continue to work to develop a system that ensures fair and equitable competition for all athletes with disabilities.

BIBLIOGRAPHY. "Classification Issues," http://edweb6.educ.msu.edu/kin866/cfissues.htm; "Functional Classification Systems." *Sports 'n' Spokes* (July 1991): 46–47; Kelley, Jerry D., and Lex Frieden. *Go For It! A Book on Sport and Recreation for Persons with Disabilities.* Orlando, FL: Harcourt Brace Jovanovich, 1989.

ADDITIONAL READING. Brasile, Frank, and Brad Hedrick. "The Relationship of Skills of Elite Wheelchair Basketball Competitors to the International Functional Classification System." *Therapeutic Recreation Journal* 30 (2000): 114–127; Dummer, Gail. "Classification in Disability Sport: Assessment Issues." *Palaestra* (Winter 1999): 58–59; Ferrara, M., and R. Davis. "Athlete Classification: An Explanation of the Process." *Palaestra* (Spring 1996): 38–44; Williamson, D. "Principles of Classification in Competitive Sport for Participants with Disabilities: A Proposal." *Palaestra* (Spring 1997): 44–48.

CODY, ANN Ann Cody always knew that she wanted to be an athlete. Growing up, she loved to play, first venturing into the world of organized sports at age 10 when she joined a softball team. Next she learned to ski, and she played volleyball, basketball, and field hockey. She began to think that she could compete at the collegiate level, and maybe even beyond.

That all changed, however, on December 16, 1979, when she awoke with pain unlike any she had ever experienced. Thinking she was just catching a bug, she took some aspirin and went back to bed. Within 12 hours, she was in the hospital fighting for her life. Transverse myelitis, a potentially deadly virus, had attacked her spinal cord, leaving her paralyzed. Devastated, she believed that pursuit of her athletic goals was no longer possible.

A discovery she made while in rehab, however, set the course for her life, though she didn't realize it at the time. It was there that she heard for the first time about the Paralympic Games, elite competition for athletes with disabilities, to be held in Holland in 1980. She had never heard of competitive sport for people with disabilities before, and she was intrigued by the possibilities. She began doing research and discovered that the University of Illinois had a groundbreaking and world renowned program for individuals with disabilities, including a disabled sports program.

Cody visited the campus in 1981 and fell in love with the school and the people. She started as a freshman in the fall of that year, and lived in the dorms next door to then fellow student Marty Morse, who would have a profound impact on her life.

Cody immediately got into the sports program, playing basketball with the then relatively new Ms. Kids women's wheelchair basketball team. When she wasn't practicing basketball, she could be found at the pool or at the wheelchair football practice. The men's and women's wheelchair basketball teams trained side by side, and it was Marty Morse who encouraged Cody to try the sport that would bring her international acclaim—track and road racing.

In her career, Cody represented the United States three times at the Paralympics, first in 1984, as a member of the U.S. women's wheelchair basketball team. Then in 1988 and

CODY, ANN

Ann Cody in Barcelona, 1992. *Copyright Chris Hamilton Photography.*

1992, she won Gold, four silvers, and a bronze as a member of the U.S. wheelchair track team. Cody held world records in multiple distances, including the 1500, 3,000, and 10,000 meters as well as the 4 by 100 meter relay. Cody also had the honor of representing the United States in the 800 meter wheelchair race at the 1988 Olympics in Seoul. Just to show the world that no distance was beyond her mastery, she also conquered the Boston Marathon, completing it in a personal best time in 1986, and coming in a close second four years later to multiple Boston winner and training partner Jean Driscoll.

Proving that she was just as capable off the field as on, Cody first earned a Bachelor of Fine Arts from the University of Illinois, initially planning to pursue a career in the arts. Her sports experience, however, convinced her to switch paths, and she followed that up with a Masters degree in Therapeutic Recreation. She worked for a time at world renowned Shepherd Spinal Center in Atlanta as a therapeutic recreation specialist, and then went on to the Atlanta Paralympics Organizing Committee, developing operating plans for 4 of the 16 events at the 1996 Games. Combining her love of sport with her exceptional advocacy skills, Cody now works for governmental relations firm B&D Consulting in Washington, D.C., as part of their health care and disability practice teams, providing planning, advocacy, and governmental affairs services in the areas of amateur sports, health, and disability.

Cody has also provided leadership to the disability sport movement, serving as the Chair of the International Paralympic Committee Commission on Women and Sport, as well as on the Women's Sports Foundation Committee on Sport for Women with Disabilities and the Marketing Committee of the International Wheelchair Basketball Association. Recently, Cody was named to the IOC Women and Sport Commission and elected to the IPC governing board.

BIBLIOGRAPHY. Against the Wind, http://will.uiuc.edu/tv/documentaries/atw/atwcody.html; Apple, Jr., David F. *Physical Fitness: A Guide for Individuals with Spinal Cord Injury*. Washington, DC: Department of Veteran's Affairs, Rehabilitation Research and Development Service, 1995; B&D Consulting LLC: Ann Cody, http://www.bakerdconsulting.com/professionals/bio.cfm?id=376; Now Foundation Women with Disabilities and Allies Forum: Speakers, http://www.nowfoundation.org/issues/disability/forum2003/speakers.html#cody; The Paralympic Newsletter 3/2002, http://paralympic.org/paralympian/20023/2002323.htm; RRDS Physical Fitness: A Guide for Individuals with Spinal Cord Injury, http://vard.org/mono/sci/scicody.htm; Steadward, Robert Daniel, E. J. Watkinson, and Garry David Wheeler. *Adapted Physical Activity*. Edmonton: University of Alberta Press, 2003.

COMMITTEE ON SPORTS FOR THE DISABLED (COSD) The Committee on Sports for the Disabled was developed by the U.S. Olympic Committee (USOC) in 1979 after passage of Public Law 95–606 (now the "Ted Stevens Olympic and Amateur Sports Act"). It was a standing committee of the USOC providing policy and procedural recommendations to the USOC Board of Directors relating to provision of services for athletes with disabilities. The COSD also provided guidance, recommended and developed policy for, and served as a representative voice within the USOC for the Disabled Sports Organization (DSO) members.

The COSD was charged with working with the National Governing Bodies (NGBs) and DSOs to involve amateur athletes with disabilities in sports programs for able-bodied athletes. For example, the COSD was instrumental in getting demonstration events for athletes with disabilities added to the summer and winter Olympics beginning in 1984, giving both the athletes and the disability sport movement added visibility and prestige. In the 1984 Olympics in Los Angeles, a women's 800 m wheelchair race and a men's 1,500 m wheelchair race were held for the first time. In subsequent Olympic Games, 1988 in Seoul, 1992 in Barcelona, 1996 in Atlanta, 2000 in Sydney, and 2004 in Athens, these events have been contested.

Additionally, the COSD, together with the former USOC Disabled Sports Services Department, was responsible for providing information on performance analysis, physical training, equipment designs, and coaching for individuals with disabilities.

In May 2001, the COSD as well as USOC Disabled Sports Services were dissolved during reorganization at the USOC. Those functions were assumed by the U.S. Paralympics, a new division of the USOC.

BIBLIOGRAPHY. Disabled Sports Services Division. *Technical Manual.* United States Olympic Committee, 1999.

COURAGE CENTER Courage Center is a nonprofit organization in Minnesota that serves over 16,000 people with disabilities annually. They offer a variety of therapeutic and recreational services, including aquatic programs such as fibromyalgia exercise class, multiple sclerosis water exercise, and a water exercise program for people who have had a stroke.

They have both competitive and recreational sports for children and adults, including archery, wheelchair basketball, boating, bowling, canoeing, competitive swimming, electric wheelchair hockey, fishing, hockey, kayaking, martial arts, quad rugby, sailing, downhill skiing, softball, tennis, track and field, trapshooting, and waterskiing. Their women's wheelchair basketball team won numerous national championships in the 1990s and many of their athletes have achieved national and international acclaim.

They also provide youngsters the chance to learn about the wide range of adapted sports and recreation available to them through a week-long youth camp. Recent additions to Courage Center programming include a goal ball team and a sled hockey program, handcycling, air guns, table tennis, and weightlifting.

BIBLIOGRAPHY. Courage Center. http://www.courage.org/.

CRASE, CLIFF Cliff Crase turned the Wheelchair Sports Hall of Fame from a list of names in a book into a permanent exhibit in Warm Springs, GA. The U.S. Air Force veteran and wheelchair user himself worked tirelessly over the years to induct scores of individuals into the Hall, yet they had nowhere to truly honor these individuals who had served the wheelchair sports movement so well.

After the Roosevelt Warm Springs Institute for Rehabilitation opened in Georgia, Crase worked with them to create a permanent exhibition. Warm Springs is now home to the Hall, where its inductees' photographs and biographies line the walls for all who visit there to see.

Crase chaired the committee for Wheelchair Sports, USA's Wheelchair Sports Hall of Fame for 28 years, beginning in 1976, spending much of his life involved in the disability sport movement. Though he retired as chair of that committee, he is still editor and publisher of both *Sports 'n' Spokes* and *Paraplegia News* magazines which provide news and information to people with disabilities nationwide about sports, recreation, advocacy, and other issues of interest.

Crase has received many honors for his contributions to the disability sport movement. He was inducted into the National Wheelchair Basketball Association Hall of Fame for his promotion of wheelchair basketball through sports columns in both *Sports 'n' Spokes* and *Paraplegia News,* as well as for his introduction of the Top 20 feature in *Sports 'n' Spokes* which ranks wheelchair basketball teams across the country.

BIBLIOGRAPHY. National Recreation and Parks Association, http://www.nrpa.org/content/default.aspx?documentId=877; "Newsroom." Paralyzed Veteran's Administration, http://www.pva.org/newsroom/FeaturesArchive/2004/f04006.htm; *Sports 'n' Spokes* (May–June 1989): 37.

CROSSBOW The crossbow is a device that can be used to enable people with disabilities to shoot archery or to hunt. It can be adapted for sip and puff technology, enabling even those with disabilities that limit their upper body strength, mobility, or dexterity to use. They can be adapted for use with a finger, a chin, or virtually any other body part that an individual still has control over.

There is an ongoing debate as to whether the crossbow should be allowed for hunting. Opponents argue that it is too efficient, and that it gives the hunter an advantage because they can hold their draw longer. Proponents, on the other hand, argue that people with disabilities are able to hunt because of the crossbow, and that it enables many people who otherwise would be unable to hunt to do so. As a result, allowing hunting with the crossbow opens the sport up to many more than might otherwise participate.

Many states offer an exemption for a hunter with a disability to use a crossbow; a special application permit and a fee are usually all that's required.

BIBLIOGRAPHY. Bow and Crossbow Rigs for the Disabled, http://residents.bowhunting.net/DisabledHunters/dis-hunters-bows2.html; Chastain, Russ. "A Question of Crossbows," http://hunting.about.com/library/weekly/aa020716c.htm; Converted Crossbow-Archery Solutions for People with Physical Disabilities, http://www.visi.com/~bluff/crossbow/about.htm.

CROSS-COUNTRY SKIING (NORDIC SKIING). *See* Skiing

CRUTCH RACING Crutch racing is another name for track and field events that certain individuals with cerebral palsy compete in. Class 5 cerebral palsy athletes generally use crutches or another assistive device to help them ambulate during competition. The most popular choice of assistive device is the forearm or Canadian crutch.

BIBLIOGRAPHY. National Disability Sports Alliance, http://www.ndsaonline.org; Paciorek, Michael J., and Jeffery A. Jones. *Sports and Recreation for the Disabled,* 2nd ed. Carmel, IN: Cooper Publishing Group, 1994.

CYCLING Cycling was first introduced as a Paralympic sport for athletes with cerebral palsy in 1984 in Stoke-Mandeville, England. It was expanded to include athletes who are blind or visually impaired in tandem cycling as well as amputee athletes in Barcelona in 1992, and most recently, a handcycle division for athletes who are wheelchair users was introduced in Athens in 2004.

Cyclists compete both on the road and on the velodrome or track. Distances range from 200 meters to 4 kilometers on the track, and 5 to 35 km road races.

For tandem riders, there is a sprint where two tandem teams compete over a distance of 1 km, an individual pursuit of 4 km for men's teams and 3 km for women and mixed teams, a 1 km time trial for men and mixed teams, and a 500 km time trial for women. Road races for men competing in tandem cycling can be as long as 100 to 135 km, and between 50 and 75 km for women.

CP sports offers both tricycle and bicycle events. Division 1 is for classes CP1–CP4, and the riders compete on tricycles. Division 2 is for CP 5 and 6, and these athletes also compete on a tricycle, primarily because they lack the balance to ride a two-wheeler. Division 3 is made of classes CP 5 and 6 who have the balance to compete on a bicycle. Division 4 is for classes CP 7 and 8, who also compete on bicycles.

For athletes with cerebral palsy, both track and road race events are available. For road races, division 4 cyclists compete at distances of 35 to 70 km. Division 3 competes at 15–70 km distances. Divisions 1 and 2 compete from 15 to 30 km. Track events are offered only for Division 3 and 4 athletes, including a standing start kilometer time trial, individual pursuit, and sprint competition.

Tandem cyclists go for the Gold. *Copyright Chris Hamilton Photography.*

CYCLING

For visually impaired cyclists, tandem cycling is offered. Other than having a sighted pilot, no real adaptation is required. Communication between the sighted pilot and the visually impaired cyclist, the "stoker," is crucial; because long hours are spent training together, a good relationship is an important factor to success. Competitors in tandem cycling are classified according to their level of vision, as a B1, B2, B3, and B4.

Cycling for amputee athletes is classified according to whether the athlete has an upper or lower limb amputation. Athletes ride with and without prostheses. Individuals who have very short residual limbs may choose not to use one; however, many athletes find that using one aids strength building and circulation in the residual limb. Balance is, of course, critical to the amputee athlete, as is a proper fitting bike.

Handcycling has been recently introduced to the international stage, for athletes who use wheelchairs or have other mobility impairments, making its Paralympic debut at Athens in 2004.

BIBLIOGRAPHY. "Cycling Tips for Leg Amputees." *Active Living.* http://www.activeliving-magazine.com/artman/publish/printer_68.shtml; National Disability Sports Alliance, http://www.ndsaonline.org; Paciorek, Michael J., and Jeffery A. Jones. *Sports and Recreation for the Disabled,* 2nd ed. Carmel, IN: Cooper Publishing Group, 1994; "Sports: Cycling." *Cerebral Palsy International Sports and Recreation Association.* http://www.cpisra.org/sports_cpisra_cycling.htm; "Sports Adaptations—Cycling." *United States Association of Blind Athletes.* http://www.usaba.org/Pages/sportsinformation/adaptations/cyclingadapt.html.

DANCING WHEELS Dancing Wheels is one of the first dance companies in the nation to integrate dancers with and without disabilities. It was created in 1980 by Mary Verdi-Fletcher, a woman who had spina bifida in 1980. Verdi-Fletcher's love of dance led to the formation of Dancing Wheels, which integrates both standing and wheeling dancers.

Dancing Wheels operates in a fully wheelchair accessible studio and offers dance classes and workshops, theater arts camps, teacher training workshops, and other specialized classes. They have inspired people with disabilities and other dance companies alike with performances around the world, including a tour to Prague, Czech Republic. They've represented the United States with performances at the International Very Special Arts Festival in Brussels and in Los Angeles, and they opened the first National Conference on Careers in the Arts for People with Disabilities at the Kennedy Center.

BIBLIOGRAPHY. Dancing Wheels, http://www.dancingwheels.org.

DEAFLYMPICS The Deaflympics, formerly World Games for the Deaf, began in Paris, France in 1924 as the International Silent Games. Prior to 1924, there were very few national federations providing sporting competitions for deaf people. France took the lead and spurred the creation of six other national federations. Together, these countries participated in the first International Silent Games. The inaugural games featured athletics, cycling, football, shooting, and swimming.

After the success of the games, an organization was created to oversee future competitions. It was called the Comité International des Sports des Sourds (CISS), or the International Committee of Sports for the Deaf. The CISS was made up entirely of European nations, until the United States joined in 1935, closely followed by Japan.

Initially, the CISS only organized summer games, which were held every four years. It wasn't until 1949, when Seefeld, Austria played host, that the first winter games were held. The games didn't move outside Europe until 1965, when they were held in Washington, D.C.

In 1961 and again in 1969, the committee changed the name of the competition. It became the World Games of the Deaf. This title remained until 2001, when the organizing committee voted to change the name to Deaflympics.

The Deaflympics are now held every other year, cycling one year after each Olympic and Paralympic Games. Like the Olympics and Paralympics, they alternate between winter and summer games. The summer games have grown from their inauspicious beginnings to a major event, with the 2005 Deaflympics in Melbourne hosting 3,000 athletes from 75 nations. The winter games have also blossomed, from the first competition in 1949, where 33 athletes from 5 nations competed, to 2003, where 253 athletes from 22 nations competed. An even larger number of athletes are expected for the 2007 Deaflympics in Salt Lake City.

BIBLIOGRAPHY. Deaflympics, http://www.deaflympics.com; National Association of the Deaf: USOC Deaflympics Letter, http://www.nad.org/sitepp.asp?c=foINKQMBF&b=17949.

DEMBY, BILL Bill Demby dreamed of playing basketball, but when he was injured in the war he thought it would never happen. Demby was a teenager, just 19, when he was drafted into the Army and shipped to Vietnam. A rocket struck the military truck he was driving, and he lost both his legs. He went through physical rehabilitation at Walter Reed Army Hospital and met Jim Withers, one of the founders of the National Handicapped Sports and Recreation Association (now Disabled Sports USA), who would later prove instrumental in his life. Demby's body healed but his psychological rehabilitation didn't come until later, after he spent years struggling with drug and alcohol addiction.

The turning point came when Demby found disability sports. He became acquainted with the Achilles Track Club International, a group that promoted sports participation for people with and without disabilities. Through Achilles, Demby began competing in 10K races and marathons. Since then, Demby has not only competed, but excelled, holding national records in the shot put, discus, and javelin.

Demby then took up Alpine skiing. His natural ability soon led to him becoming a certified ski instructor and helping to teach other people with disabilities how to enjoy the slopes. Then, in the early 1980s, Demby found out that DuPont was creating a new leg, and he volunteered to test it. DuPont then filmed a commercial with Demby in it, where he finally got his wish, playing basketball for the entire world to see.

BIBLIOGRAPHY. Admire Entertainment Speaker Profiles, http://www.admireentertain ment.com/clients/denby_b.php; Kelley, Jerry D., and Lex Frieden. *Go For It! A Book on Sport and Recreation for Persons with Disabilities.* Orlando, FL: Harcourt Brace Jovanovich, 1989; *Sports'n' Spokes* (July–August 1989): 3.

DISABLED HUNTERS OF NORTH AMERICA, INC. (DHNA) Disabled Hunters of North America (DHNA) was founded in 1989 by Norm Sauceman after he was disabled in an industrial accident. Sauceman, an avid outdoorsman before his accident, learned that people with disabilities had a hard time accessing the outdoors, especially when it came to participation in hunting. As a result, Sauceman created DHNA as a means to help hunters with disabilities by providing education and information on how to access the outdoors after an injury or disability.

DHNA provides many services, including helping hunters with disabilities connect with reputable outfitters to assist them in accessing hunting grounds and helping them better organize their hunts. DHNA also advises manufacturers on how to improve products for use by hunters with disabilities. Sauceman has written extensively on hunting for people with disabilities in *Buckmasters Online Magazine, Banta's Online Hunting Magazine, Bowhunting North America,* and *Boar Hunter Magazine.* He has also appeared on television in *Bushnell Outdoors with Dave Watson* and *The Tennessee Sportsman with O'Dell Braswell.*

BIBLIOGRAPHY. Disabled Hunters of North America. http://www.dhna.org/.

DISABLED SPORTS USA (DS-USA) Disabled Sports USA (DS-USA) was founded as the National Handicapped Sports and Recreation Association in 1967 by a group of Vietnam veterans with disabilities. While the initial purpose of the organization was to provide an avenue for disabled veterans to become reacquainted with an active lifestyle through sports and recreation, over time it has expanded to serve veterans, nonveterans, children, and adults with either congenital or acquired disabilities.

DS-USA relies on local chapters to set a programming schedule based on the identified needs of the population and the community. Existing community organizations become chapters, allowing DS-USA to expand its reach without establishing new programs.

DS-USA offers something for everyone—from the recreational athlete to the serious competitor. It remains most widely known for its work with winter sports, and in particular the Hartford Ski Spectacular in Breckenridge, Colorado. DS-USA also provides opportunities for athletes who are amputees to compete in athletics, cycling, and swimming at the elite level.

Kirk Bauer, Executive Director of DS-USA is a single leg amputee due to a war injury in Vietnam. He has received the President's Fitness Award from the President's Council on Physical Fitness and Sports and the 1986 Healthy American Fitness Leader Award.

BIBLIOGRAPHY. Joukowsky, Artemis A. W., and Larry Rothstein. *Raising the Bar—New Horizons in Disability Sport,* 1st ed. New York, NY: Umbrage Editions, 2002; Kelley, Jerry D., and Lex Frieden. *Go For It! A Book on Sport and Recreation for Persons with Disabilities.* Orlando, FL: Harcourt Brace Jovanovich, 1989.

Mono-skiing. *Photo courtesy of Rehabilitation Institute of Chicago Wirtz Sports Program.*

DRISCOLL, JEAN Jean Driscoll has won more Boston Marathons than anyone. Driscoll was born in Wisconsin in 1966, the second of five children. She was born with spina bifida, a neural tube defect, and a cleft palate. She had emergency surgery at birth, one of many to follow.

She was able to walk with the aid of braces early on, even though she had no feeling in her feet. She was aware she was different, yet longed to be "normal" like her older sister, Francie. She did her best to keep up, trying to run and play basketball.

Driscoll's mother tried to keep her away from the basketball hoop in an effort to keep her from wearing out her shoes. But in spite of repeated warnings, she couldn't stay away. Re-soling shoes, as a result, was almost a weekly event.

Walking soon became a thing of the past when Driscoll broke her leg in third grade. In a dodge ball game, she stuck her foot out to kick and instead she fell to the ground with a broken right tibia. Six weeks later, she learned the bone was not healing properly, and they had to rebreak and reset it, requiring surgery and a 12-week recuperation. Showing evidence of the determination that would later lead her to eight Boston Marathon wins, she regained the strength in her leg and was even able to ride a two-wheeled bicycle without training wheels for a time.

The next year, she broke her right leg and her left ankle, which meant more casts, more hospitals, and more surgeries. Again and again she rebounded, regaining the strength in her legs and resuming her active life, until one day when she was 14 and the path of her life changed forever.

She had won a 10-speed bicycle in a fund-raising competition and was riding her new bike home from a babysitting job. Taking a turn too sharply, she fell, crashing onto her left hip. She got up, rode home, and didn't think about it again until she got up to answer the phone that night and fell to the floor. This time, there would be no quick rebound. She would need multiple surgeries to reposition her hip and would require a body cast afterwards. In the next year, she was admitted to the hospital four times. Doctors told her that while she could use crutches for short distances such as around the house, for school and outside the house she would need to use a wheelchair.

When she returned to school, Driscoll met two boys who also used wheelchairs who invited her to play wheelchair soccer with them. She refused for months until she agreed to go in the hopes they would quit asking her. That was the beginning of Driscoll's new life.

Each week, Driscoll would come home from playing wheelchair soccer, and her wheelchair would have a new crack in it from banging into the other chairs during the games.

Driscoll soon found herself eager to try every sport available—water skiing, soccer, tennis, and ice hockey, just to name a few. Being able to be active again gave her a newfound enthusiasm, and in spite of the fact that she had missed a year of school due to her surgeries and recuperation, she was able to graduate on time. During her many hospitalizations, she had decided she wanted to become a nurse, thanks in large part to the interactions she had with her own nurses.

She enrolled at the University of Wisconsin–Milwaukee, commuting from home each day. Then, her parents divorced and Driscoll threw herself into sports, playing something every night of the week to rid herself of the guilt she felt. Neglecting her studies, she flunked out.

She found jobs and continued playing wheelchair sports in the evenings and weekends. That spring, Cindy Owens was organizing a wheelchair sports clinic, with guest speakers Brad and Sharon Hedrick. Driscoll had seen Sharon on television, competing in the Olympics in 1984, winning a Gold medal in the 800 meter wheelchair exhibition race.

At the clinic, Driscoll met Brad Hedrick, then the coach of the wheelchair basketball teams at the University of Illinois. He invited her to come to the university and join the women's team. Driscoll didn't seriously consider it after her disastrous college experience at Milwaukee, but Hedrick was persistent. When she finally made up her mind to apply, she was rejected, as she had feared, because of her poor grades.

The admissions office told her if she could pass a full semester's course load at the University of Wisconsin–Milwaukee, she would be accepted. Driscoll again showed evidence of that indomitable will; she finished the semester with Bs and Cs and headed to Champaign in the fall of 1987. It was then that her transformation to world class athlete began in earnest. Days at the University of Illinois were filled with classes in the morning, the gym after that, then basketball practice. After that, she would take to the track and road with coach Marty Morse and teammate Ann Cody.

Driscoll competed in the Paralympics in Seoul in the summer of 1988, winning Gold in the 4 by 200 relay, silver in the 4 by 100 relay, and two bronzes in the 200 and 400 meters.

Morse convinced her to turn her attention to distance races after that, and soon after Driscoll found herself in a van, driving the Boston Marathon course with Morse and teammate Cody. The plan was to take the race from Connie Hansen, the returning champion from Denmark, and keep six-time Boston champion Candace Cable out of the running. Morse's plan was for Driscoll to slow the pack down to allow Cody to make a break for the win.

Cody did make her break at the 8-mile mark, but she didn't get the win. By mile 20, Driscoll caught her, passed her and won the race in world record time, 1:43:17. From then until 1996, Driscoll was unstoppable at Boston, winning seven times in a row. It would take her until 2000 to finally secure her eighth victory, securing her place in history as the winningest athlete ever to compete at Boston.

BIBLIOGRAPHY. Crase, Nancy. "Pushing for PR's in Everything," *Sports 'n' Spokes* (September–October 1990): 18–20; Driscoll, Jean, Janet Benge, and Geoff Benge. *Determined to Win—The Overcoming Spirit of Jean Driscoll,* 1st ed. Colorado Springs, CO: WaterBrook Press, 2000; Joukowsky, Artemis A. W., and Larry Rothstein. *Raising the Bar—New Horizons in Disability Sport,* 1st ed. New York: Umbrage Editions, 2002; "Marathons and Road Racing." *Sports 'n' Spokes* (July–August 1989): 61.

DUKAT, SANDY Dukat is one of the most naturally gifted athletes anywhere. Born in Canton, Ohio with a missing femur in her right leg, she had the limb amputated above the knee at the age of 4. Growing up in a very active family, she always loved sports and was willing to try anything. It is that fearless nature that serves her well as a member of the U.S. Disabled Ski Team.

DWARF ATHLETIC ASSOCIATION OF AMERICA

Dukat got her introduction to disabled sports in 1996 when she moved to Chicago after graduating from college to pursue a job in social work, but she ended up pursuing much more. She was introduced to the Rehabilitation Institute of Chicago where she began swimming competitively. Two short years later, she set an American record in the 800 m freestyle at the 1998 World Championships in New Zealand. Dukat has also competed in running at a variety of distances, including the Chicago 10K in 2000 and 2001, and the Chicago Half Marathon in 2003.

But the sport that truly lit the flame for Dukat was not swimming or running—it was skiing. Dukat had gone with the RIC to Alpine Valley a couple of times, and one of the volunteer coaches suggested they go to the Hartford Ski Spectacular in Breckenridge. Dukat was hooked. She packed up and moved to Colorado to be able to train on the mountains, and there she joined the Winter Park Disabled Ski Team, where she remained from 1998–2001. During that time, she took 7th in the Disabled World Cup Women's Downhill and 7th in the Giant Slalom as well as 10th in downhill, 8th in Giant Slalom, and 11th in the Super G at the World Cup Salt Lake City. All her dedication paid off, and she qualified to represent the United States at the 2002 Paralympics in Salt Lake City, winning two bronze medals.

Proving to herself and the world that those bronze medals weren't just a fluke, Dukat repeated her medal winning ways at the 2003 U.S. Nationals, with silver in the downhill and bronze in Super G and slalom, winning third overall. She capped off the 2003 season with three bronze medals at the World Championships in Wildschonau, Austria. In 2004, Dukat won Gold in the slalom at the American World Cup, and in 2006 she once again represented the United States at the Torino Paralympics, adding another bronze to her medal chest.

BIBLIOGRAPHY. "Athlete Profiles: Sandy Dukat." *The Hartford Group Benefits,* http://groupbenefits.thehartford.com/usp/athletes/dukat.html; Ski Racing, http://www.skiracing.com/news/news_display.php/2697/ALPINE; Tean Ossur—Sandy Dukat, http://www.ossur.com/template110.asp?PageID=1480; United States Ski Team, http://www3.usskiteam.com/PublishingFolder/2419.htm; Women's Entertainment, http://www.we.tv/upload/html_area/1/1028/sandy_bio.html.

Sandy Dukat. *Photo courtesy of Rehabilitation Institute of Chicago Wirtz Sports Program.*

DWARF ATHLETIC ASSOCIATION OF AMERICA (DAAA)

Until 1985, dwarf athletes had no formal organization to govern sports and competition opportunities. That year, 25 athletes participated at the U.S. Cerebral Palsy Athletic Association Nationals, and the need for an organization of their own became apparent.

The Dwarf Athletic Association of America (DAAA) was

formed shortly after those games, drawing on the Little People of America for its membership. There are about 250,000 Americans who are considered little people or people of short stature, meaning they are less than 4 feet 10 inches in height. There are over 50 kinds of dwarfism, with achondroplasia the most common.

The DAAA now offers its membership events in athletics, basketball, boccia, powerlifting, swimming, skiing, table tennis, volleyball, badminton, soccer, and equestrian events.

The DAAA offers instruction, development, and organized competition at all levels—local, regional, and national for ages 7 and up. They also offer programming for children under the age of 6 which is purely recreational.

DAAA has been involved in the international scene, playing host to the first World Dwarf Games in 1993 in Chicago. The International Dwarf Athletic Federation was then formed to oversee future games, and competitions were subsequently held in 1997 in Peterborough, England, and in 2001 in Toronto. One of DAAA's athletes, Erin Popovich, was the biggest medal winner of the Athens Paralympics in 2004, winning seven Gold medals in swimming.

BIBLIOGRAPHY. Depauw, Karen P., and Susan J. Gavron. *Disability and Sport*. Champaign, IL: Human Kinetics, 1995; Dwarf Athletic Association of America, http://daaa.org.

EELS ON WHEELS SCUBA diving allows people with disabilities the chance to leave their disability behind. In 1991, Tim Skelly and Tom McCoy, SCUBA instructors in Austin, Texas, founded Eels on Wheels to share their love of diving with people with disabilities.

Eels on Wheels members are divers with and without disabilities, sharing the common desire to escape gravity and experience the underwater world. Because wheelchairs and prosthetic limbs aren't needed in the water, the adaptations required for people with disabilities to SCUBA dive are minimal. In fact, adaptations can be made so that anyone can safely learn and participate in SCUBA. Through Eels on Wheels, Skelly and McCoy have provided the opportunity to experience SCUBA to people with disabilities who previously might have thought the underwater world was out of reach.

Eels on Wheels instructors, divers, and dive buddies are certified through the Handicapped Scuba Association (HSA) at one of three levels of certification. Level A divers can dive with only one additional person. Level B divers require two divers, and while Level C divers also require two divers, one must be a certified rescue diver, ensuring a safe experience for all participants.

BIBLIOGRAPHY. Eels on Wheels, http://eels.org.

ELECTRIC WHEELCHAIR HOCKEY. *See* Power Hockey

ELIX, JAN Jan Elix spent her life working to provide sports and recreation opportunities for people with disabilities. Elix, born in 1955 in San Francisco, was an active youngster and already an accomplished diver by the age of 11. She had thoughts of collegiate or even Olympic competition on her mind, when a diving accident in 1967 rerouted her life and her plans.

As a quadriplegic from a spinal cord injury, diving was no longer an option, but a career in sport and recreation was. She attended San Jose State University, earning her B.S. in Recreation and Leisure Management, and set out to help others discover sport.

Elix went to work for the city of San Jose in the Parks and Recreation Department, where she stayed for 31 years, working to expand existing programs and implement new ones for the city's residents with disabilities. She was active on the board of Wheelchair Sports,

USA, serving as the Junior Committee Director for 21 years, and was later inducted into the WS-USA Hall of Fame in recognition of her years of dedication to the disability sport movement.

Her commitment to children with disabilities showed in everything she did. The Northern California Junior Sports Camp which began in 1983, provided opportunities for children age 5 to 21 to experience and learn activities such as water skiing, tennis, basketball, swimming, and track and field in a two-week residential setting. Her passion helped create entire new generations of athletes with disabilities. Elix died at the age of 49 in the summer of 2005 after a one year bout with bladder cancer, but the work she did to bring disability sports to the people of California, the nation, and the world will not be forgotten.

BIBLIOGRAPHY. National Wheelchair Basketball Association, http://www.nwba.org/news_index634.html; NJDC 2006: Jan Elix Memorial, http://njdc.joeywheelchairracing.com/jan.htm.

EQUESTRIAN Equestrian is one of the few sports that allow a rider to leave their disability on the sidelines. Therapeutic riding got its start in England in the 1940s, when a woman who contracted polio was told by her doctors she should no longer ride horses. She disregarded the advice and kept riding. Ultimately, she competed in the 1952 Olympics, winning a silver medal in equestrian competition.

Equestrian as a sport for people with disabilities got its start in the United States a decade later. Studies at the time showed that sitting on a horse could stretch tight leg muscles, relaxing spastic tone, and hippotherapy programs sprouted nationwide. Soon, people with disabilities were riding competitively, not just for therapy. Today, equestrian is offered as part of the Paralympic program, and is increasingly growing in popularity. In the 2000 Paralympics in Sydney, 72 riders representing 24 nations competed, the largest contingent of equestrian athletes ever.

See also North American Riding for the Handicapped Association

BIBLIOGRAPHY. Allen, Anne. *Sports for the Handicapped.* New York: Walker, 1981; International Paralympic Committee, http://www.paralympic.org/paralympian/20004/2000407.htm; Kelley, Jerry D., and Lex Frieden. *Go For It! A Book on Sport and Recreation for Persons with Disabilities.* Orlando, FL: Harcourt Brace Jovanovich, 1989.

ERGOMETER An ergometer is a fitness device that allows people to exercise their arms, legs, or both while in a stationary position, and to measure the amount of exercise being completed. Ergometers are used in rehabilitation facilities, gyms, and in the home, and are also widely used in research facilities. Stationary bikes, treadmills, and upper body ergometers are all examples of ergometers. Upper body ergometers are suitable for wheelchair users, people with lower limb disabilities, and others who are rehabbing from knee or other injuries.

Using an ergometer is an efficient means of training for many athletes with disabilities. Weather factors don't influence exercise nor do difficulties associated with transporting equipment, such as a racing chair or a handcycle to a site.

Ergometers are excellent for cardiovascular training, but can also aid in increasing strength, flexibility, and range of motion. Like other forms of cardiovascular exercise, ergometers help reduce the risk of high blood pressure, high cholesterol, and other diseases, and can help increase energy and endurance. There are many different types of ergometers available: upper body only, lower body only, and combination models which exercise both the upper and lower body simultaneously.

BIBLIOGRAPHY. UCP: Exercise and Ergometers, http://ucp.org/ucp_channeldoc. cfm/1/15/11500/11500-11500/3177.

FELLER, THOMAS A prominent figure in the world of amputee football is Thomas Feller. Born and raised in Seattle, Washington, Feller is Executive Director of the U.S. Amputee Soccer Association, as well as President of the International Amputee Football Federation.

Feller's childhood revolved around athletics. He played football, wrestled, ran track, rode bikes, swam, and hiked. Eventually he became involved in soccer, and one of his dreams was to go to Europe to play professionally.

Feller's life changed forever in the fall of 1973. He was traveling with a friend through the mountains prior to going away to college, when a pickup truck hit him head on. Feller's van went out of control, and he drove off the road down a 100-foot ravine. Feller's leg had to be amputated when gangrene developed.

After the accident, Feller thought sports and a career in physical education were no longer possible. Instead, he became a graphic artist and photographer. He avoided physical activity, finding the prosthetics difficult and uncomfortable. He withdrew from people, and from life.

Twelve years later, Feller received a call from his father telling him to go to Shoreline Stadium and to bring his camera and film. When he got to the stadium, teams from the United States and El Salvador were playing soccer, only they were all amputees like him. Within two weeks, Feller was out on the field himself playing soccer, the game he thought he would never play again.

Feller quickly rose to prominence in the sport, and he now serves as president of the International Amputee Football Federation, governing the sport he thought he would never play again.

BIBLIOGRAPHY. American Amputee Soccer Association, http://www.ampsoccer.org; International Amputee Football Federation, http://www.iaff.sport.U2/history_en.htm; Jackson, Tami Jayne. "Amputee Soccer Fielded by a Good Feller," *Active Living Magazine,* http://www.activelivingmagazine.com/artman/publish/article_18.shtml; Pan, David. "Making a Difference: Mountlake Terrace Resident Thomas Feller Guides the U.S. Amputee Soccer Association," *The Enterprise Newspaper,* http://www.enterpreisenewspapers.com/archive/2002/8/30/20021125141010.cfm.

FIELD EVENTS Field events were one of the first competitions offered for athletes with disabilities as part of athletics competition. Field events for athletes with disabilities include javelin, discus, and shot, the same implements thrown by nondisabled field athletes. Additionally, athletes with disabilities resulting in quadriplegia such as cervical spinal cord injury or cerebral palsy throw the club, which is an implement shaped somewhat like a bowling pin and weighted at one end. Amputee and visually impaired athletes also compete in both the long jump and high jump.

Field events rules are modified only slightly from those for nondisabled athletes. In classes F1 to F6, at least one part of the athlete's upper leg or buttock must remain in contact with the cushion or seat of the throwing chair until the implement is released. For classes F7 and F8, while the participant can lift out of the chair, one foot must be kept in contact with the ground inside the circle and if any part of the chair is used for leverage that too must stay within the vertical plane of the circle.

Gloves or other assistive devices are not allowed; however, substances can be applied directly to participants' hands to aid in gripping. Additionally athletes in F1–F3 classes can strap their nonthrowing hand to their chair to aid in stability.

Field events chairs have been modified over the years as well. While originally athletes competed in their everyday chairs, throwing chairs, such as those for other sports, have changed significantly. Throwing frames now usually don't have wheels, except to make transporting the chair easier. There are restrictions on seat height and footrests; these along with other rules are found in the IPC rules on athletics.

Athletes with visual impairment or amputee athletes who compete in long jump or high jump generally do not require any accommodation, except that athletes in the B1 class, who have no light perception at all, may have an individual assistant who helps them navigate the approach by using numbers to indicate left, right, or straight ahead.

BIBLIOGRAPHY. Apple, Jr., David F. *Physical Fitness: A Guide for Individuals with Spinal Cord Injury*. Washington, DC: Department of Veteran's Affairs, Rehabilitation Research and Development Service, 1995; Karp, Gary. *Life on Wheels for the Active Wheelchair User*. Sebastopol, CA: O'Reilly and Associates, 1999.

FISHING HAS NO BOUNDARIES, INC. Bobby Cammack was a fishing guide for nearly 40 years in northwestern Wisconsin, but it wasn't until he had a broken leg and had trouble getting in and out of his boat that he realized there were people with disabilities who experienced problems trying to access the outdoors. Cammack founded Fishing Has No Boundaries, Inc. in 1986 to help break down some of those barriers.

While their first event drew 80 people, Fishing Has No Boundaries has since evolved into a national organization with chapters in nine states. It is different than some of the other disability sport organizations, because any person with any disability is eligible to participate. There are no disability classifications and no age restrictions.

Fishing Has No Boundaries helps people with disabilities learn about adapted equipment available to assist them with fishing. Rod splints, reel splints, and reel mounts adapted for a wheelchair as well as electronic reels are available, as well as rod holders. The organization works to share information, create assistive technology, and provide technical support so that anyone who wants to fish can fish.

BIBLIOGRAPHY. Fishing Has No Boundaries, Inc., http://www.fhnbinc.org/.

FLOOR HOCKEY Floor Hockey was first introduced to the disability sport world at the 1970 Special Olympics World Winter Games. Adapted from the games of ice hockey and ringette, floor hockey is a team sport is played in a standard sized gymnasium.

The floor hockey rink is usually wood or concrete. The game is played in three nine-minute periods with one minute between each. Each team has six players on the floor at a time, playing with hockey sticks made of either fiberglass or wooden rods, and a circular felt disk, not the hard puck used in traditional hockey. Protective gear such as helmets and shin guards are worn by all players.

Special Olympics floor hockey is somewhat different than traditional floor hockey because it has competition in team play, individual skills, team skills, a 10-meter puck dribble, and target shot.

See also Poly Hockey.

BIBLIOGRAPHY. Paciorek, Michael J., and Jeffery A. Jones. *Sports and Recreation for the Disabled,* 2nd ed. Carmel, IN: Cooper Publishing Group, 1994; Special Olympics International, http://www.specialolympics.org.

FOUR TRACK SKIING Four track skiing is an adapted ski method commonly used by individuals with neuromuscular impairments such as cerebral palsy, muscular dystrophy, and multiple sclerosis, as well as individuals with any other disability who need additional balance and stability to ski.

Four track refers to two skis and two outriggers, which leave four tracks in the snow. An outrigger is an adapted version of a forearm crutch with a shortened ski attached to the bottom. Most outriggers are height adjustable and have a cord attached to the handgrip that flips up the ski, locking it upright for when the skier is stopped. The outrigger provides additional balance and steering maneuverability for skiers whose disabilities create the need for it.

BIBLIOGRAPHY. Paciorek, Michael J., and Jeffery A. Jones. *Sports and Recreation for the Disabled,* 2nd ed. Carmel, IN: Cooper Publishing Group, 1994.

FREEDOM INDEPENDENCE The Freedom Independence 20 is a boat designed for sailors with disabilities. It has a wider hull to make it more stable and a heavily weighted keel to keep it upright. It has full flotation supporting both the hull and keel and a foam filled mast to keep it from turning upside down.

Two counterweighted seats swing from one side of the boat to the other and remain above water even in the most extreme conditions.

The Freedom Independence costs around $20,000, and it is used by many sailing programs for people with disabilities nationwide.

FREI, HEINZ

See also Sailing for People with Disabilities

BIBLIOGRAPHY. Schroeder, David J. "Sailing into the 90's." *Sports 'n' Spokes* (July–August 1990): 34–36.

FREI, HEINZ "Mr. Marathon," Heinz Frei has been on an uphill course his whole life. The Swiss native, born January 28, 1958, injured his spinal cord when he fell while completing a mountain race in 1978. Frei has been racing now for well over two decades, and in spite of his nickname has held records and posted wins at a variety of distances both on the track and on the road.

Over the years, Frei has held world records in the 400 m (50.66 sec.), the 800 m (1:38:02 min.), and the 10,000 m (20:25:9 min.). In the marathon, he held course records for the Oita (Japan) Marathon (1:20:14), and the Boston Marathon (1:21:23), which was also a world record performance. A veteran of six Paralympic Summer Games from 1984–2004, he has earned a total of 12 Gold, 7 silver, and 8 bronze medals. Frei also competed in the men's Olympic wheelchair exhibition race, winning a bronze in Sydney in 2000.

He won his 100th marathon in the history of his racing career at Berlin in October 2005.

BIBLIOGRAPHY. "Against the Wind: Racing the Wind 2," WILL-AM, http://www.will.uiuc. edu/tv/documentaries/atw/atwwind1.html; Piltz, Dr. Reiner. "Heinz Frei—An Exceptional Wheelchair Athlete," http://www.scc-events.com/news/news003727.html.

FROGLEY, MICHAEL Mike Frogley is continuing on a long tradition of winning at the University of Illinois. He has been the head coach of the men's and women's wheelchair basketball teams since 1998.

Frogley was injured in 1986 in a car accident at the age of 17. He started playing wheelchair basketball while in rehab at the Ottawa Rehabilitation Centre in 1986, and within three years he was on the national team. He pursued his studies at the University of Wisconsin–Whitewater, where he was a member of their wheelchair basketball team from 1989-1993, and where he received his B.S. in Secondary Education and M.S. in Special Education. Frogley, a Canadian citizen, represented Canada in the Paralympic Games in Barcelona in 1992 as part of their wheelchair basketball team.

Frogley began his coaching career at University of Wisconsin–Whitewater, serving as head coach of the wheelchair basketball program from 1993–1997. He has coached the Canadian men's wheelchair basketball team various times, leading them to Gold from 1997-2000. During that time he also served as assistant coach to the Canadian women's team, helping lead them to a Gold medal at the 1996 Paralympics in Atlanta.

Frogley has earned numerous championships and medals nationally and internationally as both a player and coach, including bronze at the 1990 World Cup, Gold in 1991 at the Stoke Mandeville Wheelchair Games, Gold with the Canadian women at the 1996 Paralympics, and Gold with Canadian men at the 2000 Paralympics in Sydney and again at the 2004 Paralympics in Athens.

Nationally, he played on the Gold medal–winning Ontario team twice, coached the University of Wisconsin–Whitewater to the national collegiate title in 1996, and coached the University of Illinois men to three national collegiate titles in 1998, 2000, and 2001. He coached the University of Illinois women to their national title in 2002 and again in 2006.

BIBLIOGRAPHY. Canadian Wheelchair Basketball Association, http://www.cwba.ca/program/frogley.html; Disability Outreach Foundation, http://www.disabilityoutreach.org/Gallo032002.htm; University of Illinois Division of Rehabilitation Education Services, http://www.rehab.uiuc.edu.

GOALBALL Goalball is a Paralympic sport played solely by athletes who are blind or visually impaired. Like many other sports, it originated as an activity for blind World War II veterans. Today it is widely played in the United States and around the world.

Goalball is played on a gym floor with two three-person teams. The ball has a bell or beeper in it so players can hear where the ball is being thrown, and during competition the crowd must remain silent in order for the players to hear. The object is to get the ball past the opponent's goal line on a court 18 meters long by 9 meters wide. The court borders are marked with thick tape or cord so players can feel the boundaries with their hands or feet.

Each player has a zone that is the width of the court and three meters deep. The player must stay in their marked zone during play, whether they are the center or one of the wings. The center is usually responsible for stopping the ball and passing it to a wing. The wings use strategies such as moving around the court to surprise the defense and practice different throws to get past the opponents goal.

Defense can be played either standing, crouching, kneeling, or lying on the floor.

Equipment used in goalball is relatively inexpensive. It includes the ball itself, which is similar in size to a basketball, but specially made for goalball, including the bell or beeper inside. It also includes eyeshades, which each player is required to wear. This equalizes the field compensating for the different levels of vision players have. Players wear knee and elbow pads to protect themselves from the hard playing surface of the court. Floor tape and string is also used to mark the court— gym floor tape is most commonly used.

Goalball is played at the local, regional, national, and international level and is prominent at the summer Paralympic Games.

BIBLIOGRAPHY. Kelley, Jerry D., and Lex Frieden. *Go For It! A Book on Sport and Recreation*

Goalball. *Copyright Chris Hamilton Photography.*

for Persons with Disabilities. Orlando, FL: Harcourt Brace Jovanovich, 1989; United States Association for Blind Athletes, http://www.usaba.org.

GOLDEN, DIANA Diana Golden has been called both the Babe Zaharias and the Babe Ruth of the disability sport movement. Born in Lincoln, Massachusetts, she grew up as a typically active pre-teen who loved playing outdoors, especially downhill skiing. At the age of 12, her leg gave out when she was walking through the snow after a day on the slopes. Shortly thereafter, she was diagnosed with bone cancer and her right leg was amputated above the knee.

She learned to ski again, this time on one leg. She joined the New England Handicapped Skiing Association, and while skiing with them at Mount Sunapee, New Hampshire, decided to become a ski racer. She began competing while she was in high school at Lincoln-Sudbury High School in Lincoln, Massachusetts, continuing her competitive pursuits while earning her B.A. in English at Dartmouth College. In 1979, she became part of the U.S. Disabled Ski Team, competing from 1979–1982 and 1985–1990.

In 1980, Golden represented the United States at the Winter Paralympics in Norway. There, she competed in Alpine skiing using a method called "three-tracking," which means using one ski and two ski poles with short skis or "outriggers." Over the next decade, Golden was a seven-time world champion in downhill, earning 10 Gold medals at the World Disabled Ski Championships and 19 Gold medals at the U.S. Disabled Alpine Championships. The medal that meant the most to her, though, came during the 1988 Winter Olympics when disabled skiing was featured as a demonstration sport. There, Golden led the United States to a medal sweep in the women's slalom.

Golden continually sought new challenges, which led her to enter competitions for non-disabled athletes as well. Thanks to Golden's presence at these events, U.S. Skiing instituted what is known as "the Golden Rule," which allows disabled skiers to ski early seeds in United States Skiing Association (USSA) sanctioned events, enabling them to avoid the deep ruts that would occur later in the day.

Throughout her career, Golden was showered with awards and accolades. She was named Ski Racing's 1987–88 U.S. Alpine Skier of the Year, the first athlete with a disability to be so honored. She won the Beck Award from the U.S. Ski Association and the U.S. Ski Association Award for Outstanding Competitor of the Year. She was inducted into the U.S. National Ski Hall of Fame and the International Women's Sports Hall of Fame.

Golden was named U.S. Skier of the Year by *Skiing Magazine,* the U.S. Olympic Committee, and the North American Snow Journalists Association in 1988, again the first time an athlete with a disability had been accorded that distinction. Next, she received the Flo Hyman Award from the Women's Sports Foundation in 1991, named for Flo Hyman and presented annually on National Girls and Women in Sports Day. Golden, who died of cancer in 2001, was posthumously inducted into the U.S. Olympic Hall of Fame as part of the class of 2006, the second Paralympic athlete to receive that honor.

Before she died, Golden had essays published in *Chicken Soup for the Woman's Soul* and the *Dartmouth Alumni Magazine* as well as *Life* and *Reader's Digest* magazine. She also authored a book about losing her leg to cancer and finding self-acceptance and self-esteem through ski racing, and established the Golden Opportunities Fund to provide financial assistance to young athletes with disabilities.

BIBLIOGRAPHY. Allen, Anne. *Sports for the Handicapped.* New York: Walker, 1981; "Diana Golden Brosnihan Pacesetter: From Recreational Sport to Olympic Gold." *Palaestra* (January 2002); Kelley, Jerry D., and Lex Frieden. *Go For It! A Book on Sport and Recreation for Persons with Disabilities.* Orlando, FL: Harcourt Brace Jovanovich, 1989; Ski Racing, http://www.skiracing.com/features/news_displayFeatures.php/1672/FEATURES/news-Articles/; Sullivan, Robert. "Remembering Diana Golden Brosnihan: Love Was a Reason to Live," *Time.com,* http://www.time.com/time/samples/article/0,8599,17338,00.html.

GUIDE RUNNER. *See* Tether

GUTTMAN, SIR LUDWIG Sir Ludwig Guttman may best be known as the father of the modern Paralympic movement. After World War II, there was a large number of injured war veterans, creating the need for rehabilitation hospitals. One of these, Stoke Mandeville in Aylesbury, England, played a pivotal role in the development of disability sport, particularly for those using wheelchairs due to spinal cord injury.

Dr. Ludwig Guttman was a neurosurgeon and neurologist. A German of Jewish faith, Guttman fled his native Germany during the Nazi reign for the safety of England. There, he was appointed to the National Spinal Cord Injury Center at the Stoke Mandeville Hospital in 1944.

At that time, the life expectancy of a person with a spinal cord injury was six weeks, due in large part to the high risk of death from renal failure and complications from pressure sores.

Guttman was inspired by an incident from when he was an orderly at a hospital during World War II. A spinal cord injured soldier was brought into the ward, and was separated from the rest of the soldiers by screens. His infections were left untreated because the doctors believed he would die. Within weeks, without treatment of any kind, he did indeed die. At Stoke Mandeville, Guttman was again surrounded by individuals with spinal cord injuries who were being largely left to die from kidney failure or sepsis from pressure sores due to inactivity.

Guttman decided to treat these veterans as if they were going to live. He brought recreation into the ward, having staff toss a medicine ball to the soldiers as they lay in bed. Over time, Guttman saw the soldiers able to lift themselves out of bed and transfer to and from their wheelchairs because of the gains in strength.

He began investigating the possibility of sport, and he integrated simple ball games, such as archery, netball, and table tennis into the therapeutic program at Stoke Mandeville. The soldiers played wheelchair polo in an empty ward, then basketball, darts, table tennis, snooker, skittles, and archery. Social activity was also encouraged, with a corresponding increase in morale and a desire to return to life outside the hospital. The soldiers were no longer dying, they were surviving. From these humble beginnings, sport as recreation for people with spinal cord injuries was developed.

GUTTMAN, SIR LUDWIG

Wheelchair tennis. *Copyright Chris Hamiltion Photography.*

Guttman soon learned that people with spinal cord injuries could do more than just participate in sport. He learned that they could compete, and that they wanted to compete. He began to formulate a plan to make that happen, and it came to fruition just a few short years later.

In 1948, Guttman founded the Stoke Mandeville Games, held on the hospital grounds the same year the Olympics were being held in London. Archery was the only sport, and 14 men and 2 women competed. Over time, more sports were added to the program including slalom and obstacle races, wheelchair polo, badminton, and netball. Swimming and lawn bowls followed. Four years later, in 1952, the first international Stoke Mandeville Games took place with 130 competitors from the Netherlands contesting snooker, darts, archery, and table tennis alongside their English peers. Two years later, 14 nations were competing at the Games, including Australia, Austria, Belgium, Britain, Canada, Egypt, Finland, France, Germany, Israel, Pakistan, Portugal, The Netherlands, and Yugoslavia.

From that modest beginning, Guttman is responsible for the creation of the modern day Paralympic Games, which have grown to include thousands of athletes with many kinds of disabilities from nations all over the world.

BIBLIOGRAPHY. Joukowsky, Artemis A. W, and Larry Rothstein. *Raising the Bar—New Horizons in Disability Sport,* 1st ed. New York: Umbrage Editions, 2002; Steadward, Robert Daniel, E. J. Watkinson, and Garry David Wheeler. *Adapted Physical Activity.* Edmonton: University of Alberta Press, 2003.

HALL, BOB Bob Hall is widely considered the "grandfather" of wheelchair racing. Hall is the first wheelchair user ever to win a Boston Marathon, and he is one of the pioneers of modern day wheelchair racing. Hall's first Boston win came in 1975 in a 50-pound wheelchair, without even an official wheelchair division to compete in. Despite all that, Hall finished in a respectable 2 hours and 58 minutes, faster than many runners can complete the distance even today, 30 years later.

Hall was born in the 1950s and contracted polio as an infant. He was strong just from walking with leg braces, but there were few sports opportunities for people with disabilities like him in the 1960s. Inside, however, Hall was a competitor just waiting for an outlet. That outlet was presented to him by another pioneer in the disability sport movement, Tip Thiboutot. Thiboutot encouraged Hall to try wheelchair basketball in his senior year of high school, and despite the fact that Hall had never used a wheelchair and never played a sport, he agreed. Hall quickly discovered he had some natural ability not only for sport, but for wheelchair design.

His first "sports chair" gave the rest of the world an inkling of what Hall would become, a leader in the design and manufacture of cutting edge wheelchairs for everyday use as well as a line of sport specific wheelchairs, mono-skis, and water skis. That first chair was an old Everest & Jennings hospital wheelchair that he modified by cutting off the armrests and dropping the back. Using this chair, Hall's natural speed soon made him a force to be reckoned with.

Hall didn't start out on top, however. Using his early defeats as opportunities, he learned everything he could from his competitors in terms of technique, equipment, and training. His willingness to be a student paid off, as just a year after his first track meet, the only part of Hall his competitors saw was his back as he crossed the finish line first in the National Wheelchair Mile race in Toledo. After conquering that first mile, Hall set his sights on the marathon.

Hall, a lifelong Bostonian, had long been a fan of the granddaddy of all marathons, the Boston Marathon. There had never been a wheelchair entrant in the race, but this didn't dissuade Hall, who proposed the idea to the race director. Though he wasn't welcomed with open arms, he wasn't discouraged either, so on race day, Hall showed up and raced. Little did he know that his entry would pave the way for thousands of athletes with disabilities to enter road races of all distances worldwide.

Hall also advanced from being the first wheelchair winner of the Boston Marathon in 1975 to being the director of its wheelchair division eight years later. Since 1983, Hall has been responsible for coordinating all the arrangements for the hundreds of wheelchair athletes who have gone the distance since then.

Hall's love of tinkering with his chairs—trying new things to make them faster, lighter, better—led to the design of a prototype racing wheelchair in the late 1970s. That first chair was the start of Hall's Wheels, Hall's own wheelchair company. Hall's Wheels became known all over the United States and the world for producing the most innovative designs for some of the top racers including Paralympic medalists Candace Cable and Cisco Jeter.

As more sports were developed for people with disabilities, Hall saw an expanded marketplace and began to design adapted snow and water skis in addition to everyday and racing wheelchairs. Hall even had the foresight to reach beyond the boundaries of traditional disability marketing, and he had the first cutting edge advertising campaign featuring photography by Annie Liebovitz in mainstream magazines such as *Glamour* and *GQ*. Hall's design ingenuity was honored when his racing chairs were featured in The Museum of Modern Art in New York at a "Designs for Independent Living" exhibit in the late 1980s.

BIBLIOGRAPHY. *Sports 'n' Spokes* (July–August 1989): 4; Vogel, Bob. "Bob Hall: Farther and Faster." *New Mobility* (October 1998).

HAMILTON, MARILYN Marilyn Hamilton revolutionized the wheelchair industry almost single-handedly. She grew up in California, a lover of the outdoors, of risk, and of adventure. She lived in the foothills of the Sierra Nevada Mountains and loved nothing better than hang gliding up above her hometown. It was a hang gliding accident in 1979 that led to her spinal cord injury, and ultimately to her success in business.

While in rehab, Hamilton noticed that the wheelchairs they were using were huge and unwieldy, and yet were made out of the same diameter tubing of the hang gliders she and her friends had been flying. She and her friends Don Helman and Jim Okamoto set to work in a garage building three different wheelchairs that next year, using materials that hang gliders were built out of—lightweight, yet strong and functional. The next year, in 1980, they began selling chairs to the public as Motion Designs, renamed to Quickie Designs six years later.

Hamilton's initial interest wasn't in the business of wheelchairs. She wanted a wheelchair that gave her mobility and freedom, but most of all, one that looked good. The first chair they built weighed in at a mere 26 pounds, virtually half the weight of what people with disabilities were pushing in at the time.

Hamilton got reacquainted with sport, competing in both tennis and skiing. She won silver in 1982 at the Paralympics, and became national wheelchair tennis singles and doubles champion that same year.

Quickie grew faster than anyone could have predicted, thanks to a clever marketing campaign and Hamilton's tenacity. Within five years, sales topped a million dollars, and they were purchased by Sunrise Medical in 1986. Hamilton's experiment in the garage revolutionized the wheelchair, not only for her but for everyone who needed a wheelchair and wanted to be mobile and independent.

Hamilton's story has appeared on *60 Minutes, CBS This Morning, CBS Eye on America,* and *PBS People in Motion.* She is also featured in three books: *Companies with a Conscience,* by Mary Scott and Howard Rothman; *No Pity,* by Joseph Shapiro; and *Women Business Leaders,* by Robert B. Pile.

Hamilton has been honored numerous times for her contributions to the disability community, including being named California Business Woman of the Year and selected to the California Governor's Hall of Fame for People with Disabilities. She was a 1994 National Rehabilitation Week Award recipient and a 1992 National Victory Award recipient. Marilyn's business prowess was also recognized when she received the National Women's Economic Alliance Business Leadership Award in 1986, when she was named as the California Business Woman of the Year in 1985, and when Motion Designs Inc. received the SBA Western Regional Business of the Year award in 1984.

BIBLIOGRAPHY. "AAPD Announces Board and Officers," *ABLE Newspaper,* http://ablenews.com/archive/sept_03.htm; National Spinal Cord Injury Association, http://www.spinalcord.org/news.php?dep=8&page=2&list=544; Shapiro, Joseph. "Re-Inventing the Wheel," http://www.aliciapatterson.org/APF1403/Shapiro/Shapiro.html; Smithsonian, "Sports: Breaking Records, Breaking Barriers," http://americanhistory.si.edu/sports/exhibit/removers/wheelchair/index.cfm.

HANDCYCLING Handcycling is one of the fastest growing sports for people with disabilities in the United States today. Handcycling enables people with disabilities to participate both recreationally and competitively, and is one of the few sports people with disabilities can participate in with nondisabled family and friends. Many retired wheelchair racers have taken up handcycling as well.

Handcycling is governed by the U.S. Handcycling Federation (USHF), which has been designated the official governing body for the sport in the nation. They are working to increase both recreational and competitive opportunities for handcyclists across the country, running clinics to educate new riders, and conducting competitions throughout the year in various locations.

Handcycling is for people interested in cycling who have limited use of their lower extremities because of spinal cord injury, cerebral palsy, amputation, and other disabilities. Handcycles look somewhat different than a traditional cycle, because they are designed with three wheels instead of two. The primary difference, however, is in how the handcycle is propelled—the cyclist uses their arms to peddle instead of their legs. Just as in cycling, the handcycle rider works to maintain a pedal rhythm at a gear that can carry them the greatest distance with the least effort.

Handcycles are built with anywhere from 3 to 20 gears, and can be used for anything from touring to elite competition depending on the needs of the rider. Handcycles started out being hand built by individuals; once their popularity caught on, however, many of the major wheelchair manufacturers began building them as part of their product lines.

For handcyclists, testing several models is important before committing to the purchase, because they can cost several thousand dollars. Many models steer differently, and the seating systems put the athlete in positions that may be comfortable for one individual and completely uncomfortable for another.

Handcycles come in both upright and recumbent models. Uprights are more often used for individuals who want to pursue recreational handcycyling, because they are easier to transfer in and out of, easier to balance in, and more visible to cars and traffic. Recumbents are sleeker and sportier, more aerodynamic, and better for competition.

Handcycles offer one of two types of steering—pivot or lean. The upright handcycles pivot steer, which means the front wheel turns and the rest of the bike remains upright. Although some of the recumbents use pivot steering, most of them use lean steering. Lean steering operates much like a regular bike, with the rider leaning through turns, however, this method can be difficult for individuals whose disability causes problems with trunk stability or balance.

Once a cyclist gets comfortable with their handcycle, they may want to try one of the many competitive opportunities available. Handcyclists can participate in races similar to those offered nondisabled cyclists—road races, time trials, and criterions. Road races offer courses usually of 20 to 30 miles, involving up and down hills, tight turns, and other challenges. Time trials are run at distances of between 5 and 15 miles, and the cyclist races solely against the clock. Criterions are shorter, looped courses that last for a fixed time period such as 30 minutes. They test the athlete's ability to corner, turn, and accelerate.

As in other disability sports, handcyclists are classified in order to participate. The USHF system is based on the IPC Cycling Classification system, with handcyclists classified into the following divisions: HC Division A classes HC 1 and 2 is for cyclists who are quadriplegics because of spinal cord injury or other disability; HC division B classes HC 3, 4, and 5 are for paraplegics because of spinal injury or other disability; and HC division C classes HC 6, 7, and 8 cover individuals with other disabilities. The classification system is based on two things: the athlete's functional ability and their level of disability. In many USHF races the C division is open to individuals with and without disabilities, although most international events are for athletes with disabilities only.

Handcycling technology continues to develop, offering new and better cycles for riders. As the sport continues to grow in popularity, there are more and more options for riders, whether the goal is to ride around the neighborhood or compete in an international event.

BIBLIOGRAPHY. Cornelson, David. "The Wonderful World of Hand Cycling." *Sports 'n' Spokes* (July–August 1991): 10–12; Freedom Concepts, http://www.freedomconcepts.com; Handcycling Racing, http://www.handcycleracing.com; United States Handcycling Federation. http://www.ushf.org/links.html.

HANDICAPPED SCUBA ASSOCIATION INTERNATIONAL (HSAI) Handicapped Scuba Association International (HSAI) has become the world's foremost authority on diving for people with disabilities since its inception in 1981. They offer diver education and training, diver certification, and instructor training courses. The Professional Association of Diving Instructors (PADI) and the National Association of Underwater

Instructors (NAUI), the two major certifying agencies, recognize their programs. HSAI began offering instructor training courses in 1986, and today, their certified instructors operate in 45 countries worldwide.

HSAI teaches people with a wide variety of disabilities to SCUBA dive, including people with spinal cord injuries, amputations, cerebral palsy, brain injury, visual impairment, and intellectual disability. Divers are grouped according to three levels. "A" divers can dive with one other person. "B" divers are required to have two able-bodied divers with them, and "C" divers have to have two able-bodied divers, one of whom is trained in diver rescue.

People with disabilities themselves can be trained as SCUBA instructors. Steve Varney, a paraplegic from a car accident, was the first certified SCUBA instructor with a disability. He became a SCUBA instructor and manager of his own shop, paving the way for instructors with a variety of disabilities.

BIBLIOGRAPHY. Driessen, Paul K. "On Wings of Eagle Rays." *Sports 'n' Spokes* (July–August 1990): 10–15; Handicapped Scuba Association International, http://www.hsascuba.com/.

HEDRICK, BRAD Brad Hedrick has spent his career making others into champions. A North Carolina native, he attended the University of Illinois in the 1970s. Like many before him, he wanted to take advantage not only of the excellent academics, but also of their world renowned wheelchair sports program. Hedrick competed in basketball and track throughout undergrad and graduate school, and he had one of the best men's marathon times in the country during his tenure. In the early 1980s, Hedrick learned that the 1984 Olympics would feature a men's 800 meter wheelchair race. When he didn't make the cut, he began to pursue coaching instead.

While Hedrick was a stellar athlete, he has become more well known for his accomplishments in leading others to champion status. He was the Supervisor of Recreation and Athletics for the University of Illinois wheelchair sports programs from 1981–1995, and he has been the Director of the Division of Rehabilitation Education Services at the university since 1997. Hedrick coached 13 men's and women's wheelchair basketball teams to national titles during his tenure, and several men's and women's teams to Paralympic and world championship medals.

Hedrick is also a widely respected author in the rehabilitation field, coauthoring volumes on both wheelchair basketball and wheelchair track and field, as well as a chapter in a book on women's wheelchair basketball. He has published numerous articles on wheelchair basketball, track and field, and conditioning for athletes with disabilities.

Hedrick has also been a professor at the University of Illinois for decades. He shares his knowledge of topics such as Recreation for Individuals with Physical Disabilities, Administration of Adapted Sports and Recreation Programs, and Research Methods in Rehabilitation with students nation- and worldwide.

Hedrick's many accomplishments haven't gone unnoticed. He was 1 of 15 individuals recognized in 1999 by the Women's Division of the National Wheelchair Basketball Association for his contribution to the growth and development of women's wheelchair basketball in the United States, and he received the 1994 Jack Gerhardt Award for his contribution to wheelchair sports.

HEDRICK, SHARON

Hedrick was also instrumental in starting a junior wheelchair sports camp and a summer sports camp at the university to allow the coaches and student athletes of the program to share their wealth of knowledge with children and young adults from around the country.

BIBLIOGRAPHY. "Against the Wind: Brad Hedrick. WILL-AM," http://www.will.uiuc. edu/tv/documentaries/atw/atwhedrick.html; "Brad Hedrick's vitae." *University of Illinois Division of Rehabilitation Education Services.* http://www.rehab.uiuc.edu/staff/Brad_vita. html; Depauw, Karen P., and Susan J. Gavron. *Disability and Sport.* Champaign, IL: Human Kinetics, 1995; "16th National Women's Wheelchair Basketball Tournament." *Sports 'n' Spokes* (May–June 1990): 28–30.

HEDRICK, SHARON Sharon Hedrick made a name for herself out of being first. She was the first woman to enter the Boston Marathon alongside male wheelchair marathon pioneer Bob Hall. She was also the first female wheelchair athlete to win Olympic Gold in the 1984 800 meter exhibition race at the Los Angeles games, following that with a second Olympic Gold in the 800 meter race at the Seoul Olympics in 1988.

Hedrick, who had established a world mark in the 800 meter in 1988, slashed two seconds off her time to set a new world record in that distance in 1989 at the Prefontaine Classic in Eugene, Oregon, winning in 2:09.09. Hedrick owned world records in several other events as well, which she bested time and again. She set a world record in the 1,500 meter of 4:07.53 and 400 meter of 1:06.19 at a regional track meet in Ohio in 1989. Those records dropped just weeks later on a fast track in Johnson City, Tennessee, with Hedrick completing 800 meters in 2:08.1. While she lost the 1,500 meter to teammate Ann Cody, who out sprinted her at the end to take the race in 3:54.6, both women finished in new world record pace, with Hedrick coming in just behind her at 3:54.8. They were the first women to run 1,500 meters in under 4 minutes, setting the stage for many in the years to follow.

In addition to burning up the road and track, Hedrick was well known for her excellence on the basketball court, winning numerous national women's wheelchair basketball championships alongside her University of Illinois teammates. Hedrick was named to the first all tournament team at the National Women's Wheelchair Basketball Tournament (NWWBT) in 1989, leading the Illini with 17 points in the championship game, which they lost to the Courage Rolling Gophers of Minnesota. She was named to every all tournament team for the rest of her playing career.

Hedrick is single-handedly responsible for inspiring numerous disabled athletes who have followed in her footsteps, including other Illini standouts multitime Paralympian Scot Hollonbeck and eight-time Boston Marathon champion Jean Driscoll.

BIBLIOGRAPHY. Depauw, Karen P., and Susan J. Gavron. *Disability and Sport.* Champaign, IL: Human Kinetics, 1995; *Sports 'n' Spokes* (July–August 1989): 11; *Sports 'n' Spokes* (September–October 1989): 48+; *Sports 'n' Spokes* (May–June 1990): 28; Steadward, Robert Daniel, E. J. Watkinson, and Garry David Wheeler. *Adapted Physical Activity.* Edmonton: University of Alberta Press, 2003.

HOLLONBECK, SCOT Scot Hollonbeck has represented the United States in the 1,500 meter men's Olympic wheelchair race four times, more than any other U.S. athlete. He has held world records in the 800 meter, 1,500 meter, 4 by 400 meter relay, mile and 5K. He has competed in countless road races nation and worldwide from 10K to marathon.

Hollonbeck, of Rochelle, Illinois, was hit by a drunk driver at age 14 while riding his bike to swim practice. His introduction to the world of wheelchair sports came about while he was lying in his hospital bed watching the 1984 Olympics on the television in his room. He remembers hearing the announcer say that the women's 800 meter wheelchair race would be next. Hollonbeck, who had never before heard of wheelchair sports, watched Sharon Hedrick of the University of Illinois win and set the world record.

Having been an avid track athlete along with identical twin brother, Sean, prior to his injury, he was intrigued. He told his mom after watching the race that he'd like to try it, and the next summer he was participating in the junior sports camp at the University of Illinois. His own high school, however, wouldn't allow him to participate on the track team. Hollonbeck's family filed a lawsuit, and the result, though positive, didn't come in time for Scot, who graduated before the verdict was reached.

Hollonbeck enrolled as a freshman at the University of Illinois, where he ultimately earned a bachelor's in kinesiology and a graduate degree in sports sociology. He was extremely active in sports there, playing wheelchair basketball as well as competing in track and road racing. His talents on the court were recognized with an MVP award in 1991 and again in 1992, when he was voted the National Wheelchair Athletic Association Athlete of the Year. Although he was widely recognized for this basketball skill, his notable successes came on the track and the road.

In 1989, he won the Chicago Marathon in 1:45.20, more than 11 minutes in front of the second place finisher. In 2005, he completed the distance in 1:34.23. In 2004, he won the Grandma's Marathon in Minnesota. In 2005, he and three others beat the course record set in 1998. At the 1992 Paralympics he won Gold in the 800 m and silver in the 1,500 m. In the 1996 Olympics and Paralympics he won silver in the 1,500 m. He qualified for the 1992, 1996, 2000, and 2004 Olympic 1,500 meter exhibition events, with his best finish a silver medal in 1996.

Hollonbeck continues to travel the world competing and sharing his knowledge of track and road racing with athletes young and old.

BIBLIOGRAPHY. "Against the Wind: Scot Hollonbeck. WILL-AM," http://www.will.uiuc. edu/tv/documentaries/atw/atwtscot.html; Cross, Cecil. "Peachtree Race to Pit Wheeler against Brother." *Atlanta Journal Constitution,* http://www.ajc.com/search/content/services/ internship/story/CecilCross.html; Franco Marx, Jeanie. "Full-Fledged Stars: Despite their Disabilities Paralympic Stars Display all the Olympic Ideals." *Georgia Tech Alumni News* (Summer 1996); "Paralympian has Dream to Aid Sport for Disabled." *Atlanta Journal Constitution* (29 July 2002).

INTERNATIONAL AMPUTEE FOOTBALL FEDERATION Amputee football was established in the late 1980s, getting its start in the United States and Brazil.

The list of countries participating now includes England, Germany, Georgia, Russia, Ukraine, Moldavia, Czech Republic, Slovakia, Brazil, El Salvador, Mexico, United States, Uzbekistan, Iran, Africa, Ethiopia, Uganda, South Africa, and Zaire.

In 1988 Bill Berry, the founder of amputee football in the United States, helped establish a team in Uzbekistan. Later that same year, Moscow hosted the World Amputee Football Festival, and as a result of the festival, the International Amputee Football Federation (IAFF) was formed.

The IAFF is responsible for creating and enforcing the rules that govern amputee football and for overseeing the development of new teams and the entry of new nations into the competition.

In addition to Berry, another prominent figure in the world of amputee football is Thomas Feller. Born and raised in Seattle, Washington, Feller is Executive Director of the U.S. Amputee Soccer Association, as well as current president of the International Amputee Football Federation.

See also Feller, Thomas

BIBLIOGRAPHY. American Amputee Soccer Association, http://www.ampsoccer.org; International Amputee Football Federation, http://www.iaff.sport.U2/history_en.htm.

INTERNATIONAL BLIND SPORTS FEDERATION (IBSA) The International Blind Sports Federation (IBSA) is the primary international authority on matters relating to sports for people with visual impairments, with 108 member nations today. The IBSA was founded in Paris in 1981 and registered with the Spanish National Sports Council in March of 1996. IBSA provides a variety of assistance to its members, paying special attention to developing countries that are not able to educate and inform their citizens about the opportunities available for people who are blind or visually impaired. IBSA was a founding member of both the International Coordinating Council (ICC) and the International Paralympic Committee (IPC) together with the Cerebral Palsy International Sports and Recreation Association (CP-ISRA), the International Stoke-Mandeville Wheelchair Sports Federation (ISMWSF), and the International Sports Organization for the Disabled (ISOD).

The IBSA is responsible for regulating international sport for visually impaired athletes, planning, coordinating, organizing, and sanctioning competitions and sporting events at a national, regional, and world level. IBSA held the first World Blind Sports Championships in Madrid, Spain in July 1998, contesting swimming, judo, and goal ball.

IBSA athletes are categorized according to three classifications for the purpose of international competition. They are:

B-1 From no light perception in either eye to light perception, but inability to recognize the shape of a hand at any distance or in any direction.

B-2 From ability to recognize the shape of a hand to a visual acuity of 2/60 and/or visual field and less than 5 degrees.

B-3 From visual acuity above 2/60 to visual acuity of 6/60 and/or visual field of more than 5 degrees and less than 20 degrees.

IBSA, like other international sport federations, is governed by a General Assembly, held every four years in different nations around the world from Paris to the Dominican Republic.

BIBLIOGRAPHY. International Blind Sports Federation, http://www.ibsa.es; Steadward, Robert Daniel, E. J. Watkinson, and Garry David Wheeler. *Adapted Physical Activity.* Edmonton: University of Alberta Press, 2003.

INTERNATIONAL PARALYMPIC COMMITTEE (IPC) The International Paralympic Committee was formed in 1989 to be the international governing body of sport for persons

Sitting volleyball. *Copyright Chris Hamilton Photography.*

with disabilities. The IPC has been recognized by the International Olympic Committee, and it serves as the Paralympic sport liaison between the IOC and athletes with disabilities worldwide.

The IPC is based on the philosophy of elite disabled competition, and toward that end, it is responsible for organizing, supervising, and coordinating the Summer and Winter Paralympic Games. The IPC also sanctions and oversees multidisability regional and world championships for its 159 national members.

The IPC is comprised not only of the member nations, but of six international sport organizations for the disabled—the Cerebral Palsy International Sports and Recreation Association (CP-ISRA), International Blind Sports Association (IBSA), International Sports Federation for Persons with an Intellectual Disability (INAS-FID), International Stoke Mandeville Wheelchair Sports Federation (ISMWSF), and the International Sports Organization for the Disabled (ISOD). ISMWSF and ISOD recently merged in 2005, becoming the International Wheelchair and Amputee Sports Federation.

The IPC, in addition to promoting sport for people with disabilities worldwide is active in U.N. and other initiatives promoting health, wellness, physical activity, and human rights.

BIBLIOGRAPHY. International Paralympic Committee, http://www.paralympic.org; Joukowsky, Artemis A. W, and Larry Rothstein. *Raising the Bar—New Horizons in Disability Sport,* 1st ed. New York, NY: Umbrage Editions, 2002; Steadward, Robert Daniel, E. J. Watkinson, and Garry David Wheeler. *Adapted Physical Activity.* Edmonton: University of Alberta Press, 2003.

INTERNATIONAL SPORTS FEDERATION FOR PERSONS WITH AN INTELLECTUAL DISABILITY (INAS-FID) The International Sports Federation for Persons with an Intellectual Disability (INAS-FID) was founded in 1986 to organize and promote sports for athletes with intellectual disabilities by a group of people who believed that the needs of athletes with intellectual disabilities who were dedicated to intense training and elite performance goals were not being adequately served within Special Olympics International.

It was originally named the International Sport Federation for Persons with Mental Handicap (INAS-FMH) but changed its name to reflect more current terminology in 1999. INAS-FID was a founding member of both the International Coordinating Council (ICC) and the International Paralympic Committee (IPC) together with the Cerebral Palsy International Sports and Recreation Association (CP-ISRA), International Stoke Mandeville Wheelchair Sports Federation (ISMWSF), International Sports Organization for the Disabled (ISOD), International Blind Sports Association (IBSA), and Comité International des Sports des Sourds (CISS).

At the time of its founding, INAS-FID had 14 member nations, and by 2002, there were 86. INAS-FID, like other International Organizations of Sport for the Disabled, is structured internationally, regionally, and nationally. INAS-FID hosts sport specific world championships and oversees regional and national INAS-FID activities.

Eligibility for INAS-FID competition requires an athlete have a documented intellectual disability, with an IQ in the 70–75 range, and limitations in adaptive behavior that manifest before age 18. Unlike other disability sport organizations, INAS-FID doesn't classify its athletes other than by gender.

INTERNATIONAL SPORTS FEDERATION

Athletes with intellectual disabilities competed in the Paralympics for the first time in the 1992 Winter Games in Tignes-Albertville, France. There, they had demonstration events in alpine and Nordic skiing. Rather than continue with demonstration events in the 1992 Summer Paralympics in Barcelona, however, INAS-FID obtained approval to hold a separate Paralympic Games for athletes with an intellectual disability. In those games, 2500 athletes from 73 countries participated in athletics, basketball, soccer, swimming, and table tennis.

Paul Moran and Team USA sitting volleyball. *Photo courtesy of Rehabilitation Institute of Chicago Wirtz Sports Program.*

In 1994, INAS-FID athletes once again participated in demonstration events at the Lillehammer Winter Paralympics, competing in a 5K Nordic ski race. It wasn't until 1996 at the Atlanta Paralympic Games that INAS-FID athletes were accorded full medal status for their events—the long jump and 200 meter athletics events, and the 50m and 100 m freestyle in swimming.

In recent years, controversy has plagued INAS-FID. They were suspended from IPC membership in 2001 after an investigation disclosed that several athletes on the Spanish basketball team that competed in Sydney in 2000 did not meet the eligibility requirements. They were reinstated a year later, after creating new eligibility verification processes for athletes, however, the status of their events on the Paralympic program has yet to be decided.

BIBLIOGRAPHY. "International Disability Sports Organizations." *Michigan State University,* http://ed-web3.educ.msu.edu/kin866/orginternational.htm; Steadward, Robert Daniel, E. J. Watkinson, and Garry David Wheeler. *Adapted Physical Activity.* Edmonton: University of Alberta Press, 2003.

INTERNATIONAL SPORTS ORGANIZATION FOR THE DISABLED (ISOD) The International Sports Organization for the Disabled (ISOD) was created in 1964, primarily to serve the needs of athletes who were not being served by the International Stoke Mandeville Wheelchair Sports Federation. This included athletes with visual impairments as well as athletes who were amputees or had cerebral palsy.

The first president was Norman Acton. The second president was Sir Ludwig Guttman, who rose to prominence as the founder of the International Stoke Mandeville Wheelchair Sports Federation (ISMWSF). Over time, other disability specific organizations formed to govern sports and recreation for people with cerebral palsy (Cerebral Palsy International Sports and Recreation Association) and visually impaired athletes (International Blind Sports Federation). ISOD then became responsible for governing amputee athletes and "les autres," the athletes who did not fit into any of the existing sports organizations.

Recently, ISOD and ISMWSF have merged into IWAS, International Wheelchair and Amputee Sports Federation, and together they will govern wheelchair and amputee sports worldwide.

Wheelchair basketball. *Photo courtesy of Rehabilitation Institute of Chicago Wirtz Sports Program.*

INTERNATIONAL STOKE MANDEVILLE WHEELCHAIR SPORTS FEDERATION

BIBLIOGRAPHY. "International Disability Sports Organizations." *Michigan State University,* http://ed-web3.educ.msu.edu/kin866/orginternational.htm; Steadward, Robert Daniel, E. J. Watkinson, and Garry David Wheeler. *Adapted Physical Activity.* Edmonton: University of Alberta Press, 2003.

INTERNATIONAL STOKE MANDEVILLE WHEELCHAIR SPORTS FEDERATION (ISMWSF) The International Stoke Mandeville Wheelchair Sports Federation (ISMWSF) was formed as a result of the work of Sir Ludwig Guttman. Guttman was responsible for creating a wheelchair sports program at the Stoke Mandeville Rehabilitation Hospital. He then coordinated the first organized wheelchair sports competition in 1948, which he called the Stoke Mandeville Games. Held in Aylesbury, England, the games played a pivotal role in the development of disability sport, particularly for those using wheelchairs due to spinal cord injury.

Archery, slalom, obstacle courses, wheelchair polo, badminton, and netball were played in the early competitions, along with swimming and lawn bowls. From those beginnings came the modern Paralympic Games, which now offer competition in 19 different sports to thousands of athletes from well over 100 countries every 2 years. The Games alternate between Summer and Winter Paralympic Games and are held in the same years and in the same host cities and countries as the corresponding Olympic Games.

In addition to founding the Games, Ludwig Guttman oversaw the formation of the International Stoke Mandeville Games Federation (ISMGF), which was later renamed the International Stoke Mandeville Wheelchair Sports Federation in recognition of the broader role the organization played with regard to increasing opportunities for participation and competition. In 2000 after the General Assembly in Sydney, ISMWSF and ISOD merged, becoming the International Wheelchair and Amputee Sports federation, and will now jointly oversee development sport for wheelchair and amputee sports.

See also Guttman, Sir Ludwig

BIBLIOGRAPHY. "International Disability Sports Organizations." *Michigan State University,* http://ed-web3.educ.msu.edu/kin866/orginternational.htm; International Paralympic Committee, http://www.paralympic.org/paralympian/20004/2000407.htm; Steadward, Robert Daniel, E. J. Watkinson, and Garry David Wheeler. *Adapted Physical Activity.* Edmonton: University of Alberta Press, 2003.

INTERNATIONAL WHEELCHAIR AND AMPUTEE SPORTS FEDERATION. *See* International Stoke Mandeville Wheelchair Sports Federation

KILEY, DAVID David Kiley is considered by many to be the greatest wheelchair athlete of all time. Born on April 30, 1953, in Mooresville, North Carolina, Kiley has been a leader on and off the playing field for four decades. Kiley was a basketball star in high school, with dreams of an NBA career when he became an incomplete paraplegic with a T12-L1 injury after a tubing accident at the age of 19. He struggled with depression, drugs, and alcohol until one day when he decided to take a swim.

Sitting at the beach about 30 feet from the water on a hot day, he thought how great it would be to get in the water. Usually, he would have been worried what people would think if they saw him crawl across the beach to the water. On that day, he did not. He hopped out of his chair, covered the distance to the water and swam. Soon, he was back to the athletic life he had loved prior to his injury, and he started playing wheelchair basketball. He transferred his standing basketball skills to the wheelchair game, becoming one of the best all around players ever.

Though Kiley is best known for his basketball achievement, he also excelled in other sports. Kiley won four Gold medals in track at the 1976 Paralympics, setting three world records in the process. He also won two silver medals and two Gold at the 1992 Winter Paralympics. In fact, Kiley won eight Gold medals in three sports over five Paralympic Games. He was named All American in wheelchair basketball 19 times and was recognized as the league MVP 6 times in his career.

Along with his many contributions to the world of disability sport, Kiley will also be remembered for one of the most controversial decisions in Paralympic history. After helping the U.S. basketball team win the Gold medal at the 1992 Summer Paralympic Games in Barcelona, Kiley was drug tested. Kiley had taken a painkiller, which was on the banned substance list, resulting in a positive test. As a result, the team was stripped of their Gold medal and Kiley was banned from international competition for two years.

Despite that setback, Kiley has remained active in the disability sport world, giving back to the sports community and developing opportunities for others to excel at the levels he has achieved. Kiley was the Director of Community Wheelchair Sports, Recreation and Outdoors Program at the Casa Colina Centers for Rehabilitation in Pomona, California for 16 years before he headed south to become the director of the Adaptive Sports and Adventures Program at Charlotte Institute of Rehabilitation in Charlotte, North Carolina.

KNAUB, JIM

BIBLIOGRAPHY. International Paralympic Committee; Justice, Richard. "Wheels Can't Keep Players from Game," http://www.chron.com/disp/story.mpl/sports/justice/3666321. html; National Wheelchair Basketball Association, http://www.nwba.org; Spin Life, http:// www.spinlife.com/en/spinlifeAdvisoryBoard.cfm.

KNAUB, JIM Jim Knaub was one of the pioneers in men's wheelchair track and road racing. He posted numerous Boston Marathon wins, and he also held records at various other distances, winning the National Wheelchair 10K Championship in Torrance, California in 1990 in world record time of 22:36, hundredths of a second ahead of second place Doug Kennedy. Knaub also won the Wheelchair Race of Champions in 1990, an ultramarathon race from Purcellville, Virginia to Washington, D.C., just 29 seconds ahead of Kenny Carnes. Knaub is one of many racers who have been instrumental in creating the racing wheelchairs of today, working with companies including Cannondale and others to design and build better equipment for today's wheelchair athletes.

BIBLIOGRAPHY. *Sports 'n' Spokes* (January–February 1992): 20–21; *Sports 'n' Spokes* (May-June 1990): 28.

LARSON, DAVID Dave Larson, diagnosed with cerebral palsy at age two, never thought he would be an athlete, much less a champion athlete. He grew up like his brothers in a lot of ways, playing sports such as basketball, baseball, and tennis. But he could never forget that he was different. He ran his way through a new pair of shoes every week, thanks to hereditary spastic paraplegia, a disorder that is classified under the umbrella term cerebral palsy, which creates stiffness and spasticity in the lower limbs, affecting only about 2,500 people nationwide.

By the time he was 12, Larson had undergone four surgeries to lengthen tendons in his legs, and by age 13, problems with his hips meant he could no longer run. He turned to using a wheelchair, and, looking for ways to stay active, learned about wheelchair soccer.

Then, while attending San Diego High School, Larson ran into some Canadian wheelchair athletes working out at a track. Their coach suggested Larson give the sport a try, and he was hooked. But it wasn't until he attended Sacramento City College and met Morano Robbins, a local coach who was working with wheelchair racers, that his career really took off.

In just two short years after he began seriously training, Larson was selected to represent the United States in the Paralympics in 1988, winning bronze in both the 100 and 400 meters. At his second Paralympic appearance in 1992, he was part of a U.S. sweep in the T34 class, winning Gold medals in the 100, 200, 400, and 800 meters, setting four new world records along the way.

Then in 1994 at the IPC Athletics World Championships in Berlin, he shattered his own world records again en route to three Gold medals in the 200, 400, and 800 meter events. He followed that with yet another Gold medal, this time at home at the Atlanta Paralympics in 1996. There, he wowed the crowd with another world-record-breaking performance in the 400 meter, winning his seventh Paralympic medal and fifth Gold. He added to his medal tally with a bronze in the 100 meter.

For his accomplishments on the field, Larson was twice named the U.S. Cerebral Palsy Athletic Association male athlete of the year, in 1989 and again in 1993. He was also named the 1996 Disabled Athlete of the Year in his hometown of San Diego.

BIBLIOGRAPHY. Sheehan, Rose. "Fatherhood, the Greatest Challenge". *San Diego Family Magazine* (June 1999). http://www.stonebrew.com/cool/racing/wheelchair/indexarticle1.

html; "Sports at Lunch: Dave Larson." *San Diego Hall of Champions,* http://www.sdhoc.com/main/articles/sportsatlunch/LarsonDave.

LAWN BOWLS (BOWLS) Lawn bowls looks a lot like another disability sport, boccia. There are differences, however. Boccia is played indoors on a gymnasium floor or other hard surface; lawn bowls is played on a grass court.

The modern version of lawn bowls was developed in Scotland in the mid-1800s. It wasn't until 1930, however, that a lawn bowls event was organized specifically for people with disabilities. It took nearly 40 more years for the game to be played on the Paralympic stage when it appeared at the 1968 Paralympics in Israel. Bowls were played in every Paralympic Games with the exception of the 1992 games in Barcelona, until they were removed from the Games program in 2000.

Bowls competition is still offered at local, national, and regional competitions for both men and women with disabilities, primarily wheelchair users. It is played on a grass court that may be real or a synthetic surface. It can be played by individuals or teams of up to four, with the goal being to get the most balls closer to the white ball or "jack" than the opponent.

The bowls themselves consist of a jack or small white ball and then four bowls made of hard plastic which are shaped so as to cause the bowl to curve when it is thrown. The surface of the green and the weight of the bowl can effect the game outcome, adding an element of difficulty to the competitions.

BIBLIOGRAPHY. International Paralympic Committee: Bowles, History, http://www.paralympic.org/release/Summer_Sports/Bowls/About_the_Sport/History/.

MARTIN, CASEY Casey Martin grew up like most boys, wanting to be active, and wanting to play sports. But unlike most boys, he had a rare disability that only a handful of people in the world share with him. He was born June 2, 1972, in Eugene, Oregon. Although he couldn't compete in many sports, he found that not only was golf a sport he could play, it was one he could play well even with his disability. The problem was, whenever he did play, he ended up having severe pain and was diagnosed with Klippel-Trenaunay–Webber Syndrome, a circulatory disorder that caused his leg to swell, bleed internally, and make it extremely weak and painful.

Even with his disability, Martin quickly rose to the top in the field, winning 17 junior golf titles in his home state of Oregon. He played well enough to earn a scholarship to Stanford University, where he was teammate to Tiger Woods. He studied economics, not because of a keen interest in the subject, but because the course load allowed him to take the afternoons off to pursue his true passion—golf.

For the first two years of college, Martin walked the courses and carried his bag like the other players. As time went on, however, his leg seemed to be getting worse. He had constant pain, more swelling, and could only stand for limited periods of time. Doctors began to tell him that if he fell and broke it, it would likely have to be amputated.

Martin could no longer walk the entire 18 holes of a golf course without severe swelling and pain. He petitioned the NCAA and the PAC-10 to be allowed to use a cart to get from one hole to the next and was granted that accommodation. Together, Martin, Woods, and Notah Begay won the 1994 NCAA golf championship.

Martin graduated from Stanford, setting out to pursue his career as a professional golfer. He played on the Hooters Tour and the Tommy Armour Tour in 1996 and 1997. Both tours allowed him to use a golf cart during practice and pro-ams but not in the competition itself; meanwhile his leg continued to get worse. Even with his leg deteriorating, however, he earned his PGA Tour card by finishing in the top 15 in the 1999 Nike Tour.

Martin asked the PGA to grant the same accommodation the NCAA had provided—the right to use a cart to travel between holes. When they refused to let him use a cart in the PGA Qualifying School, he went to court, filing a suit in federal court under the Americans with Disabilities Act, alleging that the PGA Tour was discriminating against him based on his disability. Martin's suit claimed that refusing to accommodate him by modifying their policy against allowing golf carts in PGA Tour events was discriminatory.

Patrick Byrne nails the shot. *Photo courtesy of Rehabilitation Institute of Chicago Wirtz Sports Program.*

The district court in Oregon sided with Martin, and the PGA Tour appealed to the 9th Circuit Court in California. The 9th Circuit also sided with Martin. Martin was allowed to play on the Nike Tour using a cart, and subsequently qualified for the PGA Tour. The PGA then took the case all the way to the U.S. Supreme Court.

The Court issued their decision in 2001, deciding by a 7–2 margin that the PGA Tour did indeed have to allow Martin to use a cart in PGA Tour events. They dismissed the PGA's arguments that walking was fundamental to the game of golf and that a cart would give Martin an unfair advantage. The Court's decision proved to be accurate—Martin's use of a cart didn't provide him with any advantage. In fact, since winning the suit, Martin has not finished higher than the top 25.

BIBLIOGRAPHY. Moriarty, Jim. "Martin: Every Day is a Bonus." *Golf World.* http://sports.espn.go.com/golf/news/story?id=1787692; *PGA Tour Inc. v. Martin.* No. 532 U.S. 661. United States Supreme Court. 2001; "Rosaforte, Tim, Casey's Last Stand; Casey Martin Awaits the Decision that will Rule His Future in Golf." *Golf Digest* (May 2001), http://www.golfdigest.com/features/index.ssf?/features/caseys_1_d750d8lc.html.

MARTINSON, JIM Jim Martinson was a downhill skiing champion as a teen, training to qualify for the Olympics. Instead, he ended up in Vietnam, where a mine exploded, killing the four men he had been with, and tearing off his legs below the knees. When he awoke, he was in the hospital in Japan, and then he was sent back to the United States for rehabilitation.

He went through a period of drinking and using drugs, depressed and not knowing how to go on with his life. Then he met a woman, married in 1971, finished school, and then he got involved in youth ministry. The children in the ministry encouraged him to get back into athletics, so he started working out. He quickly realized, however, that the wheelchair he was using for everyday wasn't going to work for athletic activity.

He took it apart in his garage and began building a chair that weighed less than half of the original. He began training, and set his sights on the Boston Marathon. In 1981, he won that race. Others began to ask him for chairs, so Martinson began building them. He formed Magic in Motion, and began to build Shadow racing chairs.

Martinson learned that the 1984 Olympics would have a wheelchair exhibition race for the first time. The qualifier was a 1,500 meter race in New York, which he won easily. That success didn't follow him to the Olympic race, however; there, he was eighth of eight. After two months of figuring out whether to stick with it or give up, he decided to stick with racing. He took his chair back out and began once again to win race after race.

During this time his wheelchair business grew, and he began working with the athletes who bought chairs from him, providing them with training tips and racing techniques as well as the chair. Racers using his chairs began to achieve great results, getting Martinson even more acclaim. Martinson's company joined forces with Quickie Designs as part of Sunrise Medical, giving him access to the world market.

He branched out of racing chairs and began building tennis chairs, basketball chairs, mono-skis and water skis. Martinson continues to be a force in disability sport, coaching and mentoring athletes, and building and designing new and better chairs and equipment.

BIBLIOGRAPHY. International Paralympic Committee, http://www.spinlife.org; Sunrise Medical, http://www.sunrisemedical.org; Wilbee, Brenda. "What's It All About?" *Sports 'n' Spokes* (March–April 1991): 16–19.

MASTANDREA, LINDA Linda Mastandrea didn't grow up thinking of herself as an athlete. Second born of twins, she was born with cerebral palsy due to a lack of oxygen. This meant that she couldn't run, jump, and play the same as the other kids. Thinking she couldn't play sports and could never be an athlete like many of her friends, Mastandrea dedicated herself instead to academics, graduating 7th in her class from Bolingbrook High School in Bolingbrook, Illinois. Mastandrea and her twin then attended college at the University of Illinois. What Mastandrea didn't know as she packed up to begin life as a college freshman was that her life was about to change dramatically.

A sprained ankle led her to the Division of Rehabilitation Education Services, world renowned for not only its disability sports program but also for its educational support services for students with disabilities. It was there that she learned that having a disability didn't mean she couldn't participate in sports. Brad Hedrick, coach of the champion women's wheelchair basketball team, invited Mastandrea to join the women and play.

Mastandrea set off on the path that would lead her to 15 Gold and 5 silver medals in international wheelchair track competition, 4 world and 5 national records, a Paralympic championship, and a law degree. Mastandrea played basketball with the University of Illinois while earning her B.A. in Speech Communication and then returned home to Chicago where she played with the Rehabilitation Institute of Chicago Express.

While she dabbled in track and road racing during college, it wasn't until she saw former University of Illinois teammates Ann Cody and Sharon Hedrick racing in the Olympic Games in Seoul in 1988 that she thought about pursuing it seriously. Two years later, she

MASTRO, JIM

Linda Mastandrea training on rollers. *Photo courtesy of Rehabilitation Institute of Chicago Wirtz Sports Program.*

met Jeff Jones at the Rehabilitation Institute of Chicago, who invited her to join their racing team. She accepted the invitation, at the same time pursuing another dream—a law degree from Chicago-Kent College of Law.

Within the first year, Mastandrea had qualified to represent the United States at the Paralympic Games to be held in Barcelona in 1992. She took three weeks off of her second year of law school to attend the games. Unfortunately, dreams of Gold were not to be realized on that trip. Due to a lack of entrants, Mastandrea's events were deleted from the Paralympic program.

Undeterred, Mastandrea kept at it. In 1994, she graduated law school, and represented the United States at the World Championships in Berlin, where she won three Gold medals, setting world records in the 200 and 400 meters. She qualified for her second Paralympic team in 1996 going into the games heavily favored to win both the 100 m and 200 m. In a surprise upset, Mastandrea lost the 100 m to Noriko Arai of Japan. Four days later, Mastandrea got her revenge, easily cruising to Gold in the 200 m, breaking the world record she had set in Berlin in 1994 by nearly two seconds.

Mastandrea has been widely recognized for her accomplishments, being named one of Crain's Chicago Business "Forty Under 40," receiving the International Olympic Committee President's Disabled Athlete Award, and being named an Outstanding Woman Leader in Sport by the YWCA of DuPage County. Mastandrea was also a finalist for the prestigious Amateur Athletic Union (AAU) Sullivan Award, recognizing the top amateur sporting talent in the nation.

Mastandrea was also the first athlete with a disability to serve on the U.S. Olympic Committee's Board of Directors.

BIBLIOGRAPHY. "Awards of Sport," *The Sport Journal,* United States Sports Academy, http://www.thesportjournal.org/1999Journal/Vol2-No2/aos.asp; Franco Marx, Jeanie. "Full Fleged Stars: Despite Their Disabilities, Paralympic Athletes Display All the Olympic Ideals," *Goergia Tech Alumni Magazine* (Summer 1996), http://gtalumni.org/Publications/magazine/sum96/para.html; Rehabilitation Institute of Chicago Center for Health and Fitness, http://www.richealthfit.org/paralympic%20history/paralympichistorymain.htm.

MASTRO, JIM Jim Mastro, blinded as a teenager after an accident, has been in sports his whole life. He's wrestled, played baseball, competed in field events, and participated in goalball and judo. No other athlete with a disability has participated in, or medaled in, as many sports as Jim Mastro.

His sports career got its start when Mastro, a 1973 graduate of Augsburg College, competed in wrestling there, earning All Minnesota Intercollegiate Athletic Conference (MIAC) honors twice and winning the 177 pound division as a senior. He was a member of the U.S. team at the World University Games in 1973 and earned three bronze medals in international competition against nondisabled athletes. He was also an alternate for the 1976 Olympic team in Greco-Roman wrestling, the first visually impaired athlete to advance that far.

He competed in five Paralympic Games from 1976 to 2000, medaling in judo, goalball, wrestling, and track and field, winning five Gold and three silver medals as well as two bronze in international competition. Mastro was named by his U.S. teammates in 1996 as the flag bearer for the opening ceremonies in the Atlanta Paralympic Games. The next year, his alma mater inducted him into the school's Hall of Fame.

In addition to his Paralympic sports involvement, Mastro had a long career in beep baseball. He was inducted into the National Beep Baseball Association (NBBA) Hall of Fame, named to the All Tournament Team of the National Beep Baseball Association seven times, and he was selected MVP from 1978–1980, in addition to serving as the league's third president.

Mastro was a standout in the educational arena, where he was the first visually impaired student to earn a Ph.D. in physical education in the United States.

BIBLIOGRAPHY. Benson, Dan. "Augsburg Student Aaron Cross, Alum Jim Mastro to Compete in Paralympics," *Augsburg College News* (August 9, 1996), http://www.augsburg.edu/news/news-archives/1996/paralympics.html; Kelley, Jerry D., and Lex Frieden. *Go For It! A Book on Sport and Recreation for Persons with Disabilities.* Orlando, FL: Harcourt Brace Jovanovich, 1989; The National Beep Baseball Association Hall of Fame Inductees, http://halloffame.nbba.org/inductees/jim_mastro.htm; Storer, Don. "Targeting Success: No Barriers Allowed," *Augsburg Now* (Summer 2001), http://www.augsburg.edu/now/archives/summer01/barriers.html.

MENDOZA, SAUL Saul Mendoza was the first athlete with a disability in Mexico to be named Athlete of the Century. Born in Mexico City in 1967, he contracted polio before the age of one year, and discovered wheelchair sports at an early age.

His first sport was wheelchair basketball. Discovered on the court at age 15, his great speed on the court made the transition to track and road racing a natural one. He began racing in 1984 and has since completed several hundred races, winning at virtually every distance he's attempted.

Mendoza has many marathon wins to his credit, including Boston, Los Angeles seven times, London, and Japan. He has also excelled at shorter distances, capturing the Bloomsday 12K in Spokane from 1998–2005.

He has competed in five Paralympic Games, from Seoul in 1988 to Athens in 2004. He has held world records in the 5,000 and 10,000 meters and the Olympic record for the men's 1,500 meter wheelchair race winning in 3:06.75 in Sydney. He won a silver and two bronze in Seoul, a Gold in Atlanta, a Gold and a bronze in Sydney, and a silver in Athens. In the 1,500 meter race in Athens, Mendoza repeated his Gold medal performance of four years earlier, winning in 3:04.88.

MURRAY, GEORGE

While currently living in the United States, he has been named Mexican athlete of the year three times.

BIBLIOGRAPHY. Boston Marathon 2000, Boston.com, http://www.boston.com/marathon/runners/Saul_Mendoza.htm; "Saul Mendoza Takes Gold in the TS4 Men's 1500M," Paralympics.com, http://www.paralympics.com/News_articles_archive/saul_mendoza_1500 m.htm; "Saul Mendoza triunfa en NY," *Azteca 21* (July 11, 2001), http://www.azteca21.com/index.php?option=com_content&task=view&ID=23b&itemid=129.

MONO-SKI. *See* Skiing

MURDERBALL. *See* Quad Rugby

MURRAY, GEORGE George Murray was the first wheelchair racer to break the four minute mile barrier. He was also one of the first to break the 60 second barrier for the quarter mile, running a 59.2 in 1983. Murray was also one of the first Boston Marathon wheelchair division champions in 1978 with a time of 2:26:57, winning the race again in 1985 with a time of 1:45:34.

Murray was the first athlete with a disability to appear on a Wheaties box following those stand-out performances.

Murray wasn't content with just winning marathons, though. He and a friend and fellow wheelchair athlete Phil Carpenter, wanted to be the first wheelers to cross the country from coast to coast, planning a trip they called the "Continental Quest." Murray and Carpenter took 137 days to travel from Los Angeles to the United Nations Building in New York, a distance of 3,442 miles. This feat accomplished, Murray then turned his talents to wheelchair design and promotion, working with Chris Peterson to develop the Top End line of wheelchairs, which are one of the top selling wheelchairs today.

BIBLIOGRAPHY. Huber, J. H. "Boston: The 100th Marathon and the Wheelchair Athlete." *Palaestra* (21 February 2003), http://special.northernlight.com/marathon/wheelchair_palaestra.htm; Kelley, Jerry D., and Lex Frieden. *Go For It! A Book on Sport and Recreation for Persons with Disabilities.* Orlando, FL: Harcourt Brace Jovanovich, 1989.

NATIONAL BEEP BASEBALL ASSOCIATION (NBBA) There are two ways to enjoy baseball, as a fan or as a player. Only a small percentage of players actually make it into the major leagues. But thousands of people play in communities all over the country from the first days of "spring training" all through the summer. In the not-too-distant past, though, people with visual impairments were left out.

In 1964, this began to change. Charley Fairbanks, an engineer with Mountain Bell Telephone and a member of the Telephone Pioneers of America, implanted a small beeping sound module inside a normal sized softball. The Pioneers also invented a set of cone-shaped rubber bases that contained electrically powered sounding units that emitted a high pitched whistle. Initial experiments with beep baseball, as they called it, foundered due to difficulties with the equipment as well as somewhat paternalistic and restrictive rules.

A decade later, in the spring of 1975, the Minnesota Telephone Pioneers presented John Ross, Director of the Braille Sports Foundation, with a newly designed beep ball, a 16-inch ball with an improved sound module designed to withstand the impact of being hit. Ross and some of his friends began experimenting with new rule adaptations to make the game more competitive. New guidelines, known as the "Minnesota Rules," were drafted by Dennis Huberty of St. Paul, Minnesota, and Ross, and competitive beep baseball was born.

Feeling Sports, a monthly publication of the Braille Sports Foundation, started carrying accounts and results of the games. Interest grew, and an organizational meeting was held to discuss the immediate future of beep baseball. Bill Gibney, a Phoenix attorney and first president of the NBBA, provided the name that was unanimously adopted—National Beep Baseball Association.

The first World Series of Beep Baseball was held in St. Paul that same September. Over 1,500 fans filled the bleachers to cheer the local St. Paul Gorillas on to the first NBBA championship by beating the Phoenix Thunderbirds 36 to 27. Today, there are over 50 teams playing the game nationwide.

See also Beep Baseball

BIBLIOGRAPHY. National Beep Baseball Association, http://www.nbba.org.

Seven-a-side soccer. *Photo courtesy of Rehabilitation Institute of Chicago Wirtz Sports Program.*

NATIONAL DISABILITY SPORTS ALLIANCE (NDSA) Sports for athletes with cerebral palsy in the United States got their start in 1978, when the National Association of Sports for Cerebral Palsy was formed. For the first several years of its existence, the United States Cerebral Palsy Athletic Association was part of the United Cerebral Palsy Association. It became an independent nonprofit in 1987. The organization was again renamed as the National Disability Sports Alliance in 2001 to reflect the wide range of people with disabilities it serves.

Athletes with cerebral palsy have opportunities to compete at the local, regional, national, and international level. Athletes with cerebral palsy, brain injury, and stroke have competed at the 1987 Can/Am/Pacific Games for the Disabled, the 1988 Seoul Paralympics, the 1990 World Championships for the Disabled in Assen, the 1992 Paralympics in Barcelona, the 1996 Paralympics in Atlanta, the 1998 World Championships, and the 2000 and 2004 Paralympics in multidisability, multisport competition. Athletes with cerebral palsy have competed in single sport multidisability competitions like the IPC World Athletics Championships and single sport, single disability championships like the Boccia World Cup as well.

NDSA is responsible for the growth and development of recreational and elite athletes with cerebral palsy and related disabilities. They offer sports and recreation opportunities in boccia, bowling, cross-country, cycling, equestrian, powerlifting, soccer, swimming, track and field, and indoor wheelchair soccer.

NDSA athletes compete according to the classification system established by the Cerebral Palsy International Sports and Recreation Association (CP-ISRA), the worldwide governing body of cerebral palsy sport. There are eight classifications for athletes with cerebral palsy. Classes one through four are for wheelchair users; classes five through eight are for ambulatory athletes.

NDSA offers a variety of sports activities for athletes with cerebral palsy, brain injury, and stroke, along with similar disabilities.

Boccia is a game that, in the disability sport context, is played primarily by athletes with cerebral palsy, and it is open to wheelchair athletes from Classes 1 and 2. It is a game of precision and skill with the object of the game being to place balls closest to a target ball on a long, narrow indoor court. Divisions are available for athletes who can throw the ball independently and those who use assistive devices like a ramp to throw the ball onto the court.

Bowling is open to all athletes with cerebral palsy and is organized into four divisions. Divisions A and B use chutes or ramps; Divisions C and D do not. Division A is for classes 1 and 2; Division B and C are for classes 3, 4, 5, and 6; and Division D is for classes 7 and 8.

In cycling, there are four divisions; two are for tricycle and two are for bicycle. Males and females compete separately. Equestrian competition consists solely of dressage, and while the NDSA is the governing body of equestrian, athletes with a variety of disabilities participate; thus they are classified according to a functional system into one of four grades.

Indoor wheelchair soccer is a reincarnation of a sport that used to be known as wheelchair team handball. It uses a functional classification system as athletes with a range of disabilities are eligible to play. Powerlifting competition for athletes with cerebral palsy is bench press with a classification system based on weight.

Soccer is played with seven players a side, and the field is slightly smaller than FIFA regulation. Athletes in classes 5 through 8 are eligible to play, but no assistive devices are allowed. Swimming is open to all athletes within all classifications. There is also the opportunity to compete in integrated swimming events within a functional classification system, which is how swimming is conducted at the Paralympic games. Thus, swimmers may have a CP-ISRA class for CP-only competition and a functional class for IPC competition. Athletics, or track and field, offers events for athletes in all classifications. Athletes with cerebral palsy may also compete in the functional system and race against athletes with other disabilities in events sanctioned by the International Wheelchair and Amputee Sports Federation (IWAS). Cross-country is offered solely for ambulatory athletes in classes 5 through 8.

BIBLIOGRAPHY. International Paralympic Committee, www.paralympic.org; National Disability Sports Alliance, http://www.ndsaonline.org; Paciorek, Michael J., and Jeffery A. Jones. *Sports and Recreation for the Disabled,* 2nd ed. Carmel, IN: Cooper Publishing Group, 1994, 329–333.

NATIONAL FOUNDATION OF WHEELCHAIR TENNIS The National Foundation of Wheelchair Tennis was formed in 1980 by Brad Parks. It sponsors competitions, clinics, exhibitions, and camps around the nation. The Wheelchair Tennis Player's Association (WTPA) governs the rules and regulations of wheelchair tennis.

Though the sport was born in 1976, the National Foundation of Wheelchair Tennis was organized four years later in 1980. The WTPA was started in 1981 to establish rankings among the players and define competition in the seven divisions.

See also Parks, Brad; Wheelchair Tennis

BIBLIOGRAPHY. Depauw, Karen P., and Susan J. Gavron. *Disability and Sport.* Champaign, IL: Human Kinetics, 1995; "A Look at Wheelchair Tennis." *Sports 'n' Spokes* (January–February 1990): 20.

NATIONAL HANDICAPPED SPORTS. *See* Disabled Sports USA (DS-USA)

NATIONAL RIFLE ASSOCIATION (NRA) DISABLED SHOOTING SERVICES. *See* Shooting

NATIONAL SPORTS CENTER FOR THE DISABLED The National Sports Center for the Disabled was founded in 1970 when Hal O'Leary, the Winter Park Ski Resort's director, agreed to teach a group of amputee children from the Children's Hospital in Denver how to ski. Today, it is considered one of the largest outdoor recreation programs in the world for people with disabilities, offering downhill and cross-country skiing, snowboarding and snowshoeing, biking, hiking, sailing, rafting, fishing, and horseback riding, as well as camping and rock climbing. Each year thousands of children and adults come to Winter Park Resort.

The National Sports Center for the Disabled has its own adaptive equipment and staff, and it has expanded to teaching both winter and summer sports to people with both physical and mental disabilities. They also train ski racers with disabilities to prepare for elite competition in both Alpine and Nordic skiing.

BIBLIOGRAPHY. Joukowsky, Artemis A. W, and Larry Rothstein. *Raising the Bar—New Horizons in Disability Sport,* 1st ed. New York: Umbrage Editions, 2002; National Sports Center for the Disabled, http://www.nscd.org; Winnick, Joseph P. *Adapted Physical Education and Sport,* 4th ed. Champaign, IL: Human Kinetics, 2005.

NATIONAL WHEELCHAIR ATHLETIC ASSOCIATION. *See* Wheelchair Sports, USA (WS-USA)

NATIONAL WHEELCHAIR BASKETBALL ASSOCIATION (NWBA) The National Wheelchair Basketball Association (NWBA) is one of the oldest disabled sports organizations in the United States. It was formed in 1949 after an influx of disabled veterans returned home from the war looking to get involved in athletics again. The University of Illinois organized the first national wheelchair basketball tournament, which then led to the creation of a formal organization to oversee the further development of the sport of wheelchair basketball. Today, the NWBA offers divisions for men's, women's, and junior's competition nationwide, and it sanctions regional and national tournaments for each division.

Women's wheelchair basketball. *Photo courtesy of Rehabilitation Institute of Chicago Wirtz Sports Program.*

See also Wheelchair Basketball

BIBLIOGRAPHY. Depauw, Karen P., and Susan J. Gavron. *Disability and Sport.* Champaign, IL: Human Kinetics, 1995; Paciorek, Michael J., and Jeffery A. Jones. *Sports and Recreation for the Disabled,* 2nd ed. Carmel, IN: Cooper Publishing Group, 1994; Winnick, Joseph P. *Adapted Physical Education and Sport,* 4th ed. Champaign, IL: Human Kinetics, 2005.

NATIONAL WHEELCHAIR SOFTBALL ASSOCIATION (NWSA) The National Wheelchair Softball Association (NWSA) was formed in 1976 to govern wheelchair softball around the nation. Today, they sanction over 40 teams nationwide. As the official governing body for wheelchair softball, NWSA is responsible for developing the rules and regulations of the game. The official rules of 16-inch slow pitch softball approved by the Amateur Softball Association of America are the rules of the NWSA with a few modifications to accommodate the wheelchair users who play the game.

One major difference between the standing and wheelchair game is that wheelchair softball is played on a hard surface, like an asphalt parking lot, instead of on a grass field providing wheelchair users better mobility. Using the 16-inch game rules also allows wheelchair users to catch the ball without a glove, recognizing that both hands are needed to propel the wheelchair.

Many NWSA teams have aligned themselves with their city's major league counterparts such as the Chicago Cubs, Boston Red Sox, Colorado Rockies, Chicago White Sox, Minnesota Twins, New York Mets, and Philadelphia Phillies. These teams wear the official uniform of their major league team and also have a separate World Series competition in addition to the National Wheelchair Softball Association National Tournament.

See also Wheelchair Softball

BIBLIOGRAPHY. Depauw, Karen P., and Susan J. Gavron. *Disability and Sport.* Champaign, IL: Human Kinetics, 1995; National Wheelchair Softball Association, http://www.wheelchairsoftball.com.

RIC Cubs wheelchair softball player at bat. *Photo courtesy of Rehabilitation Institute of Chicago Wirtz Sports Program.*

NORTH AMERICAN RIDING FOR THE HANDICAPPED ASSOCIATION (NARHA)
The origin of therapeutic horseback riding dates back to the 1950s, when Liz Hartel of Denmark became the first person with a disability to compete in equestrian events, winning the silver medal in 1952 for Grand Prix Dressage at the Helsinki Olympics.

Her accomplishments didn't go unnoticed, and the possibility of equine therapy and riding for people with disabilities led to the creation of many centers for therapeutic riding all over Europe. Soon thereafter, the sport enjoyed a surge in popularity in North America as well, with the opening of the Community Association of Riding for the Disabled in Toronto, Ontario. Next to open was the Cheff Center for the Handicapped in Augusta, Michigan. Just eight years after Hartel's Olympic appearance, a group of people passionate about riding and people with disabilities met at the Red Fox Inn in Virginia, creating what is now known as the North American Riding for the Handicapped Association (NARHA).

NARHA received a Kellogg Foundation grant in the early 1990s, allowing it to expand its programming. It was then able to offer workshops for both riders and instructors, appear at trade shows, and develop a therapeutic riding curriculum for colleges and universities. NARHA created standards for operating centers and an accreditation for registered, certified, and master instructors.

NARHA has more than 650 program centers that serve over 30,000 individuals with disabilities in the United States and Canada. NARHA's recreational riding program offers hippotherapy, equine-assisted psychotherapy, driving, vaulting, competition, and other therapeutic and educational programs.

Individuals with many disabilities can benefit from equine therapy and activities: muscular dystrophy, cerebral palsy, visual impairment, Down syndrome, autism, multiple sclerosis, spina bifida, emotional disability, brain injury, spinal cord injury, amputation, dwarfism, learning disabilities, hearing impairments, and strokes, to name a few. Some of the physical benefits of riding include gains in balance, posture, and mobility. Muscle spasticity and paralysis make walking difficult or impossible for some individuals, but riders can experience the feel of normal walking movement while riding a horse.

NARHA works with riders from recreational to competitive and helps develop riders to compete at the Paralympic and world champion level, as well as those who just want to go out for an afternoon leaving their wheels or crutches behind.

BIBLIOGRAPHY. North American Riding for the Handicapped, http://www.narha.org.

NUGENT, TIM Tim Nugent can take credit for a number of firsts: first national wheelchair basketball tournament, first national wheelchair basketball association, and first wheelchair accessible college campus and program for students with disabilities.

Nugent, a doctoral student studying Educational Psychology at the University of Illinois, was assigned to organize a rehabilitation education program for students with disabilities, most of whom were veterans, in the 1940s. The students with disabilities were housed on a satellite campus, created from a closed Veteran's Administration Hospital in Galesburg, Illinois. When the university sought to close the Galesburg satellite, Nugent and several students staged a demonstration at the state capitol. Un-

NUGENT, TIM

successful but undeterred, the same group demonstrated on the Urbana campus. The university granted the program "experimental" status, providing it with no university funding for the first 15 years. More than 50 years later, the program, now university funded, is thriving.

One of the activities Nugent began providing for "his" students was wheelchair basketball, which was widely being played at VA hospitals at the time. Nugent created the Gizz Kids (now the Illinois Fightin' Illini), who competed in what would become the first national wheelchair basketball tournament in 1949. Six teams competed, and the Kansas City Rolling Pioneers were the first champions. Tournament director Nugent and the participating teams created the National Wheelchair Basketball Association (NWBA) at the conclusion of the tournament. The next year, Nugent was appointed technical adviser, a role he held until 1973.

Nugent was able to enlist the aid of the U.S. Armed Forces who provided teams who couldn't otherwise afford transportation a military airlift to the tournaments; housing was provided at Chanute and other military bases. Nugent was instrumental in introducing legislation regulating the types of disabilities players could have, incorporating the first classification system. He was heavily involved in creating the constitution of the NWBA, as well as in taking wheelchair basketball to the international level, where it debuted at the Paralympics in 1960.

Nugent was elected a charter member of the NWBA Hall of Fame in 1973, on the 25th anniversary of the founding of the organization.

Through Nugent's efforts, as well as the advocacy efforts of the students, new accessible housing was built, class buildings were ramped, and medical services, physical and occupational therapy, prosthetics, and sports and recreation were provided.

However, Nugent did more than bring wheelchair basketball to the university, he also built the first accessible program of post-secondary education for people with disabilities. He assembled the first fleet of wheelchair accessible buses at a university. He created the first campus housing for people with more significant disabilities. He created the first rehabilitation service fraternity, Delta Sigma Omicron.

Nugent's work had wider implications than just sport. He and his staff built a ramp, tested by students, to determine an appropriate rise that wheelchair users could independently climb. Easter Seals funded the development of the American National Standards Institute (ANSI) Standards for Accessibility, and the code for ramps was published in 1961. The ANSI standard is still used today as a basis for state and federal accessibility laws.

Nugent has received numerous awards in his career including the 1972 Individual Citation from the National Therapeutic Recreation Society, the International Wheelchair Basketball Federation's Gold Medal Triad in 1996, and the Henry Betts Laureate in 1999.

BIBLIOGRAPHY. "Capabilities." Northwestern University Prosthetics Research Laboratory and Rehabilitation Engineering Research Program, January 2000, http://www.repoc. northwestern.edu/capabilities/cap_2000_09_01.pdf; A Chronology of the Disability Rights Movements, http://www.sfsu.edu/~dprc/chronology/chron40s.html; National Wheelchair Basketball Association; University of Illinois Division of Rehabilitation Education Services, http://www.rehab.uiuc.edu.

OEHLER, DENNIS Dennis Oehler was all set to become a professional soccer player, when at the age of 24, a car accident led to amputation of his right leg.

Later that year, one of his friends took him to see the Paralympic Games in New York. It was Oehler's first exposure to such a huge number of people with disabilities, and he was impressed, not only by the athleticism he witnessed, but also by the positive attitudes of the participants. Oehler now knew what he wanted to do—compete.

Oehler had witnessed firsthand that life didn't end with disability, and began working with the Nassau County Office for the Physically Challenged to share that message with others. He spent time speaking at schools to provide youngsters with an awareness and understanding of people with disabilities, while at the same time training to participate in the next Paralympic Games.

Oehler made the team that represented the United States in Seoul in 1988. In just four years, Oehler had gone from depressed and uncertain to the fastest leg amputee in the world. He won the 100 meter that year in a world record time of 11.73 seconds, along with Gold medals in the 200 and 400 meters.

Oehler intensified his training efforts, qualifying to represent the United States again four years later. In Barcelona in 1992 he took silver in the 100 meter and won Gold in the long jump, setting a world record. He added a third Paralympic Games to his portfolio, representing the United States in Atlanta in 1996.

After the 1988 games in Seoul, Oehler and teammate Todd Schaffhauser realized they had something to share. Together, they created clinics they called "Fitness for Everyone," which they offered around the nation to amputees of all ages. In the clinics, they offered instruction in stretching, strengthening, walking, and running, and also in motivation and achieving personal goals, as well as tips on the latest in prosthetic technology.

Oehler and Schaffhauser have led hundreds of clinics around the world, helping thousands of amputees learn to become more physically active.

BIBLIOGRAPHY. Ansett, Patricia. "Getting their Lives Back: Seminars Help Amputees Learn to Use Artificial Limbs," http://www.freep.com/news/health/amp1_20040601.htm; Fitness Is for Everyone, http://www.fitnessforeveryone.com/tdbios.html.

OFF-ROAD WHEELCHAIR

OFF-ROAD WHEELCHAIR Off-road wheelchairs were first built by wheelchair users who were mountain bikers before their injuries and others who were interested in outdoor sporting activities.

Off-road wheelchairs are similar to the shape of old four-wheeled racing chairs, with big front wheels and a high degree of camber on the rear, but the similarities end there. Knobby tires, handlebars and four wheel brakes, a stronger frame, steering, and suspension complete the package. Off-road wheelchairs are considerably heavier than racing wheelchairs or even most everyday chairs, weighing about 40 pounds.

Some off-road wheelchair manufacturers have used mountain bike technology and adapted it to the wheelchair. Peter Axelson was instrumental in early off road wheelchair design. More recently, Michael Whiting, a former bike builder, has transferred his skills to building off-road wheelchairs. His chairs have hydraulic disk brakes, speed sensitive steering, and an independent suspension system, and they are made of aluminum or titanium, making them lightweight, strong, and fast, capable of speeds topping 50 miles per hour.

BIBLIOGRAPHY. Axelson, Peter, and John Castellano. "Take to the Trails." *Sports 'n' Spokes* (July–August 1990): 20–24; Cox, Jack. "Chariots of Fire." *Popular Mechanics.* http://www.popularmechanics.com/outdoors/outdoors/1277771.html.

OUTRIGGERS. *See* Skiing

PARALYMPIC GAMES The modern day Paralympic Games got their start thanks to the vision of one man, neurosurgeon, and neurologist, Sir Ludwig Guttman. Guttman fled his native Germany during the Nazi reign, emigrating to England where he joined the Stoke Mandeville rehabilitation hospital in Aylesbury, England in 1944.

Guttman believed that the war veterans returning home with spinal cord injuries could return to active lives with intense therapy including vocational and recreational therapy. Guttman devised adaptations to sport and recreation activities that the wheelchair-using veterans could play, such as games with balls, archery, netball, and table tennis.

Guttman founded the Stoke Mandeville Games in 1948, the same year the Olympics were being staged in London, England. Fourteen males and two females competed in archery during those first games, setting the stage for what was to become a worldwide movement of elite disability sport. Slalom and obstacle course events were introduced over time, as were wheelchair polo, badminton, and netball. Swimming and lawn bowls were added to the program after that.

The Games were staged annually, with an increasing number of events for a larger number of competitors. The Games went international in just four years when a contingent of athletes from the Netherlands participated. Canada, Israel, Finland, and France were the next countries to add their names to

Paralympic Games Opening Ceremonies. *Copyright Chris Hamilton Photography.*

PARALYMPIC GAMES

Opening ceremonies, Paralympic Games, 1996. *Photo courtesy of Rehabilitation Institute of Chicago Wirtz Sports Program.*

the games roster, followed by Australia, Austria, Belgium, Egypt, Germany, Pakistan, Portugal, and Yugoslavia.

A few years later, in 1958, Guttman met with Dr. Antonio Maglio of Italy to discuss the possibility of holding the next Stoke Mandeville Games in Rome. And so, in 1960, for the first time, the Games left England, and were held in the host city of the Olympics, Rome, Italy. In those games, 400 athletes from 23 countries competed in archery, basketball, swimming, fencing, javelin, shot-put, club throwing, snooker, swimming, table tennis, and pentathlon. Though the games would not be called the "Paralympics" until 1984, this event is widely considered the founding of the modern Paralympic Games.

The International Stoke Mandeville Games Committee was formed the same year the Games were contested in Rome, to promote and sanction international sport for wheelchair athletes. The Committee has undergone several name changes in the decades since its formation, to the International Stoke Mandeville Games Federation, then the International Stoke Mandeville Wheelchair Sports Federation (ISMWSF), and now, the International Wheelchair and Amputee Sport Federation (IWAS).

In 1964, the International Sport Organization for the Disabled (ISOD) was created to provide sports opportunities for athletes who did not fall under the governance of ISMWSF, namely athletes who were amputees, visually impaired, or had cerebral palsy. Athletes who were deaf or hard of hearing already had organized at the world level with CISS, the Comite Internationale des Sports des Sourds, thus they were not part of either ISOD or ISMWSF.

Separate competitions for amputee, visually impaired, and cerebral palsy athletes were held, including the First World Festival of Sport in 1974 which established rules for amputee and blind athletes. In 1976, amputee and blind athletes competed for the first time in the Paralympics in Toronto, alongside wheelchair athletes.

ISOD held another world multidisability event in 1979, the International Multi-Disabled Games of ISOD for athletes who were amputees, visually impaired, or had cerebral palsy. This event laid down the standards of selection for athletes with cerebral palsy who would compete in the Paralympics for the first time in 1980 in Arnhem, Holland. The first Winter Paralympic Games were held in 1976 in Ornskoldvik, Sweden with athletes who were amputees, visually impaired, or spinal cord injured competing.

During that time, the Cerebral Palsy International Sport and Recreation Association (CP-ISRA) and the International Blind Sports Association (IBSA) formed to promote and sanction sports for athletes with cerebral palsy and visual impairment, respectively.

With four international organizations of sport for the disabled (IOSDs) in place, the leadership of the various groups saw the need to come together to jointly organize multi-disability competitions. This desire led to the creation of the International Coordinating Committee of World Sports for the Disabled (ICC), with each international organization having representation. By 1986, the International Sports Federation for Persons with an Intellectual Disability (INAS-FID) and CISS for athletes who were deaf or hard of hearing joined IBSA, CP-ISRA, ISMWSF, and ISOD at the table.

These organizations began hosting "disability" oriented competitions and championships, refusing to allow members of the other IOSDs to compete in their games. CISS wasn't part of this conflict, however, as they had made clear when they joined the ICC that their competitions would remain separate from the other disability groups. Thus, the ICC delegates voted in 1987 to reformulate this international body to better address the needs of international disability sport. The first games of this "modern" Paralympic era were the 1988 Summer Paralympics in Seoul, Korea.

In 1989, the International Paralympic Committee (IPC), was created. The IPC took over governance of the Games right after the 1992 Paralympic Games in Barcelona, so they were first responsible for organizing the 1994 Winter Paralympics in Lillehammer.

The Paralympics have been held since 1960, but it wasn't until the 1988 Games in Seoul, Korea, that the Paralympics were held in the same host city as the Olympic Games, using the same venues and athlete's village. The games have grown to more than 4,000 athletes from 140 countries participating in Athens in 2004.

The term "Paralympic" was officially adopted by the ICC in 1985 to refer to the Games, due in large part to the IOC's insistence that the word "Olympic" not be used in conjunction with the games for athletes with disabilities. There are two different schools of thought on how the term "Paralympic" was derived. One is that the "para" stands for "paraplegic" in recognition of the early history of the Games and the fact that wheelchair users were the first competitors. The other school of thought is that "para" means "parallel" to the Olympics.

The Paralympic Games has 20 sports in summer and 3 in winter. These include archery, athletics, basketball for both intellectually disabled and wheelchair users, boccia, cycling, equestrian, fencing, goalball, judo, powerlifting, wheelchair rugby, sailing, shooting, soccer, swimming, table tennis, wheelchair tennis, and standing and sitting volleyball. The Winter Paralympics have Alpine and Nordic skiing and sled hockey, with curling introduced in 2006.

Most Paralympic sports are sports that appear on the program of the Olympic Games, such as athletics and swimming, with modifications for the particular disabilities of the competitors. However, sports such as goalball, played by visually impaired athletes, and boccia, played by athletes with cerebral palsy, do not appear on the Olympic program.

See also Classification Systems

BIBLIOGRAPHY. Joukowsky, Artemis A. W, and Larry Rothstein. *Raising the Bar—New Horizons in Disability Sport,* 1st ed. New York, NY: Umbrage Editions, 2002; Steadward, Robert Daniel, E. J. Watkinson, and Garry David Wheeler. *Adapted Physical Activity.* Edmonton: University of Alberta Press, 2003.

PARALYZED VETERANS OF AMERICA

PARALYZED VETERANS OF AMERICA (PVA) The Paralyzed Veterans of America (PVA) was founded in 1946 and has developed expertise on many issues involving the special needs of the veterans of the armed forces who have experienced spinal cord injury. The PVA, in addition to providing advocacy, education, and outreach for its membership, is actively involved in promoting sports and recreation for people with spinal cord injuries and other disabilities.

The PVA, together with the Department of Veterans Affairs, sponsor the National Veteran's Games, held annually, which offer opportunities for competition in 17 different sporting events. The games bring together more than 500 athletes for a week of competition. All competitors must be veterans of the armed forces who use wheelchairs for athletic competition.

Whether offered at the Veterans Games or not, PVA offers opportunities for recreation and competition in basketball, swimming, track and field, archery, shooting, bowling, table tennis, bass fishing, downhill and cross-country skiing, tennis, trapshooting, and other sports.

PVA sponsors a National Bass tour consisting of five tournaments that introduce anglers with disabilities to recreational fishing through competition. The PVA National Trap Shoot Circuit offers trapshooting as a competitive sport to shooters with disabilities as well as able-bodied shooters.

The PVA also produces publications that offer information, education, and resources for sports and recreation to disabled veterans and others. *Paraplegia News* is a magazine that not only provides information on sports and recreation, but on issues important to people with disabilities such as government affairs and legislation, health insurance and medical issues, and resources for daily living. *Sports 'n' Spokes* provides information and resources on topics relating to wheelchair sports, including personality profiles, results of competitions, and an annual survey of wheelchairs.

BIBLIOGRAPHY. Paralyzed Veterans of America, http://www.pva.org.

PARKS, BRAD Brad Parks is singlehandedly responsible for the success of wheelchair tennis in the United States and beyond. Parks, injured when he was 18, met Jeff Minnenbraker, a wheelchair tennis player who was also building sports wheelchairs. Beginning in the 1970s, Parks and Minnenbraker began a campaign to teach wheelchair tennis to the nation, running clinics and exhibitions across the west coast. In 1980 Parks formed the National Foundation of Wheelchair Tennis and he organized the first U.S. Open National Championship, which attracted 70 participants.

Parks understood that the key to future success was introducing youngsters with disabilities to the sport, so the next year a junior camp was held, and 25 children were added to the ranks of wheelchair tennis players. Along with youth development, the international community soon caught tennis fever and Parks was invited to Australia, Israel, and several European countries to conduct clinics and teach people with disabilities about the sport.

Parks then formed the International Wheelchair Tennis Federation (IWTF) in 1988, an organization that he served as president of for four years. Back in the United States,

Parks was instrumental in creating a solid relationship between the National Foundation of Wheelchair Tennis (NFWT) and the U.S. Tennis Association (USTA), leading to the first time a disability sport governing body was embraced by its mainstream counterpart and NFWT merged into USTA in 1997.

In addition to organizing for other players, Parks and Randy Snow teamed up to win Gold for the United States in men's doubles at the 1992 Paralympics in Barcelona, Spain. Since then, both the IWTF and the USTA have created awards in Parks's honor. Both the USTA Brad Parks Award and the IWTF Brad Parks Award are presented to an individual or group that plays, coaches, sponsors, or promotes wheelchair tennis.

BIBLIOGRAPHY. The Brad Parks Award, United States Tennis Association, http://www.usta.com/communitytennis/fullstory.sps?iNewsid=16342&itype=946&icategoryid=213; "Development of Wheelchair Tennis." *International Wheelchair Tennis Federation,* http://www.itfwheelchairtennis.com/asp/wheelchair/development/usa.asp; "Making The Dream Come True." *Sports 'n' Spokes* (May–June 1991): 42–44; Paralympic Tennis Event, Barcelona 1992, Itftennis.com, http://www.itftennis.com/paralympics/history/tennis/barcelona.asp.

PHYSICALLY CHALLENGED BOWHUNTERS OF AMERICA, INC. (PCBA) The Physically Challenged Bowhunters of America, Inc. (PCBA) began in 1993 with a group hunt at Indian Bluffs in Lexington, Mississippi. Billy Ellis, noted hunter and author, realized he had many friends with disabilities who liked to hunt, and he decided to organize an outing to include others with disabilities.

That weekend, people with spinal cord injuries, amputations, birth disabilities, and visual impairments came to hunt. Since that first weekend, the organization has grown to include several hundred individual members and over 100 corporate members.

PCBA works to provide opportunities in archery and bowhunting to people with disabilities across the United States and Canada. They can arrange and sponsor hunts and shoots, working with outfitters and guides to ensure an accessible experience. They work with other archery organizations to increase their membership of people with disabilities, and they provide technical assistance and advice to manufacturers on ways to make their equipment accessible to people with disabilities. Additionally, they work on advocacy initiatives, encouraging states to allow for hunters with disabilities to use crossbows.

PCBA will also field test equipment and make recommendations to hunters with disabilities, and they will even loan out equipment for a hunter to try to see if they can successfully use it before making an investment.

BIBLIOGRAPHY. Know Hunting (Gear Special 2003), *Bowhunter,* http://www.bowhunter.com/conservation/bn_consnews_gg03/; Physically Challenged Bowhunters of America, http://www.pcba-inc.org.

PIECES OF EIGHT AMPUTEE SKYDIVING TEAM For more than 20 years, an amputee skydiving team called Pieces of Eight has been trying to get amputees airborne, and they have had great success. They started with four divers in formation and grew to an eight

POLY HOCKEY

person star in 1993, leading to the name Pieces of Eight. Their best formation to date was with 14 divers in 1996 over North Carolina.

The group got its start in the early 1970s when Californians Chuck Anderson (a right-below-elbow amputee) and Al Krueger (left-below-elbow amputee) jumped together and got into a formation. The group still jumps today, counting among its members Dana Bowman, who rose to prominence as a member of the Army's Golden Knights parachute team.

BIBLIOGRAPHY. Pieces of Eight, http://www.flyingeyes.com/pieces_of_eight.htm; "Pieces of Eight," Parachutehistory.com, http://www.parachutehistory.com/skydive/records/poe.html.

POLY HOCKEY Poly Hockey, like floor hockey, is a Special Olympics team sport. Poly Hockey more closely resembles its ice hockey cousin, but it is played in a gymnasium, not on the ice. In poly hockey, the puck is hard plastic, and the sticks are smaller plastic versions of conventional hockey sticks.

Poly Hockey has both individual and team components to the game. Beginner athletes are offered competition in the fundamental skills of the game such as shooting, passing, and stick handling a puck through a series of cones.

Poly Hockey is played on a rink laid out on a gym floor. Teams are made of six players, and games consist of three nine-minute periods. Poly Hockey is one of the most popular winter Special Olympic sports, with over 230 athletes playing in 2005.

BIBLIOGRAPHY. Special Olympics International, http://www.specialolympics.org; Special Olympics Minnesota, http://www.specialolympicsminnesota.org/Sportsofferedpolyhocke.php.

POPOVICH, ERIN Erin Popovich did what Michael Phelps failed to do—she won Gold in every single one of her events in Athens in 2004.

Popovich was born into a family of five, the only one with a disability. Popovich has achondroplasia, the most common form of dwarfism. It is a genetic disorder of bone growth that causes abnormally short arms and legs alongside an average sized head and torso, usually evident at birth.

Popovich got into swimming in 1997 at the age of 11, and within the year she set a world record in the 100 m butterfly at her first national championship. She then competed at the World Disability Swimming Championships in New Zealand in 1998, winning four Gold medals and one bronze.

Easily qualifying for a spot on the 2000 Paralympic team that competed in Sydney, Popovich tallied three Gold and three silver medals, setting three world records in the process. Her U.S. teammates selected her to carry the flag into the closing ceremonies. She won the 2001 International Olympic Committee (IOC) President's Disabled Athlete Award presented by the U.S. Sports Academy for her successes in Sydney. Shortly thereafter, Popovich was forced to take a 6-month break after a surgery to straighten her legs.

When she returned to the pool, she was an inch taller and in a new classification swimming against new competition.

She began college at Colorado State University in 2003, swimming with the college team there. That same year, she was named the Montana Female Swimmer of the Year, and a few months later was named the Female Athlete of the Month by the U.S. Olympic Committee (USOC). For the second time in her short career, Popovich qualified to represent the United States at the Paralympic Games in Athens in 2004. There, she became the winningest U.S. athlete and the second biggest medal winner of the games overall with a total of seven Gold medals. She won five individual titles in the 200 m Individual Medley, 100 m freestyle, 100 m breaststroke, 50m butterfly, and 50m freestyle and two relay medals in the 4 by 100 m freestyle and 4 by 100 m medley relays. Additionally, Popovich set Paralympic records in the 50m freestyle, 100 m freestyle, 50m fly, and 200 m IM; world records in the 50m freestyle, 50m fly, and 200 m IM; and new American records in all five individual events as well as both relay events.

After her Athens victories, Popovich was named the 2005 Women's Sports Foundation Sportswoman of the Year alongside Cat Osterman, the youngest member of the medal-winning U.S. Olympic Softball team. She was also awarded the Little Sullivan by the Montana Amateur Athletic Union (AAU), named in honor of James Sullivan who founded the AAU, and she was named 2004 USOC Paralympian of the Year and runner up for the 2004 Olympic Committee Sportswoman of the Year. Popovich decided to forego her remaining years of NCAA eligibility, signing endorsement deals with Visa and Speedo. Future plans include graduating in 2007, qualifying for the 2008 Paralympics in Beijing, and pursuing a medical career.

BIBLIOGRAPHY. "Athlete Biographies, Erin Popovich," *The Hartford,* http://groupbenefits.thehartford.com/usp/athletes/popovich.html; Pate, Josh. "Post Paralympic Games: Record Breaking Results," http://abilitymagazine.com/Post_Paralympics_2004.html; Schank, Amanda. "Reaching Utopian Heights, Erin Popovich Named Sportswoman of the Year," http://www.collegian.com/vnews/display.v/ART/2005/10/28/4361b72fd818d.

POWER HOCKEY Power Hockey provides a means for individuals who use power wheelchairs in their daily lives to compete in sports. Power Hockey was started in the United States by a small group of friends in Minnesota who got together at the Courage Center to play. Within a couple of years, Minnesota had four organized teams with a mailing list of about 100 participants, and the organization is already expanding into Canada, Australia, and Europe.

Power Hockey is generally played on a basketball court rather than an ice rink for a very important reason—power wheelchairs generally don't combine well with ice.

Power Hockey leagues typically use hockey sticks and pucks made of plastic, because they are lighter and easier to handle than standard sticks and pucks, allowing for players with more limited upper body strength or mobility to play. Wearing a helmet, pads, and other protective gear is optional, but it is encouraged for those whose disabilities will accommodate them.

POWERLIFTING

Some modifications to the game allow people with a variety of disabilities to play. These include allowing players to tape their hockey stick to their wheelchair and inserting a dowel onto the blade of the hockey stick, which provides for greater ability to gain and retain control of the puck. Aside from these minor modifications, the rules of the game generally follow standard hockey rules, with offsides, high sticking, delay of game, and roughing resulting in a trip to the penalty box for two to five minutes per offense. Power Hockey is governed by the U.S. Electric Wheelchair Hockey Association.

BIBLIOGRAPHY. The U.S. Electric Wheelchair Hockey Association, http://www. powerhockey.com/.

POWERLIFTING Powerlifting is an official sport for athletes with physical disabilities at the Paralympic Games and for athletes with intellectual disabilities at the Special Olympics World Games.

Paralympic powerlifting competition is available to athletes with spinal cord injuries, cerebral palsy, amputations, and other physical disabilities. In addition to meeting minimum disability criteria, the athletes must be able to fully extend their arms with no more than a 20 degree loss of full extension to either elbow according to the International Paralympic Committee (IPC) rules.

In both Paralympic and Special Olympics competition, lifters are classified according to gender and body weight. Weight classes range from 40 kg to 125 kg and over. In Paralympic competition, which is cross-disability, body weights are adjusted for amputee athletes to allow for equitable competition.

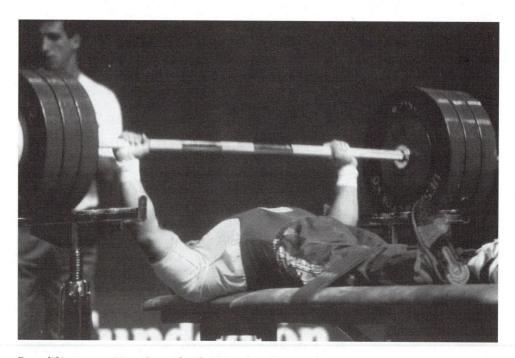

Powerlifting competition. *Copyright Chris Hamilton Photography.*

In Paralympic powerlifting competition, only the bench press is offered. In Special Olympics competition, events include the bench press, squat, deadlift, combined bench press and deadlift, and combined bench press, squat, and deadlift.

The rules of both Paralympic and Special Olympics powerlifting are based on the official rules of the International Powerlifting Federation. The lifting area or platform is 2.5 m to 4.0 m square, and must be either level or have ramp access in Paralympic competition.

For the Paralympic bench press, the athlete lies on a bench, in a modified position. The athlete must have head, trunk, legs, and both feet extended on the bench; thus, a longer bench is used for Paralympic competition than for nondisabled competition. The athlete may use strapping for stability, and athletes with cerebral palsy may compete with knees flexed with a wedge underneath them. The lift begins with the lifter holding the barbell at arms length, lowering it to the chest and pressing back up to full arm.

The equipment needed for powerlifting includes bars and collars, disc weights of 1.25 kg, 2.5 kg, 5 kg, and 10 kg which may be of any color, and 15 kg which must be yellow, 20 kg which must be blue, and 25 kg which must be red. For Special Olympics competition, a standard flat bench is used as well as the Paralympic flat bench which is 2.1 m long, 61 cm wide, and 45–50 cm high.

BIBLIOGRAPHY. Apple, Jr., David F. *Physical Fitness: A Guide for Individuals with Spinal Cord Injury*. Washington, DC: Department of Veteran's Affairs, Rehabilitation Research and Development Service, 1995; International Powerlifting Federation. http://www.powerlifting.com; Special Olympics Powerlifting, http://www.specialolympics.villanova.edu/powerlifting.htm.

POWER SOCCER Power soccer is one of a handful of sports being developed strictly for power wheelchair users. It started over 14 years ago, and today teams are being fielded in the United States, Canada, Japan, and Denmark.

Power soccer is a competitive sport designed for people with a variety of disabilities including people with cerebral palsy, spinal cord injury, and people with multiple sclerosis, muscular dystrophy, head injury, and stroke, as well as any disability that necessitates the use of a power wheelchair.

There are two divisions of power soccer, and these are based on level of ability. Division I includes players who are proficient in the game, demonstrating good technique and understanding and implementation of game strategy. Division II is for the novice player as well as players who haven't yet perfected their skills. A more formalized classification system is currently being developed.

The game is played on a standard basketball court, with a minimum court size of 84 feet by 50 feet. The goal box is 25 feet by 15 feet. The wheelchair used for play must be a four-wheeled power chair. Three-wheeled chairs and other scooters are not allowed. Teams are made up of no more than 12 players, with a maximum of 4 players on the court including the goalie. Games consist of two 20-minute periods with a half time of not more than 10 minutes. If the game is tied at the end, a shoot out determines the winner.

The game begins with a coin toss, and the offensive players can position themselves anywhere on their side of the court moving onto the other side when the referee blows the whistle signaling the start of the game. The defense has to remain at least 10 feet from the centerline until the offense contacts the ball. Contact with the ball is made solely with the wheelchairs, not with the hands or feet of the players.

Fouls can be called including the following: loss of control, where the player moves their chair without control; delay of game; charging; ramming; goal tending; illegal advantage; unsportsmanlike conduct; a goal zone violation; or a 10-foot violation, moving closer than ten feet to a hit in or free kick prior to the start of the play. The game is won by the team scoring the most goals.

BIBLIOGRAPHY. Power Soccer, http://www.powersoccer.net.

PROSTHESIS A prosthesis is a device that replaces a part of the body that is missing due to amputation or birth disorder. The earliest prostheses were made of wood and restricted the person's participation in sports and other activities.

Today, prostheses are made of plastic, carbon fiber, and composite materials which are lightweight and more functional. Knowledge of human physiology, material science, and technology has led to the production of prostheses that allow amputees to participate in almost any activity.

Prosthetic limbs power runner to victory. *Copyright Chris Hamilton Photography.*

With the increasing lifespan and more active lifestyle of today's amputees, researchers are engineering prosthetics that are specific to particular sports or activities. For example, advancements in prosthetic knee joints for artificial legs have greatly increased the speed and mobility of above the knee amputees.

World record running times have continued to fall due to prosthetic technology; for example, Marlon Shirley, a U.S. below-the-knee amputee track and field athlete, has been able to break the 11 second barrier in the 100 meter on his prosthetic leg, something no amputee has ever done before.

Prostheses are now available for a wide variety of sports, including hockey, golf, cross-country skiing, weightlifting, track and field, basketball, volleyball, and baseball. Reinforced limb sockets and the use of materials such as titanium provide the lightweight strength needed for sport use, while specialized ball and socket joints add needed flexibility. Flexible foot components, composed of laminated carbon/graphite material, simulate the natural lift and spring of foot and ankle joints allowing for more natural movement.

BIBLIOGRAPHY. "TRS, Inc., Prosthetics Research, Design, and Manufacturing," http://oandp.com/products/trs; Wikipedia, http://en.wikipedia.org/wiki/Prosthesis.

PULK Pulk is the Norwegian term for what is more commonly known as a sit-ski or ski sled used by people with mobility impairments. It was the first such device enabling people who used wheelchairs or other assistive devices to downhill ski. The pulk paved the way for the development of bi-skis and mono-skis, which are more closely related to the skis used by standing skiers. The original pulk, on the other hand, more closely resembled a toboggan.

BIBLIOGRAPHY. Allen, Anne. *Sports for the Handicapped.* New York: Walker, 1981.

QUAD RUGBY (WHEELCHAIR RUGBY, MURDERBALL) Quad rugby, or wheelchair rugby, got its start in the late 1970s when two Canadian athletes who were spinal cord injured quadriplegics decided they were tired of being token players on their local wheelchair basketball team. Together with a professor from Manitoba, they developed a hybrid of hockey, football, and wheelchair basketball played on an indoor court. Wheelchair rugby was originally called "murderball" due to the often violent nature of the game.

A team from Winnipeg played an exhibition game at Southwest State University in Minnesota in 1979, the same year Canada had their first national championship in the sport. In 1981, Brad Mikkelsen, a U.S. quad athlete, was instrumental in forming the University of North Dakota Wallbangers, the first quad rugby team in the United States. Not long after,

Quad rugby. *Photo courtesy of Rehabilitation Institute of Chicago Wirtz Sports Program.*

QUAD RUGBY

North Dakota and Minnesota played an exhibition at the 1982 National Wheelchair Games. The first international tournament was held in South Dakota later that same year, with teams from the United States and Canada competing.

Wheelchair, quad, rugby. *Photo courtesy Rehabilitation Institute of Chicago Wirtz Sports Program.*

The U.S. Quad Rugby Association was formed in 1988, governing the now more than 45 organized teams nationwide. Along with its strong national presence, quad rugby has gone global, making its Paralympic debut in 1996 as a demonstration sport. At the 2000 Paralympics in Sydney, quad rugby was integrated as a full medal sport.

In order to be eligible to play, athletes must have some impairment of both upper and lower extremities whether from a spinal injury, cerebral palsy, or another disability. Players are classified according to a point scale of 0.5 to 3.5, with a 0.5 having the most significant level of disability, comparable to a C5 quadriplegic, and a 3.5 having the least significant level of disability, more comparable to a C7/8 quadriplegic. There can be no more than eight points on the floor at a time.

Quad rugby is coed, as there are currently no gender specific teams or leagues. The game is played on a regulation basketball court using a soft sided ball such as a volleyball. Four players per team can be on the floor at any one time, subject to the eight point rule. Goals are scored when an offensive player passes the opponent's goal line while in clear possession of the ball.

Quad rugby is an intensely physical game and was the subject of a documentary film released in 2005 called *Murderball,* which chronicled the U.S. Paralympic team's quest for Gold.

BIBLIOGRAPHY. Apple, Jr., David F. *Physical Fitness: A Guide for Individuals with Spinal Cord Injury.* Washington, DC: Department of Veteran's Affairs, Rehabilitation Research and Development Service, 1995; Kelley, Jerry D., and Lex Frieden. *Go For It! A Book on Sport and Recreation for Persons with Disabilities.* Orlando, FL: Harcourt Brace Jovanovich, 1989; Yilla, Abu. "QR Classic Expands." *Sports 'n' Spokes* (July–August 1989): 40.

R

REBOLLO, ANTONIO Antonio Rebollo is a Spanish archer who achieved his 15 minutes of fame when he was selected to the light the torch in the 1992 Olympic Games for his native Spain. Rebollo had polio as a child, resulting in one leg being shorter than the other; however, he still competed in a variety of sports including archery and outdoor sports.

When the Barcelona Olympic Organizing Committee met to discuss how the torch should be lit, someone had the idea that a flaming arrow should be shot to light it. Once the decision was made, the task was to find an archer who could perform.

Once the field of eligibles was narrowed down, Rebollo was one of two who were training for the event. It wasn't until the night before the torch was to be lit that Rebollo found out that his better than 90 percent accuracy had earned him the job. Rebollo was a member of the Spanish national archery team between 1986 and 1990 and he competed in the Paralympics in Seoul in 1988 and again in Barcelona in 1992, where he and his team captured the silver medal.

Rebollo got to shoot the arrow twice that year—once to open the Olympics, and again three weeks later to light the Paralympic flame.

BIBLIOGRAPHY. Archery History, http://www.archeryhistory.com/arrows/pdf/arrowsmain.htm; The Olympic Flame and Torch Relay, Olympic Museum, Lusanne, http://multimedia.olympic.org/pdf/en_report_655; Olympic Games Torch Relay, http://olympic-museum.de/torches/torch/1992.htm; Reference.com Encyclopedia, 1992 Summer Olympics, http://www.reference.com/browse/wiki/.

ROAD RACING Road racing as a sport for people with disabilities includes events for wheelchair athletes, visually impaired athletes, amputee athletes, and athletes with cerebral palsy. Road races are usually 5,000 km or longer, though there have been wheelchair mile races staged in years past.

The marathon, a distance of 26.2 miles, was originally thought to be beyond the capability of athletes with disabilities. That changed in 1975 when Bob Hall became the first wheelchair user to complete the Boston Marathon from an everyday wheelchair weighing about 50 pounds.

Road race wheelchair division. *Copyright Chris Hamilton Photography.*

Today, it is commonplace to see athletes with a variety of disabilities competing in road race events at every distance—5K, 10K, marathon, and ultra marathon included. One of the most popular ultra long distance road races is the Midnight Sun in Alaska in which racers complete a distance of over 300 miles during the course of seven to nine days.

While each of the disability sports organizations offers programming for athletes who want to compete in road racing, one of the first organizations to promote integrated running for athletes with and without disabilities was the Achilles Track Club International. Road races generally follow the USA Track and Field rules with some modifications to accommodate the disabilities of individual athletes.

For example, there are rules relating to racing wheelchair divisions, racing wheelchair specifications and equipment, as well as integrating a wheelchair division into a road race event. There are rules that provide for blind and visually impaired runners to have a guide runner with them. Modifications for deaf and hearing impaired athletes might include a strobe light start instead of a starter pistol.

Road racing events for people with disabilities are classified into junior, adult, and master age categories, and then by disability category as well as gender. Thus, wheelchair athletes compete against wheelchair athletes of their same class, visually impaired athletes against other visually impaired athletes, and athletes with cerebral palsy may be classified into a wheelchair class or an ambulatory class depending on whether they use a wheelchair for competition or not.

Road racing provides an opportunity for athletes with and without disabilities to compete along side one another, to learn from each other, and to appreciate each other's skill and talent. Jean Driscoll with her many Boston Marathon wins over the last decade significantly raised the profile of road racing for athletes with disabilities.

BIBLIOGRAPHY. Paciorek, Michael J., and Jeffery A. Jones. *Sports and Recreation for the Disabled,* 2nd ed. Carmel, IN: Cooper Publishing Group, 1994; Road Runners Club of America, http://rrca.org/programs/programs.html; Winnick, Joseph P. *Adapted Physical Education and Sport,* 4th ed. Champaign, IL: Human Kinetics, 2005.

ROLLERS. *See* Wheelchair Rollers

RUGBY WHEELCHAIRS Quad rugby is one of many wheelchair sports that over time have developed sport-specific wheelchairs to meet the unique demands of that particular activity.

Rugby wheelchairs, like other sport specific chairs, are generally custom fit to the athlete to ensure the best performance. The U.S. Quad Rugby Association prescribes rules relating to chairs that are allowed in competition. Some of the more important rules are as follows:

Paralympic quad rugby match. *Copyright Chris Hamilton Photography.*

- The rugby chair must have four wheels.
- The length can not exceed 116 cm when including wheels.
- The maximum height allowed is 53 cm.
- The rear wheels have a maximum diameter of 70 cm and must contain a hand rim.
- The wheels must be fitted with spoke guards.
- No part of the chair is allowed to be farther out then the push rims.
- Bars or plates around the wheels are not allowed.
- Counter weights are not allowed to be added to the chair.
- Anti-tip devices are placed in the rear of the chair but cannot project past the rear wheels. The tubing used for the bumper must be smooth and free of protrusions.
- The length of the bumper must be a minimum of 20 cm edge to edge.
- There are wings on the chair to protect the area between the bumper and the back wheel. Wings must be 11 cm at all points of contact.
- One cushion on the seat is allowed with the maximum thickness being 10 cm.
- Players may have their bodies and legs strapped to the chair.
- Brakes, gears, and steering devices are not allowed to be used to help operate the chair.

See also Quad Rugby

BIBLIOGRAPHY. United States Quad Rugby Association, http://www.quadrugby.com.

SAILING FOR PEOPLE WITH DISABILITIES Sailing requires few if any rule modifications and affords athletes with disabilities the chance to compete head to head against non-disabled athletes, in addition to participating in disability-specific events. The Committee on Sailors with Special Needs was created by U.S. Sailing to promote sailing for people of all abilities, oversee the Independence Cup, select teams to compete in the Paralympic Regatta, and name sailors to the U.S. Disabled Sailing Team.

Modifications to assist sailors with disabilities include deck-mounted hydraulic pool lifts, body lifts such as Surehands or Hoyer lift for transferring, and sip and puff technology to enable individuals with limited upper body strength or mobility to control the rudder and trim the sails. Computerized equipment along with sighted guides enables visually impaired athletes to sail.

Paralympic sailing made its debut as a demonstration sport at the 1996 Atlanta Paralympic Games, where 15 nations competed. Two years later, in 1998, the U.S. Disabled Sailing Team was created by U.S. Sailing to recognize the top three teams in the chosen classes for the next Paralympic Games. Qualifying for the U.S. Disabled Sailing Team is the first step in qualifying to represent the United States at the Paralympics.

Four years later, sailing debuted as a full-medal sport in Sydney in two classes—the 23-foot Sonar, a three-person keelboat, and the 2.4 meter, a single-person keelboat. In order to qualify, countries had to be able to enter both classes.

U.S. Sailing created a Sailors with Special Needs Committee to integrate sailing for people with disabilities into its programming, although U.S. Sailing was not initially responsible for governance.

After the completion of the Sydney Games in 2000, the Sailors with Special Needs Committee and the Olympic Sailing Committee met and decided to integrate sailing for people with disabilities into U.S. Sailing. U.S. Sailing now governs sailing for athletes with disabilities including developing and selecting athletes to compete in the Paralympic Games and providing oversight for Special Olympic sailing as well as for athletes who are blind and visually impaired. Internationally, visually impaired athletes compete under the auspices of Blind Sailing International and Special Olympic athletes under Special Olympics International.

In 2004, the five U.S. Paralympic sailing team members took home silver and bronze.

BIBLIOGRAPHY. United States Sailing—Sailors with Special Needs, http://www.ussailing.org/swsn/.

SEATTLE FOOT

Paralympic sailing competition. *Copyright Chris Hamilton Photography.*

SEATTLE FOOT The Seattle Foot is a prosthetic limb, introduced in 1985, that allows amputees to engage in movements such as running. It is worn by over 120,000 amputees worldwide. The invention received the Presidential Design Award and the Washington Governor's Award for New Products.

The Seattle Foot uses a patented spring called a monolithic keel, made of a strong light-weight synthetic, designed to help the user push off when taking a step, creating a more natural springy step. This allows the user to run and jump, providing for more active sport participation than ever before with a prosthetic limb.

BIBLIOGRAPHY. Burgess, Ernest M. "The Seattle Prosthetic Foot: A Design for Active Sports: Preliminary Studies." *Prosthetics and Orthodontics International* (1985): 55; Kelley, Jerry D., and Lex Frieden. *Go For It! A Book on Sport and Recreation for Persons with Disabilities.* Orlando, FL: Harcourt Brace Jovanovich, 1989.

SHAKE-A-LEG SAILING PROGRAM The Shake-A-Leg Sailing Program, established in 1982, is best known for its adaptive sailing program for people with spinal cord and related nervous system impairments.

The Shake-A-Leg Adaptive Sailing Program was the first of its kind in the United States. Operated out of Newport, Rhode Island, they offer a fully accessible facility and five custom designed Freedom 20's and Sonars for people with disabilities to sail. They offer instruction in recreational and competitive sailing from June through September each year and they run the Millennium Regatta and the Northeast Regional competition for the Independence Cup.

BIBLIOGRAPHY. Shake A Leg, http://www.shakealeg.org.

SHIRLEY, MARLON Marlon Shirley is the world's fastest amputee. He is the first in the world to break the 11-second barrier in the 100 meters, completing the distance in an unofficial world record of 10.97. He also holds the world record in the long jump at 22 feet 3 3/4 inches.

Shirley was born April 21, 1978, and was abandoned by his birth mother, living in an orphanage until he was adopted by a Utah family at the age of nine. While living in the orphanage, an accident with a lawnmower took his left foot. Wearing a prosthetic limb, he played high school football and competed in the high jump.

In 1997, Shirley was talked into competing in a track meet, where he competed in the high jump, catching the eye of a track coach who told him about the Paralympic Games and opportunities for athletes with disabilities. Within a short time, Shirley was winning Gold at the 2000 Paralympics in Sydney, upsetting Gold medal favorite and U.S. teammate Brian Frasure to claim the title of world's fastest amputee in a world record time of 11.09 seconds. Shirley returned to the Paralympic stage in Athens in 2004, retaining his title of world's fastest amputee in a new world record of 11.08 seconds.

Shirley has signed on with several corporate sponsors, still one of only a handful of athletes with disabilities to do so, including a Reebok deal worth about half a million dollars, as well as Visa, Oakley sunglasses, Gateway, and prosthetic manufacturer Ossur. He was also part of a McDonald's promotion, with his likeness featured on bags, cups, and tray liners during the 2004 Olympics and Paralympics.

Shirley has received widespread acclaim for his accomplishments, winning an ESPY for Best Athlete with a Disability in 2003. He was named ABC News Person of the Week in 2004 for his accomplishments at the Paralympics in Athens, where he won Gold in the 100 m in world record time of 11.08, silver in the 200 m and bronze in the long jump. He also won the 2003 IOC President's Disabled Athlete Award and was named the 2000 UN Role Model of the Twenty-first Century as well as the U.S. Olympic Committee's Track and Field Athlete of the Year.

Marlon Shirley competes in the high jump. *Copyright Chris Hamilton Photography.*

SHOOTING

BIBLIOGRAPHY. Hartman, Tari Susan. "Golden Arches and Gold Medals, Paralympic Athlete Featured in McDonald's Promotion." http://www.spinalcord.org/news.php?dep=0&page=13&list=326; "Marlon Shirley, Athlete Profile," Paralympics.com, http://www.paralympics.com/athlete_profiles/marlon_shirley.htm; Muffoletto, Mary Ann. "Former Utah State Student Shines at Paralympics," http://www.hardnewscafe.usu.edu/sports/102004_paralympics.html.

SHOOTING According to a survey taken of thousands of disabled veterans, shooting and hunting rank in the top 10 most popular activities for many people with disabilities.

Shooting is a sport that can be enjoyed by individuals of any age, gender, and ability. Because of the interest expressed in the disability community, the National Rifle Association (NRA) started a Disabled Shooting Services program to provide information and resources and to research and develop modifications and accommodations to allow shooters with disabilities to participate.

Dave Baskin, past U.S. Disabled Shooting team head coach, is the manager of the program. Under his tutelage, American shooters have earned more than 250 medals and set 7 world and 16 Pan-American records in international competition.

NRA's Disabled Shooting Services programs have enabled thousands of Americans with physical disabilities to enjoy both competitive shooting events and recreational hunting. They work with shooting facilities to ensure they are accessible to shooters with disabilities, and they conduct disability awareness workshops worldwide.

Baskin has also been involved in designing a program to offer shooting as a rehabilitation tool that physical and occupational therapists can offer. Shooting can result in improved hand/eye coordination, balance, trunk control, and breathing, thus it can serve a valuable function in post injury rehabilitation for many people with disabilities.

Competitions include many local and regional events, as well as the NRA-Beeman Grand Prix Championship, a national shooting tournament, and international competitions including the Paralympic Games. Shooting has been on the Paralympic program since 1964, offering men's, women's, and mixed events in both pistol and rifle. There are two classes of competition, standing and wheelchair.

Air rifle competition allows wheelchair users to compete side by side with nondisabled competitors, since breath control, relaxation, and concentration are the primary skills required. There are three positions in air rifle competition—prone, standing, and kneeling. In prone and kneeling the athlete may use a table or a board for support; however, in the standing position, no support is allowed. For wheelchair shooters, armrests can't be used as supports, nor can any strapping be used to increase trunk stability.

There are four classifications for both men and women in rifle and pistol. SH 1 is a standing class for incomplete spinal injuries and comparable disabilities. SH II is for individuals with disabilities similar to spinal injuries in the thoracic level. SH III is for competitors with disabilities similar to C7–C8 quadriplegia, and SH IV is for athletes whose disability is more like a cervical spinal injury at C6 or higher. For SH IV athletes, assistance is allowed with loading, unloading, cocking the gun, and exchanging the target. Some athletes in this class with limited or no hand function use assistive devices like a sip and puff to activate the trigger.

BIBLIOGRAPHY. Apple, Jr., David F. *Physical Fitness: A Guide for Individuals with Spinal Cord Injury.* Washington, DC: Department of Veteran's Affairs, Rehabilitation Research and Development Service, 1995; Kelley, Jerry D., and Lex Frieden. *Go For It! A Book on Sport and Recreation for Persons with Disabilities.* Orlando, FL: Harcourt Brace Jovanovich, 1989; The Range Sport, http://www.rangeinfo.org.

SIP AND PUFF Sip and puff technology enables people with disabilities who have either no upper body movement or are extremely limited in their upper body mobility not only to navigate their world relatively independently, but also to successfully compete in sports and recreation activities.

Sip and puff technology is used by individuals who are spinal cord injured quadriplegics, or have cerebral palsy, muscular dystrophy, or other disabilities posing similar limitations. Sip and puff is used for many sports and activities including sailing, kayaking, hunting, fishing, wheelchair control, and computer control.

Sip and puff technology uses a straw-like tube attached to a transmitter at one end. The other end is used like a straw that the individual inhales from (sips) or breathes into (puffs). The transmitter is connected to the device the individual is controlling, whether a wheelchair, an environmental control system, a computer, a fishing pole, or a bow and arrow, for example. Depending on the activity the individual is performing the tube may be attached to the individual's wheelchair, attached to the sports equipment, attached to a table, or attached to a headset. Some models are designed to allow the user to activate the switch by biting rather than sipping and puffing.

Sip and puff technology can be used to enable an individual with a disability to independently power a wheelchair, including steering, moving in any direction, tilting a seat, and so forth. It has been used to enable spinal cord injured sailors to steer the rudder of a boat; it has also been used by hunters with disabilities to pull the trigger in order to shoot. Fishers with disabilities can also use sip and puff to cast and reel the line.

Technology has had a tremendous impact on disability sport participation. The addition of sip and puff technology to the tools available has enabled people whose disabilities were once thought too significant to participate in any sports and recreation activity the opportunity to enjoy the same activities their families and friends do.

BIBLIOGRAPHY. "Wheelchair Mobility for the Paralyzed," http://www.gallilaw.com.

SITTING VOLLEYBALL Sitting volleyball was first introduced in the mid-1950s in the Netherlands, originating from a game called sitzball. It was reformulated and renamed sitting volleyball by the Society of Dutch Military War Victims, with the first official competition held in 1957.

Sitting volleyball is popular because people with a variety of disabilities can play together; in fact, even people without disabilities can play, though not in Paralympic competition. It grew in popularity over the years, with European countries fielding the most teams early on. By 1980, there was enough worldwide interest in the sport to add it to the Paralympic program,

SITTING VOLLEYBALL

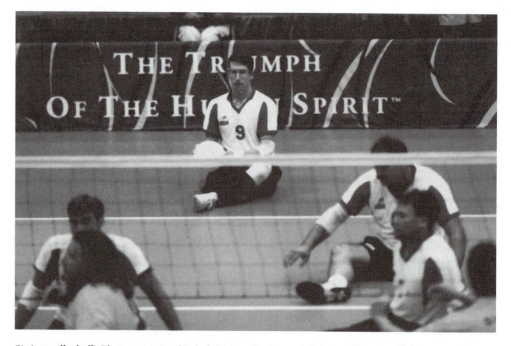

Sitting volleyball. *Photo courtesy of Rehabilitation Institute of Chicago Wirtz Sports Program.*

where seven teams participated, it has been contested in every summer Paralympics since. In the sport's first Paralympic appearance in Arnhem, the Netherlands, the Dutch team won the Gold in front of their home crowd.

The next year, European Championships were held in Bonn, Germany, followed by World Championships again in Holland in 1983. New countries join the ranks annually, such as Australia, which fielded a team in 1998 for the first time. In 2004, women's sitting volleyball was added to the Paralympic program. In the women's competition, China took the Gold with the Netherlands winning silver and the U.S. women bronze, the first volleyball medal for a U.S. Paralympic team. The U.S. men also posted their best ever finish in Athens in 2004, placing 6th overall.

Rules for sitting volleyball are virtually identical to standing play except for court size and net height. The World Organization Volleyball for Disabled established the rules including setting the court dimension at 32 feet, 8 inches by 19 feet, 7 inches. The net size is 21 feet, 7 inches by 2 feet, 6 inches and net height is 3 feet, 8 inches for men and 3 feet, 4 inches for women.

There are also a few rules specific to players with disabilities. For example, players are not allowed to sit on thick materials, and they are not allowed to wear orthopedic appliances such as braces. The sitting volleyball player must also keep their buttocks in contact with the floor when hitting the ball. Another difference from the standing game includes allowing one bounce of the ball on the court before the player hits the ball over the net. Additionally, the ball can be hit with any part of a player's body above the waist.

BIBLIOGRAPHY. Paciorek, Michael J., and Jeffery A. Jones. *Sports and Recreation for the Disabled,* 2nd ed. Carmel, IN: Cooper Publishing Group, 1994; USA Volleyball, http://

www.usavolleyball.org; Winnick, Joseph P. *Adapted Physical Education and Sport,* 4th ed. Champaign, IL: Human Kinetics, 2005.

SKI-BRA A ski-bra is a metal device that links skier's skis at the tips. It is used by people with mobility impairments, such as cerebral palsy, muscular dystrophy, or spina bifida, to downhill ski. The ski-bra enables the individual who may not otherwise be able to do so to keep their skis in a parallel position, and it gives them the ability to do a snowplow so they are able to slow down and stop independently.

BIBLIOGRAPHY. Allen, Anne. *Sports for the Handicapped.* New York: Walker, 1981.

SKIING Skiing is a popular activity for people with disabilities because accommodations enable individuals with any number of limitations to ski. Skiing can be either downhill (Alpine) or cross-country (Nordic) and either recreational or competitive. There are numerous programs coast to coast across the United States that provide instruction and opportunity for people with disabilities to ski.

Cross-country skiing is excellent cardiovascular exercise for both ambulatory and wheelchair using athletes. Cross-country skiing, also referred to as Nordic Skiing, is done over either groomed or natural terrain using either both the arms and legs, just the arms, or just the legs, depending on the disability of the individual skier.

Cross-country ski equipment includes skis, boots, and poles. Cross-country skis are usually longer than downhill skis, and the poles and outriggers may also be longer than poles used for downhill. Sit-ski options are also available for cross-country skiing.

Sit-skis have a seat balanced over a frame with two cross-country skis about 12 inches apart. Strapping can accommodate for weak muscle in the trunk or abdomen, and the legs can also be strapped for additional support.

Athletes with upper limb amputations can use adaptations such as the All-Terrain Ski Terminal Device, a prosthetic device that fits standard prosthetic wrists, enabling the athlete to hold the ski pole. Wheelchair users can

Paralympic mono-skiing. *Copyright Chris Hamilton Photography.*

participate in cross-country using sit-skis, seats mounted on skis, which the user propels using short poles called outriggers.

For downhill or Alpine skiing, bi-skis and mono-skis allow wheelchair users and others who can't ski standing to ski both recreationally and competitively. A bucket seat attached to a ski by way of a shock absorbing suspensions system along with outriggers like those used for cross-country are all it takes to get a wheelchair user down the mountain. Many mono-skis allow the skier to independently load onto the ski lifts, providing the same access other skiers have to the slopes.

A bi-ski is similar to a mono-ski, with a bucket seat, but it is attached to two skis, and either has outriggers attached to the ski, or the skier may use independent outriggers depending on their skill and ability. For leg amputee athletes, three-track skiing involves one ski and two outriggers, which are longer than the outriggers used by bi- and mono-skiers to accommodate the standing athlete.

For skiers who are blind or visually impaired, depending on the level of vision loss the skier may or may not have a sighted guide skiing with them. At the competitive level, the sighted guide and skier may communicate by two-way radio headphones to allow for communication at the high speeds attained while racing down the mountains.

For mono-skiers, amputees, and blind and visually impaired athletes, events offered include slalom, giant slalom (GS), super giant slalom (Super G) and downhill. In cross-country, events offered include 10 km and 30 km competitions for men and 5 km and 10 km for women. The winter Paralympic Games will feature athletes with physical and sensory disabilities competing in both Alpine and Nordic skiing in these events.

Special Olympic athletes also compete in Alpine and cross-country skiing, with events divided into novice, intermediate, and advanced categories. Athletes may compete in downhill, slalom, and giant slalom as well as a 10 m walk or glide for athletes with less developed ability. Cross-country events range from a 500 m to a 10K. Athletes who are deaf or hearing impaired compete in Deaflympic skiing in both Alpine and Nordic disciplines.

BIBLIOGRAPHY. Kemph, Sarah. "Cross Country Skiing Attracts New Enthusiasts," *Challenge Magazine* (Winter 2002), http://www.dsusa.org/ChallMagarchive/challmag-winter02-crosscountryskiing.html; Ski for All Foundation, http://www.skiforall.org.

SLALOM Slalom competition is conducted by wheelchair users on an obstacle course where the object is to complete the course in the fastest time with the fewest errors. Slalom, one of the first sports offered for people with disabilities, is still offered at regional and national competitions and has appeared on the CP-ISRA World Games program as recently as 2005. It offers athletes an opportunity to practice chair handling skills and provides competitive opportunities for athletes with more significant disabilities. Divisions for power chair and manual wheelchair users ensure that people with a wide range of abilities can participate.

Slalom for athletes with cerebral palsy is run according to National Disability Sports Alliance rules and is scored using the combined time of two runs, the first of which is conducted on a course with 7 obstacles over either 34 or 59 meters. The second run is the same course with the obstacles presented in a different order. Obstacles may include ramps,

turns, figure eights, and maneu-
vering the wheelchair within
tightly defined spaces. Penalties
are assessed for missed obstacles.

In Special Olympics slalom,
there is one event for manual
wheelchair users and three for
power wheelchair users. The
manual wheelchair event is a 30
meter, and the power wheelchair
events offered include 30 and
50 meter slalom and 25 meter obstacle course. Wheelchair
Sports, USA slalom for athletes
with spinal cord injury and other

Sled hockey. *Photo courtesy of Rehabilitation Institute of
Chicago Wirtz Sports Program.*

similar disabilities is much like the slalom for athletes with cerebral palsy only with more
obstacles.

BIBLIOGRAPHY. Paciorek, Michael J., and Jeffery A. Jones. *Sports and Recreation for the
Disabled,* 2nd ed. Carmel, IN: Cooper Publishing Group, 1994.

SLED HOCKEY Sled hockey got its start in Stockholm, Sweden around the 1960s when a
group of men who had played hockey prior to experiencing disabling injuries came together
to figure out a way to play again. They fashioned sleds with blades attached which allowed
the puck to pass underneath, the first "sledges," with hockey sticks made of round poles and
bike handles, and a local frozen lake served as their first rink. People with lower extremity
disabilities such as amputations, cerebral palsy, spinal cord injury, and similar disabilities all
play sled hockey today.

By 1969 there were five teams in Stockholm playing in a competitive league, with the
first international match taking place between teams from Stockholm and Oslo, Norway.
By the turn of the century, Great Britain, Canada, the United States, Estonia, Japan, Russia,
Germany, the Netherlands, Denmark, the Czech Republic, and Korea were fielding teams.
While sled hockey debuted as an exhibition game at the 1976 Paralympic Games in Sweden,
it didn't attain full medal status until the Paralympics in 1994.

Hockey rules apply to the game of sled hockey, including USA Hockey rules for U.S.
play. Specifications for the sled, hockey stick, blade, and pick can be found in the official
sled hockey rules. There are many similarities between sled hockey and hockey played by
ambulatory athletes—for example, there are six players on the ice at a time; players have
to wear protective gear including helmets, gloves, shin and neck guards, and elbow and
shoulder pads; the surface, the goal, and the pucks are the same in both games.

There are some modifications to the USA Hockey rules to accommodate the disabilities
of the players. For example, players in sled hockey play on sleds designed specifically for the
game. They are made of aluminum or steel, set on ice hockey skate blades, and have a seat

and backrest. Players can use straps to keep themselves securely in the sled during play, and the sled must sit high enough off the ice to allow the puck to pass underneath. Each player has two sticks instead of one, both of which have a metal pick on the end for propelling the player down the ice. Because many ice rinks have player benches that are inaccessible to sled hockey players, the teams sit in front of the benches, and in front of the penalty box for penalties. Sled hockey games consist of 3 15-minute periods.

The U.S. Sled Hockey Association (USSHA) is the governing body for the sport, first formed under the name American Sled Hockey Association in 1989. They changed their name in 1998 to align with their Olympic counterpart, USA Hockey. The USSHA first began participating in international competitions in 1989, but it wasn't until 1998 that the U.S. sled hockey team participated in a Paralympic Games, finishing fifth at that year's Nagano games. Just four short years later, the U.S. team reversed its fortune, winning the Gold medal in front of a home crowd at the Salt Lake Paralympics in 2002.

The USSHA offers both adult and youth competition at the national, regional, and local levels. Many teams now receive sponsorship and support from their NHL counterparts, including the Chicago Blackhawks, Colorado Avalanche, St. Louis Blues, Dallas Stars, New Jersey Devils, and the Pittsburgh Penguins.

BIBLIOGRAPHY. Paciorek, Michael J., and Jeffery A. Jones. *Sports and Recreation for the Disabled*, 2nd ed. Carmel, IN: Cooper Publishing Group, 1994; U.S. Sled Hockey Association, http://www.usahockey.com/ussha//.

SNOW, RANDY Randy Snow is the first Paralympian to be inducted to the U.S. Olympic Hall of Fame. He grew up in a middle-class suburb in Texas, working summers baling hay. At the age of 16, he was working a couple jobs to save money, one of which was driving a front-end loader retrieving bales of hay and loading them into the baler.

Snow was no stranger to this work, repeating the maneuver thousands of times without incident. One morning, however, when he was lifting a bale, the tractor he was riding went off balance and the 1,000-pound bale dislodged, crushing Snow into the steering compartment of the tractor. The accident left him with four broken ribs, a compound fracture of the left humerus, a punctured right lung, and a crushed twelfth thoracic vertebra, injuring his spinal cord and leaving him paralyzed.

After spine surgery, Snow was sent to Craig Hospital in Colorado to relearn everything he used to know how to do—among them dressing, personal hygiene, and driving. He was released back into the world 90 days later and returned to a future that seemed anything but certain.

A few years later, Snow was with his family on their ranch in Austin, Texas. Snow and his stepfather went out on a deer hunt one fall morning and Snow was dropped off at his blind. A buck came in sight, Snow took a shot and got the deer; then, he had to figure out how he was going to deal with the deer alone in the field. He managed to dress the deer, and though it took him triple the time it used to, the accomplishment made Snow see that he was still the same man he had been before his injury. Over the next decades, Snow became one of the most successful and sought after athletes with a disability in the country.

Randy Snow sets up for the shot. *Copyright Chris Hamilton Photography.*

Snow was first exposed to wheelchair sports at a University of Texas clinic in 1979. Within two short years, he was selected for the wheelchair basketball team that would represent the United States on a tour of Japan in 1981. By 1984, Snow's prowess on the track was recognized as well. He was one of a small contingent of athletes around the world who qualified to race in the men's 1,500 meter exhibition wheelchair race at the Olympic Games in Los Angeles that year, the first time the event was on the Olympic program.

Three Canadians, a German, a Belgian, and an Australian qualified as well as Randy Snow and Jim Martinson from the United States. On August 11, 1984, Snow and the others made history as the first wheelchair athletes to compete in the Olympic Games. Snow won the silver in front of 80,000 cheering fans that day.

Next, he competed in track the 1984 Paralympics shortly after his Olympic debut, winning Gold. Then he played tennis in Barcelona in 1992, again winning Gold. He made his third Paralympic appearance in Atlanta in 1996 for basketball. There, Snow hoped to become the first U.S. Paralympian to win three Gold medals in three sports in three Paralympic Games. Instead, Snow and the rest of the U.S. men's team took the bronze.

Snow was also a standout in wheelchair tennis, becoming a 10-time U.S. Open champion and an International Tennis Federation World Tennis Champion. He and teammate Steve Welch played in a wheelchair tennis exhibition at the Nuveen Masters Tennis Tournament in Florida hitting alongside John McEnroe and Mats Wilander in an "up/down" doubles tournament.

Snow has received numerous awards over his career including being the first Paralympian named to the U.S. Olympic Hall of Fame. He also was honored with an award from the Dallas Youth Foundation in 1986 where he sat alongside the legendary Walter Payton. He has also been a Jack Gerhardt Award winner, U.S. Tennis Association and a United States Professional Tennis Registry (USPTR) Player of the Year, the National Council on Disability Outstanding Disabled Citizen, the recipient of USTA Community Service Award, and Disabled Sports USA Athlete of the Year.

BIBLIOGRAPHY. Crase, Nancy. "People in Sports: Randy Snow." *Sports 'n' Spokes* (January–February 1990): 8–12; Joukowsky, Artemis A. W, and Larry Rothstein. *Raising the Bar—New*

SPECIAL OLYMPICS

Horizons in Disability Sport, 1st ed. New York: Umbrage Editions, 2002; Snow, Randy, and Bal Moore. *Pushing Forward—A Memoir of Motivation.* Dubuque, IA: Kendall/Hunt Publishing Company, 2001.

SPECIAL OLYMPICS Special Olympics are the largest worldwide sporting organization for athletes with an intellectual disability. Dr. Frank Hayden is one of the people credited with the creation of Special Olympics, beginning a fitness program in Canada with a group of intellectually disabled children and demonstrating that, with appropriate teaching, they could develop the physical skills necessary to compete in sport.

Around 1960, President John F. Kennedy's sister Eunice Kennedy Shriver started researching ways to help make life better for people with intellectual disabilities like her sister Rosemary. Dr. Hayden's work in Canada came to Kennedy Shriver's attention, and building on the foundation Hayden had laid, Special Olympics International (SOI) was formed. Kennedy Shriver wanted to create a competition along the lines of the Olympic Games, and in 1968, the first International Special Olympic Summer Games were held in Chicago, Illinois for about 1,000 U.S. athletes and a floor hockey team from Canada. The first Special Olympics Winter Games were held in 1977 in Steamboat, Colorado for over 500 athletes.

The games have grown in size and scope, and now nearly a million athletes from over 160 countries participate in 26 sports in both the Summer and Winter Special Olympic Games. Nearly 30 million people worldwide have an intellectual disability, and about 7 million in the United States alone. Special Olympics International, headquartered in Washington, D.C., is both the international governing body for Special Olympic sport and the national governing body for Special Olympic sport in the United States.

Special Olympic athletes must have a primary intellectual disability and may or may not have physical or sensory disabilities. Athletes are grouped or "divisioned" according to age, sex, and ability.

SOI sanctions 14 individual and 5 team sports and recognizes 7 national sports which have high participation rates in parts of the world but aren't offered internationally.

Special Olympics rules require that Special Olympic competition divisions consist of a minimum of three and a maximum of eight competitors, and that every participant receive an award, with medals for first to third place and ribbons for fourth to eighth. Another important distinction between Special Olympic and other competitions is the presence of huggers at the finish lines of races and on the sidelines of other competitions, volunteers who give hugs and high fives to all participants at the end of the competition.

The Special Olympics Summer games offer training and competition in the following sports: Aquatics, Athletics, Badminton, Basketball, Bocce, Bowling, Cycling, Equestrian Sports, Football (Soccer), Golf, Gymnastics (Artistic & Rhythmic), Powerlifting, Rollerskating, Sailing, Softball, Table Tennis, Team Handball, Tennis, and Volleyball. Special Olympic Winter Sports Include: Alpine Skiing, Cross-Country Skiing, Figure Skating, Floor Hockey, Snow Boarding, Snow Shoeing, and Speed Skating.

BIBLIOGRAPHY. Henriod, Lorraine. *Special Olympics and Paralympics.* New York: Watts, 1979; Steadward, Robert Daniel, E. J. Watkinson, and Garry David Wheeler. *Adapted Physical Activity.* Edmonton: University of Alberta Press, 2003.

SPINA BIFIDA Spina bifida is a congenital birth defect of the spinal column. It is caused when the neural arch of a vertebra fails to close properly around the spinal cord. There are three types of spina bifida: myelomeningocele, meningocele, and occulta. Myelomeningocele is when the spinal cord, cord membrane, and the spinal fluid protrude through the vertebra in a sac. Surgery is the only means to correct this form of spina bifida, which is the most severe of the three. Meningocele occurs when the cord membrane and spinal fluid protrude in a sac through the vertebra. As with myelomeningocele, surgery is the only way to correct this condition. In the occulta form of spina bifida, one or more vertebra is improperly formed. It is usually undetected until an x-ray discloses the condition.

While the cause of spina bifida is not known, increased folic acid intake in pregnant women reduces the risk of having a child with the condition. Individuals with spina bifida may have paralysis, loss of sensation, and loss of bladder, or bowel control.

BIBLIOGRAPHY. Steadward, Robert Daniel, E. J. Watkinson, and Garry David Wheeler. *Adapted Physical Activity.* Edmonton: University of Alberta Press, 2003.

SPINAL CORD INJURY Spinal cord injury is a paralysis of the upper or lower extremities resulting in impaired muscle function, sensation, or both. Paraplegia results with an injury at or below the thoracic level of the spine, impacting the lower limbs and part of the trunk. Quadriplegia results when a cervical spinal injury occurs, causing paralysis to upper and lower limbs.

Spinal cord injury can be either traumatic, resulting from an accident or injury, or caused by illness like transverse myelitis, a virus that attacks the spinal cord.

BIBLIOGRAPHY. Steadward, Robert Daniel, E. J. Watkinson, and Garry David Wheeler. *Adapted Physical Activity.* Edmonton: University of Alberta Press, 2003.

SPORTS 'N' SPOKES *Sports 'n' Spokes* is published by the Paralyzed Veteran's Administration and has been the major source of information on wheelchair sports activities, athletes, and resources for active wheelchair users for decades. It has worldwide circulation to thousands of people with disabilities, family members, and sports and recreation professionals worldwide.

Cliff Crase, member of the Wheelchair Sports, USA Hall of Fame, publishes the magazine.

BIBLIOGRAPHY. PVA Publications—*Sports 'n' Spokes,* http://www.pvamagazines.com/sns/.

SWIMMING Swimming is one of the most popular sports and recreation activities worldwide for people with and without disabilities. It has been part of the Paralympic program since the first Games in 1960, with more than 80 countries fielding competitors in the sport today. At the Paralympic Games, the swimming competition is routinely held before capacity crowds.

SZOTT, KEVIN

Swimming is offered for athletes in every disability group, including athletes who have cerebral palsy, visual impairment, spinal injury, amputation, and hearing impairment. Special Olympics also offer swimming in their summer games competitions.

Swimming was one of the first sports to integrate a functional classification system for Paralympic competition, where athletes compete across disability categories. The system is still evolving since its implementation in the

Stephanie Brooks swims at the Paralympics. *Photo courtesy of Rehabilitation Institute of Chicago Wirtz Sports Program.*

early 1990s. Classifications are S1 to S10 for the freestyle, backstroke, and butterfly. S1 is a high level quadriplegic, and S10 swimmers have lower limb disabilities. For the breaststroke, swimmers are classified SB1–SB10, and for the individual medley SM1–SM10.

Swimming for athletes with disabilities is held in the same 50-meter pools as their nondisabled counterparts use, and the events contested are also the same. Swimming for athletes with disabilities, in addition to being categorized by disability, is separated by gender. FINA (the Federation International de Natation Amateur) rules apply, with some modifications. For example, some athletes start on the platform; others start in the water due to limitations imposed by their disability. Swimmers with visual impairments can use tappers, an individual standing at the end of the pool who taps them on the head with a stick or pole to indicate they are approaching the wall. No prosthetics or assistive devices are allowed for swimming competition.

Some of the most decorated Paralympic athletes have been swimmers, such as Trischa Zorn, a visually impaired U.S. swimmer, who won 55 medals in Paralympic competition during her career, and Erin Popovich, a swimmer who won seven Gold medals in Athens in 2004.

BIBLIOGRAPHY. Apple, Jr., David F. *Physical Fitness: A Guide for Individuals with Spinal Cord Injury.* Washington, DC: Department of Veteran's Affairs, Rehabilitation Research and Development Service, 1995; Paralympic Swimming." United States Olympic Team, http://www.usolympicteam.com/paralympics/swimming_teams.html; USA Swimming, http://www.usaswimming.org/.

SZOTT, KEVIN Kevin Szott is the only U.S. athlete to ever medal in four different Paralympic sports. He holds over 30 national titles in wrestling, powerlifting, shot put, discus, javelin, and judo.

Kevin became visually impaired at age 10 from retinitis pigmentosa and macular disease. Despite his visual impairment, he became a stellar athlete, competing in football through college. In 1983, he earned First Team All-East Honors and was an NCAA Division III All

American in football. He didn't compete in disability sports at all until his college career was done.

His first Paralympic games came soon after. He competed in the 1984 Long Island Paralympic Games where he earned two Gold medals in wrestling and goalball, and a silver medal in the shot put. Since then he has competed in five Paralympic games, compiling numerous titles in many sports.

His most recent success has come in judo, a sport in which he won the Gold medal at the 2000 Sydney Paralympic Games. For the 2004 Paralympic Games in Athens, Greece he was chosen as the U.S. team's flag bearer for the opening ceremony. Kevin concluded his career by winning a bronze medal in judo in the men's 100-kg division in Athens. Kevin is now lending his expertise to helping others as the president of the USABA board of directors.

BIBLIOGRAPHY. Jomantas, Nicole. "10 Questions with Kevin Szott." US Olympic Team, http://www.usolympicteam.com; "US Paralympics Athlete Profiles—Kevin Szott." *The Hartford Financial Services,* http://www.groupbenefits.thehartford.com/usp/athletes/szott.html.

SZYMAN, BOB Bob Szyman has made a career out of building champion wheelchair basketball players. Szyman, a Chicago native, graduated from Mount Carmel High School and quickly earned his B.A. and M.A. at Chicago State University. His first exposure to wheelchair sports, however, was at the University of Illinois, where he earned his Ph.D. in Leisure Studies in the 1970s. It was there he coached the University of Illinois women to victory in 1978. He took what he learned there to Minnesota, leading the Courage Rolling Gophers women's wheelchair basketball team to national championship victory three times in 1987, 1988, and 1989.

Next, he turned to the international stage, coaching the U.S. women to medal after medal. The U.S. women's team won the bronze at the 1977 International Stoke Mandeville Games, the 1978 Pan American Wheelchair Games, and the 1980 Paralympic Games in Arnhem, Holland. In 1983, he coached the U.S. women to silver at the International Women's Wheelchair Basketball Tournament, and his team finally struck Gold in 1990 at the Pan American Games. Szyman most recently coached the Rehabilitation Institute of Chicago Express to their first national championship in the history of the National Women's Wheelchair Basketball Tournament in 2005.

Szyman isn't just a coach, however. He has been involved in wheelchair sports at the administrative level for decades, serving on various committees of Wheelchair Sports, USA since the 1970s. He was on the International Stoke Mandeville Wheelchair Sports Federation's Executive Committee from 1988–1998. He served as Team Leader for the U.S. Wheelchair Athletic Team at the 1984 and 1988 Paralympic Games, as well as the 1982 and 1986 Pan American Games and five appearances at the International Stoke Mandeville World Games. His leadership to the sport of wheelchair basketball led to his selection as International Wheelchair Basketball Federation Secretary General where he served for several years.

BIBLIOGRAPHY. "Szyman Leaves IWBF," *Sports and Recreation,* http://www.pvamagazines.com/pnnews/magazine/article.php?art=278; *Paraplegia News,* http://www.disability.uiuc.edu/ARCN/campuslife/guide2000/general.html.

TABLE TENNIS Table tennis is one of the few Paralympic sports that can be played by people with and without disabilities together. It is offered recreationally and on a competitive basis for athletes with a variety of disabilities. At the Paralympic level, athletes compete in table tennis in 1 of 11 classifications, where table tennis has been part of the Paralympic program since the first Games were held in Rome in 1960. Today, athletes in more than 100 countries participate in table tennis worldwide.

Table tennis athletes are grouped into one of three classifications: wheelchair, standing, and intellectual disability categories. The classification system is a functional one, with the classification based on the player's level of impairment. Classes 1 through 5 compete in wheelchairs. Class 1 is comparable to a C6 spinal injury. Class 2 is similar to a C7. Class 3 compares to a C8–T7 with no sitting balance or trunk rotation and Class 4 is most like a T8–L1 spinal cord injury. Class 5 players have disabilities that are comparable to L2–S2 spinal cord injuries. Classes 6 through 10 compete standing.

Table tennis is governed by the International Paralympic Table Tennis Committee (IPTTC). The rules of the International Table Tennis Federation (ITTF) also apply to the Paralympic Table Tennis competitions with slight modifications for wheelchair athletes, since table tennis is easily adapted for play by athletes with disabilities, it is one of the most popular racquet sports.

Table tennis is an official activity of the American Wheelchair Table Tennis Association (AWTTA), the Dwarf Athletic Association of America (DAAA), National Disability Sports Alliance (NDSA) Special Olympics International (SOI), the United States of America Deaf Sports Federation (USADSF), and the U.S. Cerebral Palsy Athletic Association (USCPAA).

For wheelchair athletes, the AWTTA is the governing body; they follow USA Table Tennis (USATT) rules. For DAAA table tennis competition, USATT rules are followed, with the exception of using risers or platforms that are 1 foot high to enable players to see and reach above the table. Special Olympics also offer table tennis competition in singles, doubles, and wheelchair and individual skills contests, as well as doubles competition. USCPAA (now National Disability Sports Alliance [NDSA]) and the USADSF also follow USATT rules.

The major equipment for play includes the table, net, and balls. There are U.S. and international standards for the equipment which must be met in order to have an event sanctioned either by the U.S. Table Tennis Association (USTTA) or the ITTF. To accommodate athletes with disabilities, unobstructed space of 15 feet by 35 feet should be allotted for each table. Barriers should be placed between tables to contain balls, and flooring should be firm.

There are rules regarding table dimension, net dimension, and paddle configuration also published by USATT and ITTF allowing for consistent and equitable competition. Modifications are made to the table for wheelchair users, removing the support bar from the frame. Paddles can also be modified, with tape, strapping, and cuffs to assist in strapping the paddle to the playing hand.

The wheelchair the player uses must conform to certain specifications also found in USTTA and ITTF rules. Individual strength and balance come into play as well when configuring a wheelchair for table tennis competitions with wheel size and cushion height remaining constant sources of experimentation for the wheelchair table tennis athlete.

Table tennis offers something for every level of interest from the most recreational to the most elite level on the Paralympic stage.

BIBLIOGRAPHY. Apple, Jr., David F. *Physical Fitness: A Guide for Individuals with Spinal Cord Injury*. Washington, DC: Department of Veteran's Affairs, Rehabilitation Research and Development Service, 1995; "Summer Sports—Table Tennis." International Paralympic Committee, http://www.paralympic.org/release/Summer_Sports/Table_Tennis/index.html.

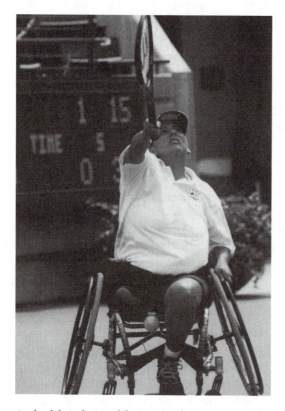

A wheelchair designed for tennis. *Photo courtesy of Rehabilitation Institute of Chicago Wirtz Sports Program.*

TANDEM CYCLING. *See* Cycling

TENNIS WHEELCHAIR Wheelchairs are designed like shoes, specific to each sport the athlete may participate in, and tennis is no exception. In the 30 years since wheelchair tennis has been played in this country, the tennis wheelchair has evolved along with the sport. Players used to use their everyday wheelchairs, which were made of heavy stainless steel, weighing as much as 50 pounds. Athletes took to modifying their own chairs, trying to make them faster and better on the court. Today, the manufacturers have done it for them, creating chairs that are strong, lightweight, and maneuverable.

Tennis wheelchairs used by today's players come in three- and four-wheeled models. Whatever the number of wheels, however, a rigid framed chair is a must, as it allows for stability and maneuverability.

Most tennis wheelchairs will also have a high degree of camber in the rear wheels, giving the chair a wider wheelbase and allowing for faster and tighter turns, essential for the athlete to quickly move from one side of the court to the other. It is primarily for this reason that the tennis wheelchair is not functional as any everyday chair; while its lightweight and sporty look may make it an appealing choice for everyday use, the wide camber of the wheels will prevent the user from getting through most doorways.

BIBLIOGRAPHY. "All About Wheelchair Tennis Chairs—3 or 4 Wheels," International Paralympic Committee, http://www.paralympics.com/wheelchairs/tennis_wheelchairs. htm; "Wheelchair Tennis." Alta Foundation, http://www.altafoundation.org/wheelchair_ tennis.html.

TETHER A tether is an adaptive device that allows a blind or visually impaired runner to compete in track and running events. The tether, according to rule, cannot be longer than 50 cm, or about a foot in length. It can be made of anything, even shoestring, as long as it is nonelastic. The purpose of the tether is to allow the runner and guide to have contact yet allow independent movement for both.

During training or races, the guide runner and the athlete will both have one end of the tether either in their hands or wrapped around their wrist, while keeping in mind that the guide runner cannot ever be in front of the visually impaired athlete. Racers have, in fact, been disqualified in events where they crossed the finish line behind their guide runner. Guide running isn't easy. In order to be an effective guide runner, the guide has to be able to run about 20 percent faster than the visually impaired athlete. This means that a guide runner should be able to complete a marathon within one half hour faster than the runner with the disability without strain.

Running on a tether takes a great deal of practice and skill, and requires excellent communication between the guide and the athlete. Using a guide runner, a visually impaired athlete can attain great success, like Tim Willis, U.S. Paralympian and multiple medalist.

BIBLIOGRAPHY.International Paralympic Committee, http://www.paraplympic.org; United States Association for Blind Athletes, http://www.usaba.org.

THIBOUTOT, TIP Armand "Tip" Thiboutot has spent a lifetime on wheelchair basketball. He began his career as a wheelchair athlete, advocate, and administrator with the New England Clippers in 1968, and went on to found another team, the Boston Mustangs in 1972.

Thiboutot transferred the skills he learned on the court into a successful career as a wheelchair basketball coach and classifier, where his credits include coaching the 1984 men's U.S. Paralympic wheelchair basketball team and the 1988 men's team that competed in the Paralympics in Seoul, Korea.

He has long been recognized as a leader in the wheelchair basketball movement, serving as first vice president of the National Wheelchair Basketball Association (NWBA) for 15 years. He also served internationally on the executive committee of the International Wheelchair Basketball Federation and was both President and Vice President of the International

Wheelchair Basketball Federation (IWBF) technical commission. Thiboutot was inducted into the National Wheelchair Basketball Association Hall of Fame in 1993.

Thiboutot shares his passion for the sport through his writing as well. His articles have been published in *Basketball News, Paraplegia News,* and *Sports 'n' Spokes,* including "Talented Enough for Wheelchair Basketball?" *Sports 'n' Spokes,* 15, no. 2 (July/August 1989): 23.

BIBLIOGRAPHY. International Wheelchair Basketball Federation, http://www.iwbf.org; National Wheelchair Basketball Association, http://www.nwba.org.

THREE-TRACKING Three-tracking is a method of skiing for skiers who have use of one leg and two arms. It is usually practiced by leg amputees, but it may also be used by individuals with weakness in one leg due to a disability. One of the most popular adaptations in skiing for people with disabilities, it is called three-tracking after the number of tracks left in the snow by the skier—one for the ski, and two for the outriggers.

Three trackers use one standard ski and two outriggers, which are forearm crutch-style ski poles. Outriggers are used to help steer, add balance, and assist with slowing and stopping. They are height adjustable, and they may be locked in an upright position to be used as a walking crutch. If the skier has two legs but only functional use of one leg, the weaker leg may rest on an adaptive support that is attached to the ski. More highly skilled three track skiers may choose to use regular ski poles rather than outriggers, and three trackers can be seen everywhere from the local ski hill to the Paralympic stage.

See also Skiing

BIBLIOGRAPHY. Adaptive Adventures, http://adaptiveadventures.org; Paciorek, Michael J., and Jeffery A. Jones. *Sports and Recreation for the Disabled,* 2nd ed. Carmel, IN: Cooper Publishing Group, 1994.

UNITED STATES AQUATIC ASSOCIATION OF THE DEAF. *See* USA Deaf Sports Federation (USADSF)

UNITED STATES ASSOCIATION FOR BLIND ATHLETES (USABA) The United States Association for Blind Athletes (USABA) was founded in 1976 as the organization to oversee sport for athletes with visual impairments in the United States. Blind athletes competed for the first time in the 1976 Olympiad for the Physically Disabled in Toronto, Canada (the Paralympic Games predecessor), which led to the creation of an organization to administer and oversee sports opportunities for blind athletes in the future. In the nearly 30 years since its formation, USABA has served more than 100,000 people.

USABA provides opportunities for athletes at the local, regional, national, and international levels, and currently has over 3,000 athlete members competing in activities including goalball, gymnastics, judo, powerlifting, outdoor recreation, swimming, tandem cycling, athletics, bowling, cycling, golf, wrestling, Alpine skiing, Nordic skiing, and speedskating.

Athletes compete in one of four classifications based on their degree of visual impairment:

Class B1: No light perception in either eye up to light perception, but inability to recognize the shape of a hand at any distance or in any direction.

Class B2: From ability to recognize the shape of a hand up to visual acuity of 20/600 and/or a visual field of less than 5 degrees in the best eye with the best practical eye correction.

Class B3: From visual acuity above 20/600 and up to visual acuity of 20/200 and/or a visual field of less than 20 degrees and more than 5 degrees in the best eye with the best practical eye correction.

Class B4: From visual acuity above 20/200 and up to visual acuity of 20/70 and a visual field larger than 20 degrees in the best eye with the best practical eye correction.

BIBLIOGRAPHY. Depauw, Karen P., and Susan J. Gavron. *Disability and Sport.* Champaign, IL: Human Kinetics, 1995; United States Association for Blind Athletes, http://www.usaba.org.

UNITED STATES CEREBRAL PALSY ATHLETIC ASSOCIATION (USCPAA). *See* National Disability Sports Alliance (NDSA)

UNITED STATES DISABLED ATHLETES FUND (USDAF) The 1996 Atlanta Paralympics, in addition to providing top competition and a once in a lifetime experience for athletes around the world, left behind a legacy called the United States Disabled Athletes Fund (USDAF). In 1997, Blaze Sports Georgia was rolled out in cooperation with the Georgia Parks and Recreation Association.

Blaze Sports provides children and adults with a wide range of disabilities with the opportunity to participate in sports competitions, camps, and clinics. They are working in partnership with other community-based organizations such as the Shepherd Center and Roosevelt Warm Springs Sports Training Complex to provide athletes interested in swimming, wheelchair basketball, and track and field the opportunity to learn and to compete.

The USDAF launched Blaze Sports Clubs of America in 2002, where community organizations nationwide partner with USDAF to offer programs to athletes with disabilities in sports such as wheelchair tennis, wheelchair basketball, wheelchair racing, wheelchair rugby, swimming, and field events. There are now 43 Blaze Sports Clubs operating in 22 states.

USDAF sponsors events to educate people with disabilities and others about adapted sports and recreation, such as Blaze Sports Days, one-day events that serve to introduce children to a host of adapted sports and recreation; weekend-long Blaze Sports coaches training clinics; an annual disability sports conference; and coaches training on adaptive sports methods to those coaching nondisabled sports.

BIBLIOGRAPHY. Blaze Sports, http://www.blazesports.com/.

UNITED STATES DISABLED SKI TEAM (USDST) The United States Disabled Ski Team (USDST) got its start when the National Handicapped Sports and Recreation Association (NHSRA), now Disabled Sports, USA, began conducting ski competitions in the 1970s. A regional race qualifying system was developed to take the sport from a mostly recreational event to something on par with competitive downhill skiing for nondisabled athletes.

In 1985, a special seeding provision for ambulatory skiers with disabilities was created in U.S. Skiing Association (USSA) races. Disabled alpine skiing became a full medal sport in the 1988 Pan American Winter Games in Argentina and was offered as an exhibition event at the 1988 Winter Olympics in Calgary, Alberta, Canada.

The USDST was one of the first disability sport organizations to be integrated into the sport's national governing body when it came under the jurisdiction of the U.S. Ski and Snowboard Association. This integration provided the athletes with access to sponsorship and media opportunities previously unavailable to athletes with disabilities. They've had great success internationally over two decades, topping the medal count and Gold medal tally in virtually every appearance at a World Cup or Paralympic competition.

BIBLIOGRAPHY. Robbins, Paul. "US Disabled Ski Team Still Strong But the Rest of the World is Catching Up." *Ski Racing.* http://www.skiracing.com/features/news_displayFeatures.php/1562/FEATURES/newsArticles; *Sports'n' Spokes* (May–June 1989): 11.

ADDITIONAL READING. Batcheller, Lori J. *Alpine Achievement A Chronicle of the United States Disabled Ski Team.* Bloomington, IN: 1st Books, 2002.

UNITED STATES ELECTRIC WHEELCHAIR HOCKEY ASSOCIATION (USEWHA). *See* Power Hockey

UNITED STATES OLYMPIC COMMITTEE (USOC) The United States Olympic Committee (USOC) is charged with the responsibility for oversight of Olympic, Pan American, and Paralympic sport in the United States. Their authority derives from the Ted Stevens Olympic and Amateur Sports Act, legislation spearheaded by Ted Stevens, U.S. Senator from Alaska. U.S. Paralympics, a division of the USOC, was created to govern Paralympic sport specifically.

BIBLIOGRAPHY. United States Olympic Committee, http://www.olympic-usa.org.

UNITED STATES QUAD RUGBY ASSOCIATION (USQRA) In 1988, because of the popularity of the sport of quad rugby, the USQRA was formed to provide oversight, including developing rules, a classification system, certification for officials, and sanctioning of events.

See also Quad Rugby; Wheelchair Rugby

BIBLIOGRAPHY. United States Quad Rugby Association, http://usqra.org.

USA DEAF SPORTS FEDERATION (USADSF) The USA Deaf Sports Federation (USADSF) got its start when the Akron Club of the Deaf in Ohio sponsored a national basketball tournament for deaf and hard of hearing athletes in 1945. After the success of the tournament, an organization was formed to create rules of competition and a more formalized structure. Originally called the American Athletic Association of the Deaf, the organization was created to sanction and provide competitions and to assist in preparing U.S. teams for competition, as well as to provide social activities for athletes who were deaf and hearing impaired.

The organization changed its name to the USA Deaf Sports Federation (USADSF) in 1998. Today, USADSF is made up of 18 national sports organizations. In order to be eligible to participate in USADSF sanctioned competition, athletes must have a hearing loss of 55 dB or greater. Hearing aids are not allowed in competition. Unlike other disability sport organizations, there are no classifications in deaf sport; no separate rulebook is used. Athletes who are deaf and hearing impaired have the opportunity to qualify internationally for the Deaflympics, an international competition held every other year, the year following each Summer and Winter Olympic and Paralympic Games.

Affiliated sports include aquatics, baseball, basketball, bowling, cycling, golf, ice hockey, martial arts, orienteering, shooting, ski and snowboard, soccer, team handball, tennis, track and field, volleyball, and wrestling.

BIBLIOGRAPHY. Disability Sport Organizations," http://edweb6.educ.msu.edu/kin866/orgusadsf.htm; USA Deaf Sports Federation, MSU Disability Sports Web Site, http://edweb6.educ.msu.edu/kin866/orgusadsf.htm; USA Deaf Sports Federation, http://www.usdeafsports.org.

USA DEAF VOLLEYBALL ASSOCIATION. *See* USA Deaf Sports Federation

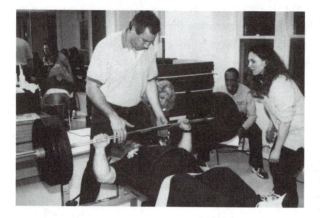

Powerlifting practice. *Photo courtesy of Rehabilitation Institute of Chicago Wirtz Sports Program.*

U.S. PARALYMPICS U.S. Paralympics is a division of the United States Olympic Committee (USOC), formed in 2001 to increase support for Paralympic sport in the USA. U.S. Paralympics coordinates the preparation and selection of athletes to U.S. Paralympic teams, both summer and winter, in 23 different sports, in conjunction with national governing bodies (NGBs), disabled sport organizations, and other partner organizations. U.S. Paralympics also works with national and locally focused sport organizations that offer Paralympic programs to children and other developing athletes.

U.S. Paralympics also promotes the Paralympic Academy, a program designed to introduce the Paralympics and disability sport to children with and without disabilities through education, instruction, and activities, and the Paralympic Military Program, designed to introduce disabled war veterans to Paralympic and disability sport.

BIBLIOGRAPHY. United States Paralympics, http://www.usolympicteam.com/paralympics/.

UNITED STATES SAILING ASSOCIATION SAILORS WITH SPECIAL NEEDS (USSA-SWSN). *See* Sailing for People with Disabilities

UNITED STATES SLED HOCKEY ASSOCIATION. *See* Sled Hockey

UNITED STATES WHEELCHAIR WEIGHTLIFTING FEDERATION. *See* Powerlifting

UPPER BODY ERGOMETER (UBE). *See* Ergometer

VERTICAL INTEGRATION Vertical integration is a concept and a philosophy relatively new to the disability sport movement. It derives from the notion that athletes with disabilities should be integrated, not based on disability, but on the sport in which they participate.

It is premised on the notion that the national governing bodies for particular sports should assume the responsibility for development, coaching, training, and support of athletes with disabilities instead of parallel functions being performed by disability specific sport organizations.

Two of the earliest sport national governing bodies in the United States to operate under the model of vertical integration are the U.S. Tennis Association incorporating wheelchair

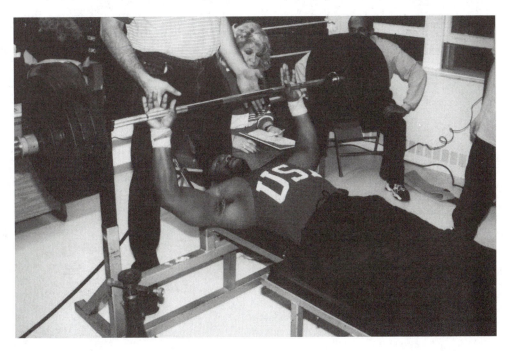

Lifting practice. *Photo courtesy of Rehabilitation Institute of Chicago Wirtz Sports Program.*

tennis into its programming and the U.S. Ski and Snowboard Association assuming responsibility for the U.S. Disabled Ski Team.

Vertical indicates the notion of games organized around the sport, and integration describes the assimilation of elite, professional athletes with disabilities into mainstream competitions, without necessarily having direct competition between persons with and without disabilities. Instead of establishing separate associations for disability, amputee, or wheelchair sports, vertical integration operates under the premise that all athletes participating in a given sport are governed by the same association, with governance focused on the sport, not the disability.

BIBLIOGRAPHY. Ragged Edge, http://www.raggededgemag.com.

VOLPENTEST, TONY Tony Volpentest, a quadruple amputee track sprinter, won the title of world's fastest not once, but twice. Volpentest, born without hands and feet, sprinted 100 meters to gold at the 1992 Paralympics in Barcelona, setting a world record of 11.63 seconds. He repeated four years later at the 1996 Paralympics in Atlanta, winning another gold medal and setting a new world record of 11.36 in the process. Volpentest also won a gold medal and set a world record in the 200 meter in Barcelona.

Volpentest was the youngest of six children, and although he was active, he wasn't too interested in sports. In fact, he joined the track team as a sophomore in high school not to run but to try and learn to overcome his shyness.

Shriner's Hospitals in Portland helped Volpentest obtain his racing prosthetics, and his carbon-graphite feet bolted to carbon-composite sockets catapulted him to victory.

Volpentest's story was the subject of a documentary entitled *Dreams of Gold* which itself won gold at the New York Film Festival and a CINE Golden Eagle from the Council on International Nontheatrical Events.

Tony Volpentest at the start. *Copyright Chris Hamilton Photography.*

BIBLIOGRAPHY. Joukowsky, Artemis A. W, and Larry Rothstein. *Raising the Bar—New Horizons in Disability Sport,* 1st ed. New York: Umbrage Editions, 2002; "Shriner's Hospitals Patient and Double Amputee Wins Double Gold at 1996 Paralympic Games." *Shriner's Hospital for Children,* http://www.shrinershq.org/patients/tony9-96.html.

WADDELL, CAMILLE Camille Waddell was born to be in the water. She grew up in Pascagoula, Mississippi, in a family who loved to swim, ski, and sail. Waddell, born with achondroplasia, was no different. She loved the freedom of the water and like the rest of her family, she was an excellent swimmer. She didn't turn to competition, though, until much later, learning about disability sports well into adulthood.

Waddell graduated from the University of Southern Mississippi in 1983; her first international competition wasn't until nearly a decade later. She was selected to represent the United States at the Paralympics in Barcelona in 1992, where she was the first little person in U.S. history to win a Paralympic Gold, which she did en route to setting a world and Paralympic record in the 100 meter breaststroke. She also won silver in the 50 meter freestyle.

In 1993, she was named the Dwarf Athletic Association of America's (DAAA) female athlete of the year for her outstanding performances, which continued over the next two years. She set national records in short course meters in the 50 m breast stroke, 50 m fly, 100 m freestyle, and 100 m individual medley. She also set national records in short course yards in four events.

Back on the Paralympic stage in 1996, Waddell repeated her 1992 performance, breaking her 100 m breast stroke world record by over a second and winning a Gold medal in a time of 1:53.48. She added to her medal tally with a silver medal in the 4 by 50 m medley relay alongside U.S. teammates Sue Moucha, Jill Nelson, and Stephanie Brooks, and a bronze medal in the 200 m freestyle relay.

Waddell has won numerous honors and accolades, including one from her home state of Mississippi. In 1997, the Mississippi legislature honored her with House Resolution 40 commending and congratulating her for her honors and medals won in swimming competition.

Now retired from competition, Waddell has translated her skill in the pool to the creation of Swim-n-Stuff, a retail swim store with locations in Pensacola, Florida and Mobile, Alabama.

BIBLIOGRAPHY. "DAAA Swim Records." *Dwarf Athletic Association of America.* http:// www.daaa.org/swim_recm.htm; Depauw, Karen P., and Susan J. Gavron. *Disability and Sport.* Champaign, IL: Human Kinetics, 1995; "Paralympic Results—Swimming." *International*

WADDELL, CHRIS

Paralympic Committee, http://www.paralympic.org/release/Main_Sections_Menu/Sports/ Results/paralympics_results.html?event_id=1209.

WADDELL, CHRIS According to many, Waddell is the man who revolutionized mono-skiing. Waddell, born in 1968 in Granby, Massachusetts, was on skis by age three. Growing up, he wanted nothing but to be a ski racer, and he was well on the way to achieving his goal. He was training with his college team at Middlebury as a freshman, but never got to race—at least not with them. While he was on Christmas break, December, 20, 1988, skiing at Berkshire East, a binding released, he fell, and he doesn't remember much else except that his dreams of skiing appeared over.

Within a year, however, his dreams were once again within reach, this time from a mono-ski. Within a couple weeks of his first time on the monoski, he was competing. Not too long after that, he was winning.

Waddell has represented the United States in seven Paralympic Games, four winter and three summer. He swept his events in mono-skiing in Lillehammer in 1994, winning Gold in the slalom, Super G, downhill, and Giant Slalom. Later that year, he won silver at the Athletics World Championships in Berlin. Four years later he won Gold and silver at the Nagano Paralympics, and he followed that with a Gold and bronze at the World Athletics Championships in Birmingham, England. In the 2000 Paralympics in Sydney, he won another silver on the track in the 200 m.

During the off season, Waddell and fellow U.S. Disabled Ski Team member Sarah Will founded the Chris Waddell and Sarah Will Monoski Camp, where they've taught hundreds of people with disabilities to ski.

Waddell's story, good looks, and easygoing manner have made him a media favorite. He has appeared on Dateline and Oprah, and has been featured in *Skiing Magazine, Outside Magazine, Vertical Reality,* and *Olympian Magazine.*

He was named one of *People* magazine's 50 Most Beautiful People in 1998, and he has some acting credits to his name as well, including a stint on the soap opera *Loving.*

BIBLIOGRAPHY. Joukowsky, Artemis A. W., and Larry Rothstein. *Raising the Bar—New Horizons in Disability Sport,* 1st ed. New York: Umbrage Editions, 2002; Wallace, Bevin. "Top 25 Skiers: Chris Waddell." *Skiing Magazine,* http://www.skiingmag.com/skiing/face_ shots/article/0,12910,328910,00.html.

WELLMAN, MARK Mark Wellman is considered by many to be the "grandfather" of adventure sports for athletes with spinal cord injuries. Wellman climbed and lit the Paralympic torch in 1996 to start the Atlanta games that year; but in spite of the fact that he held the torch between his legs with only flame retardant pants between him and the flame, that was not his most challenging climb.

Wellman started climbing in the 1970s, at the age of 17, with his uncle John. After hundreds of uneventful climbs, Wellman fell in 1982 while he was on a climb with long-time friend and climbing partner, Mike Corbett. That day, he fell from 13,000 feet up in the Sierras, landing after about a hundred feet. After seven and a half months in the hospital, Wellman wasn't sure what he would do—but he definitely didn't think he'd be climbing again.

That all changed when Wellman saw a disability magazine featuring a paraplegic woman being lowered down a rock face on a rope. Wellman thought if she could do it, so could he, so he and partner, Corbett, set to work devising a system to enable them to climb together. After months of trial and error, they cemented their place in the history books with a 1989 climb up the face of El Capitan in Yosemite. Wellman climbed by doing one pull up at a time, completing over 7,000 repetitions from bottom to top of the 3,000-foot rock face.

The seven-day climb received national coverage, with Tom Brokaw providing daily updates on the evening news. Two years later, Corbett and Wellman climbed again, this time up Half Dome in Yosemite, a climb that took 13 days and is one of the subjects covered in detail in Wellman's book *Climbing Back*. In 1999, Wellman and Corbett celebrated the tenth anniversary of their climb up El Capitan by returning to the scene and climbing the nose of the mountain, calling it "Return to the Challenge."

Wellman earned a degree in Park Management from West Valley College in Saratoga, California and worked for seven years as an interpretive ranger and Director of the Disabled Access Program at Yosemite National Park. In addition to climbing, Wellman has been a member of two Paralympic teams, competing in cross-country skiing for the U.S. Disabled Ski Teams that competed in Albertville in 1992 and Lillehammer in 1994.

Wellman operates a business, No Limits, out of his Truckee, California home, serving as a film maker, motivational speaker, and adventure sports camp operator. He has created three documentary videos, *No Barriers, Beyond the Barriers,* and *Wheels of Fire,* featuring athletes with disabilities participating in adventure sports such as climbing, kayaking, and hang gliding.

BIBLIOGRAPHY. No Limits, http://www.nolimitstahoe.com.

WHEELCHAIR ATHLETICS OF THE USA (WAUSA) Wheelchair Athletics of the USA (WAUSA) is the governing body for wheelchair track and field in the United States. It is a member organization of Wheelchair Sports, USA and is affiliated with USA Track and Field. WAUSA sanctions events in athletics, slalom, and road racing and is involved in selecting athletes to represent the United States in international athletics competition.

WAUSA drafts the rules relating to wheelchair divisions in road races and track meets and prescribes rules for equipment including wheelchair specifications. These rules are taken from the International Association of Athletics (IAAF), International Paralympic Committee (IPC), and USA Track and Field (USATF) rules with modifications for the wheelchair and the athlete's disability related needs.

See also Wheelchair Track and Field

BIBLIOGRAPHY. Depauw, Karen P., and Susan J. Gavron. *Disability and Sport.* Champaign, IL: Human Kinetics, 1995; Wheelchair Sports USA, http://www.wsusa.org.

WHEELCHAIR BASKETBALL

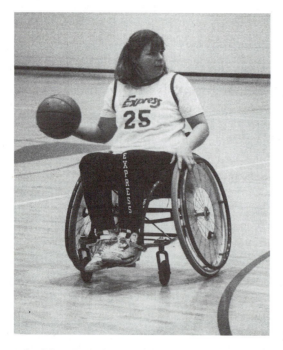

Wheelchair basketball. *Photo courtesy of Rehabilitation Institute of Chicago Wirtz Sports Program.*

WHEELCHAIR BASKETBALL Wheelchair basketball is the most well-known sport for people with disabilities worldwide. It rose to popularity after disabled veterans began returning from World War II. Veteran's hospitals began offering therapeutic recreation for these veterans, mostly active young men who wanted to do more than just sit in a wheelchair the rest of their lives. They started playing table tennis, bowling, and swimming, then added sports like water polo softball, football, and finally basketball.

Wheelchair basketball started with the New England and California chapters of the Paralyzed Veteran's Administration (PVA) in the early 1940s. VA hospitals across the nation soon offered programs, and by 1948 there were six teams across the United States as well as teams in Canada and England. The PVA organized a national championship in 1948, won by the Flying Wheels of California. A short time later, the National Wheelchair Basketball Association (NWBA) took over governance of the sport, and community and collegiate teams began forming outside the VA system.

Tim Nugent, director of the Division of Rehabilitation Education Services at the University of Illinois, was instrumental in creating the first National Wheelchair Basketball Tournament outside the VA hospital system. The Kansas City Pioneers were the first tournament champions, followed by St. Louis the next three years, and then the Illinois Gizz Kids. After that first tournament, Nugent and the other teams created the NWBA which now governs men's, women's, intercollegiate, and junior wheelchair basketball programs nationwide. The NWBA men's division has grown to include nearly 200 teams in 22 divisions around the country.

Wheelchair basketball has been a force on the international disability sport scene since the early years as well, since Montreal, Canada sent a team to the National Wheelchair Basketball Tournament in 1954, loosely recognized as the first "international" tournament. Wheelchair basketball has been offered on the Paralympic program since early in the Games history, and has added Gold Cup and World Championship play to the international competition opportunities.

For the first 30 years in U.S. wheelchair basketball's history, the sport was played only by men. Finally in the 1970s the University of Illinois established the Ms. Kids, the first women's wheelchair basketball team in the nation. The team spent the first four years playing nondisabled opponents. Four years later in 1974, history was made with the first wheelchair basketball game between two organized women's teams, the Ms. Kids and the Southern Illinois University Squidettes. Detroit added a team the next year, and Canada joined in after that.

Southern California, the Courage Rolling Gophers (now Timberwolves) and the Rehabilitation Institute of Chicago Express came next. Internationally, U.S. women started competing in 1976; four years later they won their first Paralympic medal with a bronze. In 1988 the U.S. women took home Paralympic Gold for the first time.

Wheelchair basketball is played according to NCAA rules with a few modifications. Traveling in wheelchair basketball, for example, occurs when the player takes more than two pushes of the wheelchair without bouncing or passing the ball. However, most highly skilled players use a traditional dribble.

Another difference between the standing version of the game and wheelchair basketball is the physical advantage foul. When a player stands up out of their wheelchair, if they place their foot to the ground to boost themselves, or if one or both buttocks comes up off the seat cushion, this is considered a physical advantage foul.

Classification in wheelchair basketball ensures that individuals with various levels of disability can play. Basketball on the national level in the United States has three classes, I, II, and III, while at the international level there are more.

Class I players have complete motor loss at or above T7 that limits trunk mobility, balance, arm strength, and range of motion. Class II is disability comparable to a T8–L2 spinal injury or double hip amputee, with limited forward, backward, and sideways trunk mobility and balance. Class III includes all players with motor loss originating at L3 or below, as well as those with amputations and orthopedic disabilities. Each player has a point value depending on their classification (i.e., 1, 2, or 3). A team may have no more than 12 points on the floor at a time, and may never have more than three class III players on the floor at a time.

The wheelchairs used in the game generally are specifically designed for basketball, quite different from the heavy stainless steel wheelchairs that players used a few decades ago. Basketball wheelchairs are lightweight, rigid framed, and designed to keep opposing players at a distance. The high degree of camber most players use in their wheels ensures the chair will be highly maneuverable, able to spin and turn easily.

Wheelchair basketball is a sport enjoyed by people of all ages and all levels of ability and interest around the nation and around the world.

BIBLIOGRAPHY. Apple, Jr., David F. *Physical Fitness: A Guide for Individuals with Spinal Cord Injury*. Washington, DC: Department of Veteran's Affairs, Rehabilitation Research and Development Service, 1995; Kelley, Jerry D., and Lex Frieden. *Go For It! A Book on Sport and Recreation for Persons with Disabilities*. Orlando, FL: Harcourt Brace Jovanovich, 1989; International Paralympic Committee, http://www.paralympic.org; National Wheelchair Basketball Association, http://www.nwba.org; United States Paralympics, http://www.usolympicteam.com/paralympics/.

WHEELCHAIR DANCE SPORT Wheelchair dance sport was introduced in 1977 in Sweden and became an official IPC sanctioned sport in 1998, with the first World Championships held in Japan. Today more than 5,000 dancers practice in over 40 countries, though European nations predominate. In North America, Mexico is the only country actively participating—the United States and Canada have never had an organized program for wheelchair dance sport. There are, however, many dance troupes and adapted dance programs throughout the United States.

WHEELCHAIR FENCING

In wheelchair dance sport, there are divisions for wheelchair users dancing with standing partners (combo style) and for two wheelchair users dancing together (duo). In the combo style, the wheelchair dancer is the most important part of the couple; they can't be there merely to complement the standing dancer. The couple must dance in harmony, in time to the music. They have to express a sense of rhythm, demonstrated by push and pull on the wheels, stops, and turns. Originality, expression, use of space, interpretation of the music, bodywork, body lines, connection, balance, leading and position are all important parts of the wheelchair dance performance. There are also formation dances for four, six, or eight couples on the floor together at one time. Dances performed include standard dances like the waltz, tango and Viennese waltz as well as Latin dances like the samba, rumba and cha-cha.

Wheelchair users are classified according to their level of function into one of two classes, LWD1 or LWD2, based on their trunk control and rotation, and ability to push, pull, stop, and accelerate. The wheelchair can be either manual or a battery powered wheelchair depending on the individual's level of disability.

The IPC Wheelchair Dance Sport committee is working to encourage the worldwide growth of wheelchair dance sport, to improve training for the sport for athletes, judges, and coaches.

BIBLIOGRAPHY. International Paralympic Committee, http://www.paralympic.org/paralympian/20004/2000407.htm; "Summer Sports—Wheelchair Dance Sport." International Paralympic Committee, http://www.paralympic.org/release/Summer_Sports/Wheelchair_Dance_Sport/.

WHEELCHAIR ERGOMETER. *See* Ergometer

WHEELCHAIR FENCING Fencing has been popular in Europe since the 1940s, although it has been slower to catch on in the United States. In disability sport, fencing is offered for wheelchair users only. Unlike the standing version, the wheelchair fencer is stationary, locked into an adjustable fencing frame. With the exception of that modification, the rules are virtually identical.

The first set of rules for wheelchair fencing were created in the 1970s, a slightly modified version of the rules drafted by F.I.E., Federation Internationale d' Escrime, the international governing body for fencing.

Classification in wheelchair fencing has changed from a disability specific system to the present-day functional system, allowing athletes with different disabilities such as spinal cord injury, cerebral palsy, and polio to compete against each other equitably. The functional classification system was introduced at the Seoul Paralympics in 1988, with athletes classified 1A, 1B, 2, 3, or 4 depending on the functional abilities and limitations they display.

Class 1A and 1B athletes have disabilities such as spinal injury or cerebral palsy resulting in upper body impairment. Tape and strapping can be used to assist these athletes in handling their weapons and keeping them attached to the hand. Class 2 athletes have disabilities similar to a spinal injury of T1 to T8, but no impairment to the competition arm. Class 3 athletes have disabilities similar to a spinal injury of T9 to L1, and class 4 have disabilities similar to L4 injury or lower.

Wheelchair fencers compete in epee, saber, and foil. The foil has a flexible rectangular blade, weighs about a pound, and is usually around 35 inches in length. The target for foil

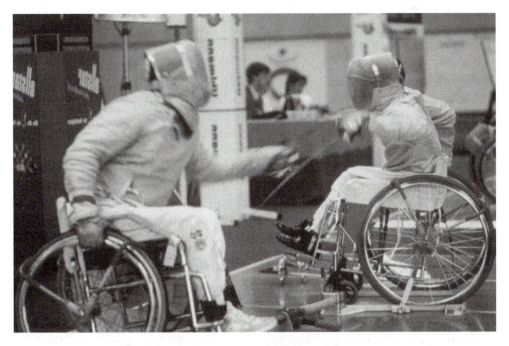

Wheelchair Fencing Competition. *Copyright Chris Hamilton Photography.*

is the torso, shoulders to groin, front, and back and during competition the fencer wears a vest over the target area, allowing points to be scored electronically.

The epee weighs about two pounds with a large hand guard and a stiffer blade than the foil. The whole upper part of the fencer's body, including the part of the wheelchair extending above that line, is the target for epee.

The saber is similar in weight and length to the foil, but it is a slashing weapon. The target area is from the bend of the hips to the top of the head front and back, simulating a cavalry rider on a horse. In saber the fencer wears not only a jacket but a protective head covering as well, since for this weapon, the head is a target.

In addition to the weapons, equipment needed to participate includes protective clothing such as a lamé apron, helmet, mask, padded gloves, vest, jacket, and leg covering. While most of the equipment is available through commercial suppliers, the fencing frame is not.

Because wheelchair fencers don't have identical-sized wheelchairs, nor are they all the same height with the same length of arms, the fencing frame must be adjustable. The frame should be adjustable to the widths of various wheelchairs as well as adjustable forward and back to accommodate the length of the fencer's arm and reach. The front casters as well as the back wheels of the wheelchair are locked into the frame.

In fencing, the object of the sport is to score 15 points in direct elimination or 5 points in preliminary pool play against your opponent. Points are awarded each time the fencer touches an opponent in the target area.

BIBLIOGRAPHY. Apple, Jr., David F. *Physical Fitness: A Guide for Individuals with Spinal Cord Injury.* Washington, DC: Department of Veteran's Affairs, Rehabilitation Research and Development Service, 1995; "Fencing." Michigan State University. Disability Sports, http://edweb6.educ.msu.edu/kin866/spfencing.htm; International Wheelchair Fencing, http://www.iwfencing.com/.

WHEELCHAIR FOOTBALL Football is one of the most popular sports in America, with a few modifications wheelchair users can play. Played in a gym on a 60- by 30-yard playing field with 8-yard end zones, each team has six players on the field at a time. A two-hand touch takes the place of the tackle, but the rest of the play is similar with sweeps, screen, and deep passes.

While wheelchair football was played in the early years at the University of Illinois, women didn't play until the 1970s, and large scale tournaments didn't take place until the 1980s, when in 1981 Brad Hedrick started a tournament between the University of Illinois and neighboring teams.

Other universities got on the wheelchair football bandwagon with University of Wisconsin–Whitewater and University of Wisconsin–Milwaukee forming an intramural league. University of Wisconsin–Madison and University of Wisconsin–LaCrosse formed teams soon after, followed by Racine.

Across the country, Santa Barbara, California was the first place in the west coast to embrace wheelchair football. Andy Fleming, who was then the coordinator of the Santa Barbara Park District's adaptive programs division, created the Blister Bowl wheelchair football tournament to provide options other than the wheelchair basketball and track programs they offered.

In February 1980, the first Blister Bowl was held between Santa Barbara police officers and the local wheelchair football team, the Santa Barbarians. By 1988 and 1989, eight teams nationwide competed. Today, the Blister Bowl is an international event, attracting teams from as far away as Australia and New Zealand.

BIBLIOGRAPHY. Hamilton, Bill. "Pigskin Progress, Wheelchair Football and the Blister Bowl." *Sports 'n' Spokes* (January–February 1990): 32–34; Kelley, Jerry D., and Lex Frieden. *Go For It! A Book on Sport and Recreation for Persons with Disabilities.* Orlando, FL: Harcourt Brace Jovanovich, 1989.

WHEELCHAIR RACQUETBALL Wheelchair racquetball arrived on the international scene in 1990, debuting at the 5th World Championships in Caracas, Venezuela. Five athletes demonstrated it at the 1992 Paralympics in Barcelona, and it appeared again as an exhibition event at the 1996 Paralympics in Atlanta.

Racquetball was developed as a variation on paddleball in the 1940s and 1950s, but it didn't become popular with wheelchair users until the 1980s, largely due to the fact that racquetball courts were mostly inaccessible. David Hinton, Chair of the International Stoke Mandeville Wheelchair Sports Federation (ISMWSF) Racquetball Division and the International Racquetball Federation's Committee for Athletes with Disabilities, brought wheelchair racquetball to the world stage, introducing it at the Stoke Mandeville Games in England in 1993.

Wheelchair racquetball, like its counterpart for athletes without disabilities, is played on a smooth floored, smooth walled court. Racquets, balls, and protective eye wear are the only equipment needed.

A few modifications to the game enable wheelchair users to play. In wheelchair racquetball, players are allowed two bounces of the ball before they must hit it again instead of the one bounce allowed in the standing game. Points are scored only on the serve, and matches consist of the best two out of three games played to a score of 15.

A second modification relates specifically to wheelchair use, and provides that players cannot stand up out of their wheelchair to hit or serve a ball. The rear wheels cannot cross service and fault lines during play, but the players front casters can cross the lines without penalty. Wheelchair racquetball, like wheelchair tennis, is a sport that can be played by people with and without disabilities.

BIBLIOGRAPHY. Kelley, Jerry D., and Lex Frieden. *Go For It! A Book on Sport and Recreation for Persons with Disabilities.* Orlando, FL: Harcourt Brace Jovanovich, 1989; *Sports 'n' Spokes* (July–August 1990): 52.

WHEELCHAIR ROLLERS Wheelchair rollers are modeled after wind trainers for cycling, which allow wheelchair users to exercise in a stationary manner. Various models of wheelchair rollers allow users to exercise from an everyday chair, a racing wheelchair, or a handcycle.

Rollers allow athletes with disabilities who live in climates with difficult weather conditions to stay fit and healthy, as well as to train for competitive events. Rollers are excellent for speed training as well as long, steady-state workouts.

There are a few different models of wheelchair rollers on the market; some require the athlete to supply the momentum, and others are computerized, allowing the athlete to prescribe a particular race course or set of conditions to train.

The Bug wheelchair roller by McLain Cycle Products was one of the early rollers in the late 1980s. It had a ramp for easy access, locks to secure the wheelchair in place, and a flywheel for momentum. Eagle Sportschairs and Sportaid have since come up with their own rollers. Although none of the models currently available are easily portable, they provide a means for athletes and others to stay in shape no matter what the weather.

BIBLIOGRAPHY. Eagle Sportschairs, http://www.eaglesportschairs.com; Sportaid, http://www.sportaid.com.

WHEELCHAIR SOFTBALL Wheelchair softball has been played in the United States, like many other wheelchair sports, since the time many disabled veterans were returning from World War II. The University of Illinois offered it to their disabled students as an activity as early as the 1950s, but it wasn't widely played until 1975 with the first national tournament held in 1977. The National Wheelchair Softball Association (NWSA) was founded that same year and serves as the governing body for wheelchair softball in the United States. Over 40 teams throughout the nation compete regularly in local and regional competition, with the top teams qualifying for the annual National Wheelchair Softball Tournament.

WHEELCHAIR SPORTS, USA

Wheelchair softball is played according to the official rules for 16-inch slow pitch softball, with one major difference. Wheelchair softball is played on parking lots or other hard paved surfaces, not on grass, with the diamond painted onto the parking lot or hard surface for the game. The first dedicated wheelchair softball field in the nation was built by the city of Chicago and opened in 2003.

Wheelchair softball players must use manual wheelchairs; no power wheelchairs are allowed in the game.

The wheelchairs used for wheelchair softball are similar to those used for basketball, tennis, and other sports, though no chair is built specifically for this sport. Players choose lightweight, rigid-frame chairs that have a high degree of camber in the wheels so they can round the bases quickly.

Wheelchair softball uses a classification system to ensure equitable play for the people with spinal cord injuries, amputations, cerebral palsy, and other mobility disabilities who are eligible to play. The classification system is similar to wheelchair basketball classification, with Class I, II, and III players, however, instead of 12 points, a maximum of 22 points can be on the field at any one time, with each team having at least one class I player on the field at all times.

Many wheelchair softball teams around the nation have been successful in partnering with their local Major League Baseball (MLB) team counterparts, such as the Minnesota Rolling Twins, Colorado PVA Rockies, Chicago RIC Cubs, Chicago White Sox, Boston United Spinal Association Red Sox, and the New York United Spinal Association Mets. These teams wear the official Major League Baseball uniform and receive varying amounts of support from the franchise, which has helped increase wheelchair softball's popularity and visibility.

BIBLIOGRAPHY. Kelley, Jerry D., and Lex Frieden. *Go For It! A Book on Sport and Recreation for Persons with Disabilities.* Orlando, FL: Harcourt Brace Jovanovich, 1989; National Wheelchair Softball Association, www.wheelchairsoftball.com.

WHEELCHAIR SPORTS, USA (WS-USA) Wheelchair Sports, USA was founded in 1956 as the National Wheelchair Athletic Association to provide organized sports opportunities for people with spinal cord injuries and other disabilities, primarily injured war veterans. They changed their name to Wheelchair Sports, USA in 1994.

The organization's main focus has been on providing opportunities to athletes who use wheelchairs, whether due to spinal cord injury, amputation, or other disabilities.

In order to be eligible to compete in WS-USA sanctioned competition, the individual must have a disability such as spinal cord injury, spina bifida, poliomyelitis, or other lower limb impairment. Athletes are classified in WS-USA competition based on a functional system, taking into account the activities performed in the particular sport and the muscles needed to participate.

WS-USA offers athletes the opportunity to participate in archery, athletics, basketball, fencing, handcycling, pool, powerlifting, racquetball, shooting, swimming, table tennis, water skiing, wheelchair rugby, and sled hockey.

Wheelchair Sports, USA operates in regions around the country, which offer sports competitions to athletes in their geographic area, qualifying them to advance to national and international competitions.

In addition to providing regional opportunities for competition in all these sports, WS-USA also conducts national championships and fields teams to international competitions like the International Stoke Mandeville Games, the Pan-American Games, and the Paralympics.

Wheelchair Sports, USA was based in New York, before moving to Colorado Springs, where they stayed for 20 years. The move to Colorado Springs enabled WS-USA to establish a relationship with the U.S. Olympic Committee, creating new opportunities for wheelchair athletes to train and compete, such as the 1984 addition of wheelchair exhibition races on the program of the Olympic Games.

In recent years, Wheelchair Sports, USA has redirected its energies because of the recognition that nearly a third of its membership is under the age of 18. Junior focused programming allows children with disabilities the opportunities to develop skills and abilities in both a recreational and competitive environment, creating not only future elite sport athletes but healthy and fit adults.

BIBLIOGRAPHY. Disability Sports Web Site, Michigan State University, http://edweb6.educ.msu.edu/kin866/orgwsusa.htm; Wheelchair Sports, USA, http://www.wsusa.org.

WHEELCHAIR TENNIS Brad Parks and Jeff Minnebraker brought tennis to wheelchair users throughout the United States beginning in 1976, but the real growth spurt happened throughout the 1980s. The first U.S. Open was held in 1980, with 70 participants competing in Irvine Park, California.

Along with U.S. development, Parks was instrumental in bringing the sport to the international stage. Between 1980 and 1985, Australia, Japan, Israel, Germany, France, Holland, and Switzerland brought Parks and fellow players Rick Slaughter and Ron Hastings to their countries to conduct clinics and expand development of wheelchair tennis.

The Wheelchair Tennis Player's Association (WTPA) was formed in 1981 and organized the first Grand Prix Circuit of wheelchair tennis in the United States, including four nationally sanctioned tournaments and the U.S. Open. A French athlete attended the U.S. Open in 1981 and brought wheelchair tennis back to his country, developing a circuit of tournaments and the first

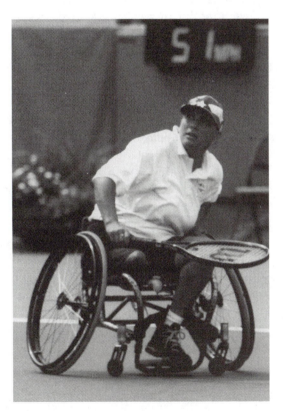

Wheelchair tennis match at the Paralympics. *Photo courtesy of Rehabilitation Institute of Chicago Wirtz Sports Program.*

French championship in 1983. From there, wheelchair tennis spread throughout the rest of Europe.

Then, in 1984, the Everest & Jennings Grand Prix Circuit was created, named after one of the major wheelchair manufacturers of the time. By the next year, there were over 60 wheelchair tennis tournaments across the United States and over 250 participants at the U.S. Open. The Japan Open, Israel Open, and French Open followed, further expanding the sport across the globe.

The International Wheelchair Tennis Federation Committee of Management met for the first time in 1988 and established five world regions and an eight-tournament international circuit. In 1990, there were 10 member nations. Just three years later there were 33 and by 1995, 45 countries were participating internationally in wheelchair tennis.

Not only were the 1980s the period that saw the largest growth in wheelchair tennis, they were pivotal to the sport for another reason. The NFWT formed an alliance with the U.S. Tennis Association (USTA), the national governing body for tennis, and after a decade of working together, the NFWT formally merged with USTA, making USTA only the second NGB to formally integrate a disability sport into its governance.

In the early years of wheelchair tennis, tournaments were organized with two divisions— open and novice. As the sport grew, it became clear that further subcategories were needed to reflect the differing abilities of the players. New divisions A–D were added, along with women's, junior's, and quadriplegic divisions. By the year 2000 there were 130 tournaments offered in 37 countries on the NEC Wheelchair Tennis Tour. Today, there are more than 10,000 people actively participating in wheelchair tennis worldwide.

While the men's and women's divisions experienced quick growth, the quad division did not. Because there were a lot of quad players in the United States but no where else, the Stoke Mandeville Games in 1993 encouraged countries to enter tennis players in the quad division, which resulted in 12 entries. Three years later, in 1996, two of the top U.S. quad players were invited to Europe to conduct clinics at the Dutch and British Open tournaments, but it took nearly 10 more years for the quad division to appear at the Paralympic Games in Athens in 2004. The first victory for the division was awarded to the U.S. team of Nick Taylor and David Wagner, who beat Great Britain for the Gold medal.

Wheelchair tennis is played on standard tennis courts, with no modification made to the net or court configuration, the tennis racquet, or balls. While players are allowed two bounces to return the ball, the best players never use the second bounce.

BIBLIOGRAPHY. Apple, Jr., David F. *Physical Fitness: A Guide for Individuals with Spinal Cord Injury.* Washington, DC: Department of Veteran's Affairs, Rehabilitation Research and Development Service, 1995; International Foundation of Wheelchair Tennis, http://www.ifwt.com; Paciorek, Michael J., and Jeffery A. Jones. *Sports and Recreation for the Disabled,* 2nd ed. Carmel, IN: Cooper Publishing Group, 1994.

WHEELCHAIR TRACK AND FIELD As with many other sports for wheelchair users, wheelchair track and field events were participated in as early as the 1940s. It wasn't until 30 years later, however, that the sport really took off. Athletes with spinal cord injury, amputation, spina bifida, polio, cerebral palsy, and other disabilities compete in wheelchair track and field under Wheelchair Sports, USA (WS-USA), National Disability Sports Alliance (NDSA), and DS-USA.

With advances in technology and training, athletes competing in wheelchair track and field and road racing have seen race times drop dramatically in the years since the sport began. Marathons are routinely completed by men in under an hour and a half, and women in less than two hours.

In early years, wheelchair racing was restricted to 60 meters for women and 100 meters for men. It wasn't until the Olympiad for the Disabled held in Toronto in 1976 that longer events were offered, and still it took until after 1980 for an event longer than 400 meters to be offered for athletes with spinal cord injuries up to the T10 level, although for those whose injury was below T10, events up to the 1,500 m were offered. Today, events ranging from the 100 m to the marathon are offered for individuals regardless of disability classification.

The first wheelchair athletes competed in marathons in the 1970s, with Bob Hall the first entrant in the Boston Marathon in 1975. He completed the race in 2:58 in a modified everyday wheelchair. In 1993, Jim Knaub won the Boston in a time of 1:24, and in 2004 Ernst van Dyk won in a world record time of 1:18:27.

Similar gains have been seen for women wheelchair athletes on the road and on the track. In 1977, Sharon Hedrick competed in Boston, winning in a time of 3:46. Jean Driscoll, subsequent eight-time winner of the women's wheelchair division of Boston, ran a world record of 1:34 in 1993. Sharon Hedrick set a world record in the 800 meter at the Olympics in 1984, completing the distance in 2:16. In 1993, Louise Sauvage of Australia completed the distance in 1:52.

Racing wheelchairs have evolved from modified hospital or everyday wheelchairs to highly sport specific, aerodynamic machines. Rules governing the sport specify the maximum length of the racing wheelchair as well as the maximum diameter of the inflated wheels. The rear wheels can be no larger than 70 cm, with one push rim and no gears, levers, or cranks attached. No devices can serve the sole purpose of aiding the aerodynamic function of the chair except for the area within the outside edges of the rear wheels. This particular rule has been the subject of contention time and again as athletes have made modifications that other athletes have argued aided the aerodynamics of the particular chair.

Positioning in the chair is critical, and when purchasing a racing chair it is important to have the chair fitted by someone knowledgeable. The athlete sits much lower in the racing wheelchair than in other sport-specific wheelchairs, with arms able to touch the ground at full extension. Two seating positions—one with legs tucked under, the other with legs extended in front, have both been used with success by various athletes.

Racing wheelchairs, like other sport specific chairs, have camber, which is a tilt to the wheel so that it is set out wider at the bottom than at the top. This allows the racer to sit lower in the chair and reach the bottom of the smaller push rim, as well as providing a stable wheelbase for the chair. Racing wheelchairs also typically have a compensator, a device attached to the front wheel of the wheelchair which the athlete can "set" for varying degrees of turns on a track. Then, while training or racing, the athlete merely taps the compensator to enter the turn and taps it back when entering the straight.

Equipment needed includes a racing chair, helmet, gloves, tires and tubes, a compressor or air pump, various Allen wrenches, and other tools. Wheels may be spoked, carbon fiber, or disk wheels. Chairs weigh from 10 to 15 pounds.

Helmets are worn, as in cycling, for both aerodynamics and safety. They are not required on the track in sprint distances of 100 to 400 meters, but they are mandatory for distances of 800 meters and above. In road races, helmets are always required.

Pushing techniques in the racing chair have evolved over time. Racers first wore handball or racquetball gloves, pushing the racing chair much as they did the everyday chair, grasping and releasing the rim. Athletes would spend hours taping their gloves, which would wear out in as little as one workout. As speeds increased, pushing technique was refined leading to the creation of specialized gloves that allow athletes to push the rim with a closed fist, minimizing the drag induced from gripping the wheel on each push. The University of Illinois Para Backhand has become the pushing technique used by most athletes worldwide.

BIBLIOGRAPHY. Apple, Jr., David F. *Physical Fitness: A Guide for Individuals with Spinal Cord Injury.* Washington, DC: Department of Veteran's Affairs, Rehabilitation Research and Development Service, 1995; Depauw, Karen P., and Susan J. Gavron. *Disability and Sport.* Champaign, IL: Human Kinetics, 1995; Paciorek, Michael J., and Jeffery A. Jones. *Sports and Recreation for the Disabled,* 2nd ed. Carmel, IN: Cooper Publishing Group, 1994.

WHITTAKER, TOM Tom Whittaker, born to a Welsh army officer, grew up playing rugby, trying out for the Welsh national team at 17. He came to the United States as a young adult in 1976 and took up rock climbing. Eventually he began to climb mountains, not just rocks. He ascended the North Face of Matterhorn, Mt. McKinley, and the Nose of El Capitan in Yosemite from 1976 to 1979. An accident on Thanksgiving Day, 1979, changed the direction his life would take.

He was involved in a head on car crash while driving home for the holidays. His legs were shattered and one foot amputated. He gave up climbing and returned to school for a second master's degree. He got married and had a family. Finally he decided to return to the mountains, this time wearing a prosthetic limb.

He first attempted to climb Mount Everest in 1989. Six years later, he made the attempt again; this time, he was 1,500 feet from the summit when he had to turn back. Three years after that, Whittaker and a team of five others with various disabilities finally made it to the summit of Everest. A documentary of the expedition *A Footprint on Everest* was renamed and aired on *48 Hours* with Dan Rather as *Against All Odds.* Whittaker now has his sights set on being the first amputee to climb the highest peaks on the seven continents.

BIBLIOGRAPHY. Moran, Mark. "Tom Whittaker and Everest: A Disabled Climber Reflects," http://classic.mountainzone.com/features/whittaker/; Tom Whittaker, http://www.tomwhittaker.org/.

WILLIS, TIM Tim Willis has always loved to run. As a runner with a visual impairment, Willis uses a guide runner who is tethered to him by a shoe string. In high school, Willis had to educate the Georgia High School Association, teaching them that the guide didn't give advantage in races so that he could compete alongside nondisabled runners using his guide.

Willis went on to attend Georgia Southern University, where he continued to race with his college team. He was introduced to disability sport, began running against other visually impaired athletes, and quickly rose to the top. Willis competed in three world championships—1990, 1994, and 1998. He also represented the United States on two Paralympic teams, Atlanta in 1996 and Sydney in 2000.

Willis won silver in the 10,000 meter and bronze in the 1,500 m and 5,000 m in Atlanta, as well as a relay bronze for the 4 by 400 meter. He won bronze in the 10,000 m in Sydney, and silver in both the 5,000 and 10,000 at the 1998 World Championships in Madrid.

Willis received much acclaim during his career. He was chosen as the Georgia Blind Person of the Year in 1992, and he received the Georgia Sports Hall of Fame Achievement Award in 1995. His 1996 medals and racing spikes are on display in the Georgia Sports Hall of Fame.

BIBLIOGRAPHY. Joukowsky III, Artemis A.W., and Rothstein, Larry. *Raising the Bar—New Horizons in Disability Sport,* 1st ed. New York, NY: Umbrage Editions, 2002; Success Stories, Recording for the Blind and Dyslexic, http://www.rfbd.org/media_4C.htm.

WORLD GAMES FOR THE DEAF. *See* Deaflympics

Tim Willis. *Copyright Chris Hamilton Photography.*

WRESTLING (BLIND) Wrestling is one of many sports that people who are blind or visually impaired can compete in. The rules are the same as for nondisabled athletes except for one. In wrestling for blind athletes the wrestlers must "touch up" or maintain constant contact while standing. This is accomplished by the wrestlers touching fingertips, one wrestler's hand up, the other wrestler's hand down. If they break contact, the referee stops the match and the wrestlers have to "touch up" before they can start again.

Wrestling for visually impaired athletes is organized by weight class, generally from 103 to 275 pounds. Matches last for a total of 6 minutes, and they are broken up into two 3-minute periods. It is an extremely demanding sport, not only physically, because athletes who compete must be in peak condition, but also mentally, because wrestling is as much about strategy as it is about physical strength.

Wrestling for athletes who are blind or visually impaired was included in the Paralympic Games in 1984; however, due to a lack of participation by the requisite number of countries it hasn't been offered since. Over the last several years, however, there have been national championships in 15 countries, and world championships were held in the Netherlands and in the United States. Because of to the renewed interest, there is a movement to get wrestling for blind individuals reinstated on the Paralympic program, this bid has not yet been successful.

WRIST SUPPORT (CUFF)

BIBLIOGRAPHY. "Sports and Activity Rules for those with Visual Impairments," http://www.recreationtherapy.com/tx/txblind.htm#wrestling; United States Association for Blind Athletes, http://www.usaba.org.

WRIST SUPPORT (CUFF) The wrist support cuff, also referred to as the handgrip, is a piece of equipment worn by individuals with limited hand function. It fits around the hand and wrist to afford support and control over the manipulation of objects. It is specially designed to grasp bars, polls, rails, racquets, cues, bats, and paddles, enabling participation in a vast range of activities. The cuff enables an improved range of extension and flexion in the hand, wrist, and arm, allowing for enhanced control, and overall, manipulative factors. Use of the cuff is advantageous for athletes with hand/wrist disabilities looking to expand object manipulation and control skills.

BIBLIOGRAPHY. Inclusive Fitness Initiative, http://www.inclusivefitness.org.

WYETH, DUNCAN Duncan Wyeth has been an advocate both on and off the field of play in disability sport for over 30 years. Born in 1946 with cerebral palsy, Wyeth didn't have much of an opportunity to compete in sports and recreation activities while growing up. He loved downhill skiing and cycling, but competitive opportunities for people with disabilities weren't available. After graduating from Michigan State University, Wyeth became involved in the Mid-Michigan Tri-County Bicycle Association, regularly participating in long distance rides. It wasn't until he was 32, however, that he participated in his first competition organized for people with disabilities, the Michigan Regional Cerebral Palsy Games.

Wyeth moved to international competition, winning the first U.S. medal at the Cerebral Palsy Games in Denmark in 1982. Over the years, he earned many more medals in both cycling and track and field. After representing the United States at the Paralympic Games in Seoul in 1988 in cycling, Wyeth was named the Male Athlete of the Year by the U.S. Olympic Committee (USOC) and the Cerebral Palsy Male Athlete of the Year by the Colorado Amateur Sports Corporation.

Wyeth then turned his energies toward the administrative side of sport, serving as staff to the U.S. team in Barcelona in 1992 and as chef de mission to the U.S. team in Atlanta in 1996. He served on the Atlanta Paralympic Organizing Committee Board of Directors as well as the USOC Board of Directors.

Wyeth has received many honors and awards, including the 1996 Michigan Rehabilitation Association Outstanding Achievement Award, the 1998 UCPA National Volunteer Award, the 1998 National Leadership Award from the National Council on Disability and the 2001 UCPA National Achievement Award. He was also inducted into the Michigan Athletes with Disabilities Hall of Fame in 2001, and in 2000, the American Academy on Cerebral Palsy and Developmental Medicine established the "Duncan Wyeth Award" to annually recognize an individual who contributes significantly to the health and wellness of persons with disabilities through sport and recreation.

BIBLIOGRAPHY. Athletes with Disabilities Hall of Fame, http://www.athleticachievement.org/adhof/famers/bios/wyeth.html; Depauw, Karen P., and Susan J. Gavron. *Disability and Sport*. Champaign, IL: Human Kinetics, 1995.

YILLA, ABU Abu Yilla, eight-time All National Tournament pick in wheelchair basketball, was born in Freetown, Sierra Leone, West Africa, but spent most of his years growing up in England. Yilla had polio as a child, but this didn't deter him from pursuing either sports or an education.

Yilla has earned multiple degrees—two bachelors degrees, a masters degree, and a PhD. He started out his career as an accountant in England, making the switch to physical education when he moved to the United States. His first job, as Wheelchair Sports Coordinator for the Dallas Rehabilitation Institute led him to the Dallas Wheelchair Mavericks, the multi-time national champion wheelchair basketball team in town.

Yilla joined the team, where he played for fifteen years, leading Dallas to several national titles with his skills and leadership on the court. But basketball wasn't his only interest; in fact, Yilla has years of experience as a coach, player and administrator of various disability sports, including quad rugby, the sport featured in the recent documentary *Murderball*. Yilla was founding president of the USQRA, and also spent time coaching both a local Dallas team and the 1990 U.S. national team. Yilla also has two Paralympics and three World Championships to his credit, medaling in track in 1988 as part of the Great Britain contingent.

Yilla has retired from competition, and is now an assistant professor of kinesiology at the University of Texas–Arlington where he teaches courses such as adapted exercise and sport, sociocultural aspects of sport, and theory and application in motor development. Yilla is also widely published in the field of disability sport, with articles appearing in *Adapted Physical Activity Quarterly, Sports 'n' Spokes, Palaestra,* and *Wychowanie Fizyczne I Sport (Physical Education and Sport)*, as well as book chapters for various volumes on disability sport.

BIBLIOGRAPHY. Dallas Wheelchair Mavericks, http://www.wheelmavs.org/journey/yr1997/abune.html.

ZORN, TRISCHA Trischa Zorn is the most decorated Paralympian in the history of the games, with an outstanding total of 55 medals to her credit (41 Gold, 9 silver, and 4 bronze). Zorn is legally blind, born with a condition called aniridia, meaning she has no iris in her eyes. Zorn didn't let her poor eyesight deter her from anything, least of all sports.

She began swimming in 1971 at the age of seven at Mission Viejo, California, widely known as one of the top swimming programs in the country, competing against sighted swimmers. She was the first visually impaired swimmer to win a Division I scholarship, which covered her education at the University of Nebraska, where Zorn earned All-American honors four times.

Zorn was introduced to disability sport first competing at the 1980 Paralympics in Arnhem, Holland at age 16, the same year she missed a spot on the U.S. Olympic team by a mere 1/100 of a second. She took home seven Gold medals and set seven world records that year. At the Seoul Paralympics in 1988, Zorn won 12 Gold medals, setting 9 world records. In front of a capacity crowd in Barcelona in 1992, she added 10 Gold medals to her collection. At the 2004 Summer Paralympic games in Athens, Zorn concluded her athletic career by winning a bronze medal in the 100-meter breaststroke bringing her total medal count to 55.

In Athens, Zorn's U.S. teammates honored her accomplishments by nominating her to carry the flag at the closing ceremonies of the 2004 Paralympic Games.

BIBLIOGRAPHY. Allen, Anne. *Sports for the Handicapped.* New York: Walker, 1981; The Hartford, Athlete Profiles, Trischa Zorn, http://groupbenefits.thehartford.com/usp/athletes/zorn.html; Joukowsky, Artemis A. W., and Larry Rothstein. *Raising the Bar—New Horizons in Disability Sport,* 1st ed. New York: Umbrage Editions, 2002.

Appendix: Disability Organizations

American Association of Adapted Sports
  Programs (AAASP)
PO Box 538
Pine Lake, GA 30072
(404) 294-0070
aaasp@bellsouth.net

American Association of Challenged
  Divers
P.O. Box 501405
San Diego, CA 92150
(619) 597-8798
pinnacle@cts.com

American Blind Bowling Association
315 North Main Street
Houston, PA 15342
(412) 745-5986

American Blind Skiing Foundation
2228 Grand Pointe Trail
Aurora, IL 60504
www.abssf.org

American Competition Opportunities for
  Riders with Disabilities (ACORD)
5303 Felter Road
San Jose, CA 95132
(408) 261-2015

American Wheelchair Bowling
  Association (AWBA)
2912 Country Woods Lane
Palm Harbor, FL 34683-6417
(727) 734-0023
www.awba.com

America's Athletes with Disabilities
8630 Fenton St. Suite 920
Silver Spring, MD 20910
(800) 238-7632
www.americasathletes.org

Association of Disabled American
  Golfers
P.O. Box 280649
Lakewood, CO 80228-0649
(303) 922-5228
http://www.golfcolorado.com/adag/

Buckmasters Quadriplegic Hunters
  Association (BQHA)
Jeff Lucas
P.O. Box 117
Hyde Park, NY 12538
(914) 229-4131
www.buckmasters.com

Capable Partners
P.O. Box 27664
Golden Valley, MN 55427-0664
(763) 439-1038
www.capablepartners.org

Cerebral Palsy International Sports and
  Recreation Association (CP-ISRA)
Secretariat-CP-ISRA
Trudie Rombouts
P.O. Box 16
666 Zgheteren
The Netherlands
+31 26 47 22 593
www.cpisra.org

APPENDIX

Disabled Sports USA (DS-USA)
451 Hungerford Drive, Suite 100
Rockville, MD 20850
(301) 217-0960
www.dsusa.org

Dwarf Athletic Association of America
  (DAAA)
418 Willow Way
Lewisville, TX 75077
(972) 317-8299
www.daaa.org

Eastern Amputee Golf Association
2015 Amherst Drive
Bethlehem, PA 18015-5606
(888) 868-0992
www.eaga.org

Eels on Wheels Adaptive Scuba Club
8024 Mesa Drive, #17
Austin, TX 78731
www.eels.org/home/

Handicapped Scuba Association
  International
1104 El Prado
San Clemente, CA 92672-4637
(949) 498-4540
http://www.hsascuba.com

International Blind Sports Federation
  (IBSA)
Michael Berthezene, Secretary General
42 rue Louis Lumiere
75020 Paris
France
+33 1403 145 15
www.ibsa.es

International Disabled Self-Defense
  Association (IDSA)
22-C New Leicester Hwy.—259
Asheville, NC 28806
(828) 683-5528
www.defenseability.com

International Paralympic Committee (IPC)
Adenauerallee 212-214
53113 Bonn
Germany
+49 228 2097 0
www.paralympic.org

International Wheelchair and Amputee
  Sports Federation
Olympic Village
Guttman Road
Aylesbury, Buckinghamshire HP21 9PP
United Kingdom
+44 1296 436179
www.wsw.org.uk

International Wheelchair Aviators
PO Box 2799
Big Bear City, CA 92314
(909) 585-9663
www.wheelchairaviators.org

International Wheelchair Basketball
  Federation (IWBF)
109, 189 Watson St.
Winnepeg, Manitoba
Canada R2P 2E1
www.iwbf.org

Lakeshore Foundation
4000 Ridgeway Drive
Birmingham, AL 35209
(205) 313-7500
www.lakeshore.org

National Ability Center
PO Box 682799
Park City, UT 84068
(435) 649-3991
www.nac1985.org

National Disability Sports Alliance
  (NDSA)
25 West Independence Way
Kingston, RI 02881
(401) 792-7130
www.ndsaonline.org

National Rifle Association Disabled
  Shooting Services
11250 Waples Mill Road
Fairfax, VA 22030
(703) 267-1450
www.nrahq.org

National Sports Center for the Disabled
PO Box 1290
Winter Park, CO 80482
(970) 726-1540
www.nscd.org

National Wheelchair Basketball
  Association (NWBA)
6165 Lehman Drive
Suite 101
Colorado Springs, CO 80918
(719) 266-4082
www.nwba.org

National Wheelchair Softball Association
  (NWSA)
6000 W. Floyd Avenue
Denver, CO 80227
(303) 936-5587
www.wheelchairsoftball.com

North American Riding for the
  Handicapped Association (NARHA)
PO Box 33150
Denver, CO 80233
(800) 369-7433
www.narha.org

Paralyzed Veterans of America (PVA)
801 Eighteenth Street, N.W.
Washington, DC 20006-3517
(800) 424-8000
www.pva.org

Physically Challenged Bowhunters of
  America
2152 Route 981
New Alexandria, PA 15670
(724) 668-7439
www.pcba-inc.org

Physically Challenged Golf Association
10 East View Drive
Farmington, CT 06032
(860) 676-2035
www.townusa.pcga

Rehabilitation Institute of Chicago Wirtz
  Sports Program
710 N. Lake Shore Drive 3rd Floor
Chicago, IL 60611
(312) 238-5001
www.richealthfit.org

Skating Association for the Blind and
  Handicapped
1200 East and West Road
West Seneca, NY 14224
(716) 675-7222
www.sabahinc.org

Special Olympics
1133 19th St. N.W.
Washington, DC 20036
(202) 628-3630

United Foundation for Disabled Archers
PO Box 251
20 NE 9th Avenue
Glenwood, MN 65334
(320) 624-3660
www.uffdaclub.com

United States Aquatic Association of the
  Deaf
2211 South Road
Baltimore, MD 21209
(410) 664-3727 V/TTY
http://members.tripod.com/USAAD

United States Association for Blind
  Athletes (USABA)
33 N. Institute St.
Colorado Springs, CO 80903
(719) 630-0420
www.usaba.org

United States Deaf Cycling Association
Bobby Skedsmo, Secretary Treasurer
247 London Court
Pittsburg, CA 94565
www.usdeafcycling.org

United States Deaf Ski and Snowboard
  Association
1772 Saddle Hill Drive
Logan, UT 84231
(435) 752-2702
www.usdssa.org

United States Disabled Athletes Fund
280 Interstate North Circle
Suite 450
Atlanta, GA 30339
(770) 850-8199
www.blazesports.com

United States Electric Wheelchair Hockey
  Association
7216 39th Avenue North
Minneapolis, MN 55427
(763) 535-4736
www.powerhockey.com

APPENDIX

United States Handcycling Federation
PO Box 3538
Evergreen, CO 80437
(303) 679-2770
www.ushf.org

United States Olympic Committee
  (USOC)
One Olympic Plaza
Colorado Springs, CO 80909-5760
(719) 632-5551
www.usoc.org

United States Paralympics
One Olympic Plaza
Colorado Springs, CO 80909-5760
(719) 866-2030
www.usparalympics.org

United States Quad Rugby
5861 White Cypress Drive
Lake Worth, FL 33467
(561) 964-1712
www.quadrugby.com

United States Sailing Association—Sailors
  with Special Needs
PO Box 1260
Portsmouth, RI 02871-0917
(401) 683-0800
www.ussailing.org/swsn

United States Sled Hockey Association
2236 E. 46th St.
Davenport, IA 52807
(563) 344-9064
www.usahockey.com/ussha

United States Tennis Association (USTA)
110 Turnpike Road
Westborough, MA 01581
(508) 366-3450
www.usta.com

United States Wheelchair Weightlifting
  Federation
39 Michael Place
Levittown, PA 19057
(215) 945-1964
www.wsusa.org

USA Deaf Sports Federation
102 N. Krohn Place
Sioux Falls, SD 57103-1800
(605) 367-5760
(605) 367-5761 TTY
www.usdeafsports.org

Western Amputee Golf Association
11323 Ringtail Road
Penn Valley, CA 95946
(530) 432-9283
www.wagagolf.org

Wheelchair Athletics of the USA
2351 Parkwood Road
Snellville, GA 30278
(770) 972-0763
www.wsusa.org

Wheelchair Sports, USA
1668 320th Way
Earlham, IA 50072
(515) 833-2450
www.wsusa.org

Wilderness on Wheels
PO Box 1007
Wheat Ridge, CO 80034
(303) 403-1110
www.wildernessonwheels.org

Bibliography

ABLE Data. "Amputee Golf Grip." http://www.abledata.com/abledata.cfm?pageid=19327&top=12690&productid=10903.

Able Newspaper. Positively For By and About the Disabled. http://ablenews.com/archive/sept_03.htm.

About the Alicia Patterson Foundation. http://www.aliciapatterson.org/APF_Info/About_APF.html.

Achilles Track Club International. http://achillestrackclub.org.

ADA Portal. http://adaportal.org.

Adaptive Adventures. http://www.adaptiveadventures.com.

"Against the Wind." *Interview with Ann Cody.* http://www.will.uiuc.edu/tv/documentaries/atw/atwcody.html.

"Against the Wind." *Interview with Brad Hedrick.* http://will.uiuc.edu/tv/documentaries/atw/atwhedrick.html.

"Against the Wind." *Interview with Scot Hollonbeck.* http://www.will.uiuc.edu/tv/documentaries/atw/atwtscot.html.

"Against the Wind." *Racing the Wind 2.* http://www.will.uiuc.edu/tv/documentaries/atw/atwwind1.html.

Allen, Anne. *Sports for the Handicapped.* New York: Walker, 1981.

American Amputee Soccer Association. http://www.ampsoccer.org.

American Association of Adapted Sports Programs. http://www.aaasp.org.

American Hearing Impaired Hockey Association. http://www.ahiha.org/index.html.

American Wheelchair Bowling Association. http://www.awba.com.

American Wheelchair Table Tennis Association. http://www.atta.org.

Amputee Golf Grip. http://oandp.com/products/trs/sports-Recreation/golf.asp.

Andrews, Tina. "Coach?? I Don't Even Play Golf." United States Blind Golf Association. http://blindgolf.com/articles_tina_coach.htm.

Ansett, Patricia. "Getting their Lives Back: Seminars Help Amputees Learn to Use Artificial Limbs." http://www.freep.com/news/health/amp1_20040601.htm.

Apple, Jr., F. David. *Physical Fitness: A Guide for Individuals with Spinal Cord Injury.* Washington, DC: Department of Veteran's Affairs, Rehabilitation Research and Development Service, 1995.

ARGO. "World Leader in Amphibious Vehicles." http://www.argoatv.com.

Athens 2004 Olympic Games. http://www.athens2004.com.

"Athlete Profiles, Cheri Blauwet." *The Hartford.* http://groupbenefits.thehartford.com/usp/athletes/blauwet.html.

BIBLIOGRAPHY

"Athlete Profiles, Sandy Dukat," *The Hartford*. http://groupbenefits.thehartford.com/usp/athletes/dukat.html

"Athlete Profiles, Trischa Zorn." *The Hartford*. http://groupbenefits.thehartford.com/usp/athletes/zorn.html.

"Awards of Sport." *The Sport Journal* 2, no. 2 (Spring 1999). http://www.thesportjournal.org/1999Journal/Vol2-No2/aos.asp

Axelson, Peter, and John Castellano. "Take to the Trails." *Sports 'n' Spokes* (July–August, 1990): 20–24.

Azteca 21. http://www.azteca21.com/noticias/deportes/saul-mendoze-triunfa-en-ny.

Barker, Tony. "Revised Legislation to Help Athletes With Disabilities." *Ball State University News Center* (1988). http://www.bsu.edu/news/article/0,1370,-1019-366,00.html.

Batcheller, Lori J. *Alpine Achievement, "A Chronicle of the United States Disabled Ski."* Bloomington, IN: 1st Books, 2002.

Bauman, J. "How Changing Ads in Health and Fitness can Change Attitudes." (2001). http://www.ncpad.org.

Bensen, Dan. "Augsburg Student Aaron Cross, Alum Jim Mastro to Compete in Paralympics." *Ausburg College News* (1996). http://www.augsburg.edu/news/news-archives/1996/paralympics.html.

Blauwet, Cheri. "2005 Runners Bios." *Boston Runners Marathon*. http://www.boston.com/marathon/runners/2005_runners/blauwet.htm.

Blauwet, Cheri. "A Broad View Magazine." *Retrospective* (Fall, 2004). http://www.abroadviewmagazine.com/archives/fall_04/blauwet.html.

Blaze Sports. http://www.blazesports.com.

Bloomsday 12K Run. http://www.bloomsdayrun.org/1985WheelchairOpenStats.htm.

Bloomsday 12K Run. http://www.bloomsdayrun.org/1986WheelchairOpenStats.htm.

Bow and Crossbow Rigs for the Disabled. http://residents.bowhunting.net/DisabledHunters/dis-hunters-bows2.html.

Bowman, Dana. http://www.danabowman.com.

Boy Scouting. http://www.cacbsa.org/Boy%20Scouting.htm.

Brad Hedrick's vitae. University of Illinois Division of Rehabilitation Education Services. http://www.rehab.uiuc.edu/staff/Brad_vita.html.

The Brad Parks Award, United States Tennis Association. http://www.usta.com/communitytennis/fullstory.sps?iNewsid=16342&itype=946&icategoryid=213.

Brasile, Frank, and Brad Hedrick. "The Relationship of Skills of Elite Wheelchair Basketball Competitors to the International Functional Classification System." *Therapeutic Recreation Journal* 30 (2000): 114–127.

Breckenridge Outdoor Education Center. http://www.boec.org/.

Buckmaster's American Deer Foundation. http://www.badf.org/.

"Buddhism Plus Disability: One Step Closer to Nirvana." *New Mobility* (November, 1999). http://www.newmobility.com.

Burgess, Ernest M. "The Seattle Prosthetic Foot: A Design for Active Sports: Preliminary Studies." *Prosthetics and Orthodontics International* (1985): 55.

Canadian Wheelchair Basketball Association. http://www.cwba.ca/program/frogley.html.

Candace Cable. http://www.candacecable.com.

"Capabilities." *Northwestern University Prosthetics Research Laboratory and Rehabilitation Engineering Research Program* (January. 2000). http://www.repoc.northwestern.edu/capabilities/cap_2000_09_01.pdf.

Cerebral Palsy International Sports and Recreation Association. http://www.cpisra.org/.

Chafee, Ella. http://www.geocities.com/expressbasketball/roster/echafee.htm.

Challenged Athlete's Foundation. http://challengedathletes.org.

Chicago Blackhawks in the Community. http://www.chicagoblackhawks.com/community.

A Chronology of the Disability Rights Movements. http://www.sfsu.edu/~dprc/chronology/chron40s. html.

Classification Issues. http://edweb6.educ.msu.edu/kin866/cfissues.htm.

Cody, Ann. "IPC Sets Focus on Women in Sport." *The Paralympian Newsletter* (2000). http://www. paralympic.org/paralympian/20023/2002323.htm.

Colorado Discover Ability. http://coloradodiscoverability.org/summer/bicycling.cfm.

"Converted Crossbow." Archery Solutions for People with Physical Disabilities. http://www.visi.com/ ~bluff/crossbow/about.htm.

Cornelson, David. "The Wonderful World of Hand Cycling." *Sports 'n' Spokes* (July–August, 1991): 10–12.

Courage Center. http://www.courage.org/.

Cox, Jack. "Chariots of Fire." *Popular Mechanics.* http://www.popularmechanics.com/outdoors/ outdoors/1277771.html.

Crase, Cliff. "Cliff's Corner." *Sports 'n' Spokes* (September–October, 1989): 5.

Crase, Nancy. "People in Sports: Randy Snow." *Sports 'n' Spokes* (January–February, 1990): 8–12.

Crase, Nancy. "Pushing for PR's in Everything." *Sports 'n' Spokes* (September–October, 1990): 18–20.

Crase, Nancy. "Wheelchair Specialized Bowling Equipment." *Sports 'n' Spokes* (1975): 16–17.

Cross, Cecil. "Peachtree Race to Pit Wheeler against Brother." *Atlanta Journal Constitution.* http:// www.ajc.com/search/content/services/internship/story/CecilCross.html.

"Cycling Tips for Leg Amputees." *Active Living.* http://www.activelivingmagazine.com/artman/ publish/printer_68.shtm.

"DAAA Swim Records." *Dwarf Athletic Association of America.* http://www.daaa.org/swim_recm.htm.

Dallas Wheelchair Mavericks. http://www.wheelmavs.org/journey/yr1997/abune.html

Dancing Wheels. http://www.dancingwheels.org

"Deaf and Hard of Hearing Children Participate in Hockey Program." http://http://abclocal.go.com/ wls/story?section=community&id=3361917.

Deaflympics. http://www.deaflympics.com.

The Deak Group. http://www.deakgroup.com/ccable.html.

Depauw, Karen P., and Susan J. Gavron. *Disability and Sport.* Champaign, IL: Human Kinetics, 1995.

"Development of Wheelchair Tennis." *International Wheelchair Tennis Federation.* http://www. itfwheelchairtennis.com/asp/wheelchair/development/usa.asp.

"Diana Golden Brosnihan Pacesetter From Recreational Sport to Olympic Gold." *Palaestra* (January, 2002): 9.

Disability Outreach Foundation. http://www.disabilityoutreach.org/Gallo032002.htm.

"Disability Sports Organizations." *Michigan State University.* http://edweb6.educ.msu.edu/kin866/ orgwsusa.htm.

Disabled Sports Technical Manual. "United States Olympic Committee," (1998).

Disabled Sports USA. "Cross Country Enthusiasts Attract New Enthusiasts." http://www.dsusa.org/ ChallMagarchive/challmag-winter02-crosscountryskiing.html.

Driessen, Paul K. "On Wings of Eagle Rays." *Sports 'n' Spokes* (July–August, 1990): 10–15.

Driscoll, Jean, Janet Benge, and Geoff Benge. *Determined to Win: the Overcoming Spirit of Jean Driscoll* (1st ed.). Colorado Springs, CO: WaterBrook Press, 2000.

Dummer, Gail. "Classification in Disability Sport: Assessment Issues." *Palaestra* (Winter, 1999): 58–59.

Dwarf Athletic Association of America. www.daaa.org.

Eagle Sportschairs. www.eaglesportschairs.com.

Eels on Wheels. http://www.eels.org.

BIBLIOGRAPHY

"Fencing." *Michigan State University*. http://edweb6.educ.msu.edu/kin866/spfencing.htm.

Ferrara, M., and R. Davis. "Athlete Classification: An Explanation of the Process." *Palaestra* (Spring, 1996): 38–44.

Fields, Cheryl D. "Casters." *Team Rehab Report* (April–May, 1992). http://www.wheelchairnet.org/WCN_ProdServ/Docs/TeamRehab/RR_92/9203ar t2.PDF.

Fishing Has No Boundaries, Inc. www.fhnbinc.org/.

Fitness Is for Everyone. http://www.fitnessforeveryone.com/tdbios.html.

Franco Marx, Jeanie. "Full-Fledged Stars: Despite their Disabilities Paralympic Stars Display all the Olympic Ideals." *Georgia Tech Alumni News* (Summer 1996). http://gtalumni.org/publications/magazine/sum96/para.html.

"Freedom Concept." Creating a Cycle of Mobility. http://www.freedomconcepts.com.

"Functional Classification Systems." *Sports 'n' Spokes* (July 1991): 46–47.

Giambaccini, Peter. "Blauwet: Hell on Wheels." http://www.villagevoice.com/news/0344,jockbeat,48214,3.html.

Hamilton, Bill. "Pigskin Progress, Wheelchair Football and the Blister Bowl." *Sports 'n' Spokes* (January–February, 1990): 32–34.

Hamilton, Marilyn." Breaking The Record. *Smithsonian*. http://americanhisotry.si.edu/sports/exhibit/removers/wheelchair/index.cfm.

Handicapped Scuba Association International. http://www.hsascuba.com/.

Hartman, Tari Susan. "Golden Arches and Gold Medals, Paralympic Athlete Featured in McDonald's Promotion." http://www.spinalcord.org/news.php?dep=0&page=13&list=326.

"Hearing Loss Can't Silence these Skills." *Hearing Loss News and Reviews*. http://www.4hearingloss.com/archives/2005/02/hearing_loss_ca.html.

Henriod, Lorraine. *Special Olympics and Paralympics*. New York: Watts, 1979.

"Highlights." *Craig Blanchette*. http://craigblanchette.com.

History of Bowls, International Paralympic Committee. http://www.paralympic.org/release/Summer_Sports/Bowls/About_the_Sport/History.

Huber, J. H. "Boston: The 100th Marathon and the Wheelchair Athlete." *Palaestra* (February, 2003). http://special.northernlight.com/marathon/wheelcahir_palaestra.htm.

IFI Background. Inclusive Fitness Initiative. http://www.inclusivefitness.org.

International Amputee Football Federation. http://www.iaff.sport.U2/history_en.htm.

International Blind Sports Federation. http://www.ibsa.org.

"International Disability Sports Organizations." *Michigan State University*. http://ed-web3.educ.msu.edu/kin866/orginternational.htm.

International Foundation of Wheelchair Tennis. www.ifwt.com.

International Paralympic Committee. http://www.paralympic.org/paralympian/20004/2000407.htm.

International Wheelchair Basketball Federation. www.iwbf.org.

International Wheelchair Fencing. http://www.iwfencing.com.

ISAF International Association for Disabled Sailing. International Sailing Federation. http://www.sailing/disabled.org.

Jackson, Tami Jayne. "Amputee Soccer Fielded by a Good Feller." *Active Living Magazine* (2004). http://www.activelivingmagazine.com/artman/publish/article_18.shtml.

Jackson, Tami Jayne. *Amputation Doesn't Derail Soccer Dream*. The O & P Edge (April, 2003). http://www.oandp.com/edge/issues/articles/2003-04_08.asp.

Jomantas, Nicole. "10 Questions with Kevin Szott." *US Olympic Team*. www.usolympicteam.com.

Joukowsky, Artemis A. W., and Larry Rothstein. *Raising the Bar New Horizons in Disability Sport* (1st ed.). New York: Umbrage Editions, 2002.

Karp, Gary. *Life on Wheels for the Active Wheelchair User*. Sebastopol,CA: O'Reilly and Associates, 1999.

Kelley, Jerry D., and Lex Frieden. *Go For It! A Book on Sport and Recreation for Persons with Disabilities*. Orlando, FL: Harcourt Brace Jovanovich, 1989.

"Know Hunting Gear Special." *Bowhunter* (2003). http://www.bowhunter.com/conservation/bn_consnews_gg03/.

Lipman, J. "Disabled People Featured in More Ads." *Wall Street Journal* (28 February 1990): B6.

"A Look at Wheelchair Tennis." *Sports 'n' Spokes* (January–February, 1990): 20.

"Making The Dream Come True." *Sports 'n' Spokes* (May–June 1991): 42–44.

"Mansfield Announced Recipient of USA Hockey's Disabled Athlete of the Year." *Deaf Today*. (12 November 2005). http://www.deaftoday.com/v3/archives/2005/05/mansfield_annou.htm.

"Marathons and Road Racing." *Sports 'n' Spokes* (July–August, 1989): 61.

Marlon, Shirley. "Marlon Shirley Athletic Profile." *Athletics, Track & Field* (2004). http://www.paralympics.com/athlete_profiles/marlon_shirley.htm.

Mono & Bi-Ski Manufacturers Page. http://www.sitski.com/manufac.html.

Moran, Mark. "Tom Whittaker and Everest: A Disabled Climber Reflects." http://classic.mountainzone.com/features/whittaker/.

Moriarty, Jim. "Martin: Every Day is a Bonus." *Golf World* 22. http://sports.espn.go.com/golf/news/story?id=1787692.

"MSU Disability Sports Website." Law-Olympic and Amateur Sports Act. http://edweb6.educ.msu.edu/kin866/lawoasa.htm.

Muffoletto, Mary Ann. "Former Utah State student shines at Paralympics." http://www.hardnewscafe.usu.edu/sports/102004_paralympics.html.

Murderball Quad Rugby Central. http://www.quadrugby.com/toc.htm.

National Association of the Deaf. http://www.nad.org/site/pp.asp?c=foINKQMBF&b=91587.

National Beep Baseball Association. http://www.nbba.org.

National Disability Sports Alliance. www.ndsaonline.org.

National Recreation and Parks Association. http://www.nrpa.org/content/default aspx?documentId=877.

The National Spinal Cord Injury Association. http://www.spinalcord.org/news.php?dep=8&page=2&list=544.

National Sports Center for the Disabled. http://www.nscd.org.

National Wheelchair Basketball Association. http://www.nwba.org/news_index634.html.

National Wheelchair Softball Association. http://www.wheelchairsoftball.com.

NBBA Hall of Fame Inductees. The National Beep Baseball Association Hall of Fame. http://halloffame.nbba.org/inductees/jim_mastro.htm.

NCAA Washington Review. http://www.ncaa.org/databases/reports/3/199810mc/199810_d3_mc_agenda_s18.html.

New Sports Olympic Page. http://www.adr.org/SportsOlympic.

"Newsroom." *Paralyzed Veteran's Administration*. http://www.pva.org/newsroom/FeaturesArchive/2004/f04006.htm.

No Limits. http://www.nolimitstahoe.co.

North American Riding for the Handicapped. http://www.narha.org.

"Now Foundation: Women With Disabilities & Allies Forum Speakers." National Organization for Women Foundation. http://www.nowfoundation.org/issues/disability/forum2003/speakers.html#cody.

Nunnekamp, B. "Bowling from a Wheelchair." *Sports 'n' Spokes* (February–March, 1976): 17–19.

Paciorek, Michael J., and Jeffery A. Jones. *Sports and Recreation for the Disabled* (2nd ed.). Carmel, IN: Cooper Publishing Group, 1994.

BIBLIOGRAPHY

"Paralympian has Dream to Aid Sports for Disabled." *Atlanta Journal Constitution* (29 July 2002). http://www.invacare.com/cgi-bin/imhqprd/inv_newsArticleOnly.jsp?=0&passedchildOID=536965911&from=Home.

"Paralympic Results—Swimming." *International Paralympic Committee.* http://www.paralympic.org/release/Main_Sections_Menu/Sports/Results/paralympics_results.html?event_id=1209.

"Paralympic Swimming." *United States Olympic Team.* http://www.usolympicteam.com/paralympics/swimming_teams.html.

Paralyzed Veterans of America. http://www.pva.org.

Pate, Josh. "Post Paralympic Games: Record Breaking Results." http://abilitymagazine.com/Post_Paralympics_2004.htm.

"Performance: How About a Boost?" *Sports 'n' Spokes* (May 2001). http://www.pvamagazines.com/sns/magazine/article.php?art=502.

PGA Tour Inc. v. Martin. No. 532 U.S. 661. United States Supreme Court. 2001.

Physically Challenged Bowhunters of America. http://www.pcba-inc.org.

Pieces of Eight. http://www.flyingeyes.com/pieces_of_eight.htm.

"Pieces of Eight." Parachute History.com. http://www.parachutehistory.com/skydive/records/poe.html.

Popovich, Erin. *The Hartford.* http://groupbenefits.thehartford.com/usp/athletes/popovich.html.

"Powerhockey.com." U.S. Electric Wheelchair Hockey Association (U.S. EWHA). http://www.powerhockey.com.

Power Soccer. http:// www.powersoccer.net.

PVA Publications–Sports 'n' Spokes. http://www.pvamagazines.com/sns/.

"A Question of Crossbows." http://hunting.about.com/library/weekly/aa020716c.htm.

Radocy, Bob. "Upper Extremity Prosthetics: Considerations and Designs for Sports and Recreation." *Clinical Prosthetics and Orthotics* 11, no. 3 (1987): 131–153.

Ragged Edge. http://www.raggededgemag.com.

The Range Sport. http://www.rangeinfo.org.

Rehabilitation Institute of Chicago Center for Health and Fitness. http://www.richealthfit.org/paralympic%20history/paralympichistorymain.htm.

Road Runners Club of America. http://rrca.org/programs/programs.html.

Robbins, Paul. "US Disabled Ski Team Still Strong But the Rest of the World is Catching Up." *Ski Racing.* http://www.skiracing.com/features/news_displayFeatures.php/1562/FEATURES/newsArticles/.

"Rosaforte, Tim, Casey's Last Stand; Casey Martin Awaits the Decision that will Rule His Future in Golf." *Golf Digest* (May 2000). http://www.golfdigest.com/features/index.ssf?/features/caseys_1_d750d8lc.htm.

Saul Mendoza Wins 1500m. Paralympics.com. http://www.paralympics.com/News_articles_archive/saul_mendoza_1500m.htm.

Schank, Amanda. "Reaching Utopian Heights, Erin Popovich named Sportswoman of the Year." http://www.collegian.com/vnews/display.v/ART/2005/10/28/4361b72fd818d.

Schroeder, David J. "Sailing into the 90's." *Sports 'n' Spokes* (July–August 1990): 34–36.

"Scouts with Disabilities and Special Needs Fact Sheet." Boy Scouts of America, 2002.

Shake-A-Leg. http://www.shakealeg.org

Sheehan, Rose. "Fatherhood, the Greatest Challenge" *San Diego Family Magazine* (June 1999). http://www.stonebrew.com/cool/racing/wheelchair/indexarticle1.htm.

"Shriner's Hospitals Patient and Double Amputee Wins Double Gold at 1996 Paralympic Games." *Shriner's Hospital for Children.* http://www.shrinershq.org/patients/tony9-96.html.

Silicon Valley/San Jose Business Journal. http://sanjose.bizjournals.com/sanjose/stories/1998/08/03/editorial5.html.

Ski Racing. http://www.skiracing.com/features/news_displayFeatures.php/1672/FEATURES/news-Articles/.

Ski Racing. http://www.skiracing.com/news/news_display.php/2697/ALPINE.

Smith, Mark E. "Get it Straight: A Wheelchair Junkie's guide to Sports chair Alignment." http://www.wheelchairjunkie.com/alignment.html

Snow, Randy, and Bal Moore. *Pushing Forward A Memoir of Motivation*. Dubuque, IA: Kendall/Hunt Publishing Company, 2001.

Special Olympics International. http://www.specialolympics.org.

Special Olympics Minnesota. http://www.specialolympicsminnesota.org/Sportsofferedpolyhocke.php.

Special Olympics Powerlifting. http://www.specialolympics.villanova.edu/powerlifting.htm.

"Spinlife.com." Experts in Motion. http://www.spinlife.org.

Spokes 'n' Motion. Products. http://www.spokesnmotion.com/products_shop/product_detail.asp?product_id=1029.

Sportaid. http://www.sportaid.com.

"Sporting Events: Table Tennis." *ICan Online*. http://www.icanonline.net/news/fullpage.cfm?articleid=8476B92D-692D-48AF-B3738E3D76FA8449&cx=sports.get_active.

"Sports Adaptions-Cycling." *United States Association of Blind Athletes*. http://www.usaba.org/Pages/sportsinformation/adaptions/cyclingadapt.html.

"Sports and Activity Rules for those with Visual Impairments." http://www.recreationtherapy.com/tx/txblind/htm#wrestling.

"Sports and Leisure: Boccia." *United Cerebral Palsy Association*. http://www.ucpa.org/ucp_channeldoc.cfm/1/15/11383-11383-11383/2819.

"Sports at Lunch: Dave Larson." *San Diego Hall of Champions*. http://wwwsdhoc.com/main/articles/sportsatlunch/LarsonDave.

"Sports: Boccia." *International Paralympic Committee*. http://www.paralympic.org/sports/sections/bo.asp.

"Sports: Cycling." *Cerebral Palsy International Sports and Recreation Association*. http://www.cpisra.org/sports_cpisra_cycling.htm.

Sports 'n' Spokes (May–June, 1989): 11.

Sports 'n' Spokes (May–June, 1989): 37.

Sports 'n' Spokes (July–August, 1989): 11.

Sports 'n' Spokes (July–August, 1989): 3.

Sports 'n' Spokes (July–August, 1989): 4.

Sports 'n' Spokes (September–October, 1989): 48+.

Sports 'n' Spokes (May–June, 1990): 28.

Sports 'n' Spokes (July–August, 1990): 52.

Sports 'n' Spokes (September–October, 1990): 54.

Sports 'n' Spokes (January–February, 1991): 23.

Sports 'n' Spokes (January–February, 1992): 20–21.

Steadward, Robert Daniel, E. J. Watkinson, and Garry David Wheeler. *Adapted Physical Activity*. Edmonton: University of Alberta Press, 2003.

Stoner, Don. *Targeting Success, No Barriers Allowed*. Ausburg College News (2001). http://www.augsburg.edu/now/archives/summer01/barriers.html.

BIBLIOGRAPHY

Sullivan, James. "Hot Lanes in Florida." *Sports 'n' Spokes* (September, 1991): 26.

Sullivan, Robert. "Remembering Diana Golden Brosnihan: Love Was a Reason to Live." *Time.com* (31 August 2001). http://www.time.com/time/samples/article/0,8599,17338,00.html.

"Summer Sports—Wheelchair Dance Sport." *International Paralympic Committee.* http://www.paralympic.org/release/Summer_Sports/Wheelchair_Dance_Sport/.

"Summer Sports—Table Tennis." *International Paralympic Committee.* http://www.paralympic.org/release/Summer_Sports/Table_Tennis/index.htm.

Sunrise Medical. http://www.sunrisemedical.org.

"Table Tennis: Sports and Team Games." *United Cerebral Palsy.* http://www.ucp.org/ucp_channeldoc.cfm/1/15/61/61-61/358.

Team Rehab Report. http://www.wheelchairnet.org/WCN_ProdServ/Docs/TeamRehab/RR_96/9606art1.PDF.

"UCP Exercise Cycles and Ergometers." UCP United Cerebral Palsy. http://www.ucp.org/ucp_channeldoc.cfm/1/15/11500/11500-11500/3177.

United Cerebral Palsy Association. http://www.ucp.org/ucp_channeldoc.cfm/1/15/61/61-61/3564.

United States Association for Blind Athletes. http://www.usaba.org.

United States Blind Golf Association. http://www.blindgolf.com/articles_real_team_players.htm.

United States Blind Golf Association. History. http://www.blindgolf.com/history.htm.

United States Blind Golf Association. A Modification of the USGA "Rules of Golf" for Golfers with Disabilities. http://www.blindgolf.com/usga_blind_golf_rules.htm.

United States Handcycling Federation. http://www.ushf.org/links.html.

United States Olympic Committee. "Ted Stevens Olympic and Amateur Sports Act." http://www.usoc.org/12699_12720.htm.

United States Olympic Committee. http://www.olympic-usa.org.

United States Paralympics. http://www.usolympicteam.com/paralympics/.

United States Quad Rugby Association. http://usqra.org.

United States Sailing—Sailors with Special Needs. http://www.ussailing.org/swsn/.

United States Ski Team. http://www3.usskiteam.com/PublishingFolder/2419.htm.

University of Illinois Division of Rehabilitation Education Services. http://www.rehab.uiuc.edu.

U.S. Department of Justice ADA Home Page. http://www.usdoj.gov/crt/ada/adahom1.htm.

"US Paralympics Athlete Profiles—Kevin Szott." *The Hartford Financial Services.* http://www.groupbenefits.thehartford.com/usp/athletes/szott.html.

US Sled Hockey Association. http://www.usahockey.com/ussha//.

USA Deaf Sports Federation. http://www.usdeafsports.org.

USA Swimming. http://www.usaswimming.org.

USA Volleyball. http://www.usavolleyball.org.

Vogel, Bob. "Bob Hall: Farther and Faster." *New Mobility* (October, 1998). http://newmobility.com/review_article.cfm?id=132 & action = browse.

Vogel, Bob. "Shouldering the Load." *New Mobility* (September 2005). http://newmobility.com/review_article.cfm?id=1055&action=browse.

Wallace, Bevin. "Top 25 Skiers: Chris Waddell." *Skiing Magazine.* http://www.skiingmag.com/skiing/face_shots/article/0,12910,328910,00.html.

Welcome to DRES Division of Resources and Educational Services, University of Illinois at Urbana-Champaign. http://www.disability.uiuc.edu.

Welcome to PN/Paraplegic News. *Sports and Recreation.* http://pvamagazines.com/pnnews/magazine/article.php?art=278.

Welcome to Jackie Chan.com. http://www.jackiechan.com/news/news20050530.

Welcome to Recording for the Blind and Dyslexic. http://www.rfbd.org/media_4C.htm.

What is Adaptive Skiing and Sports. http://www.sitski.com/whatisit.htm.

"Wheelchair Mobility for the Paralyzed." http://www.gallilaw.com.

Wheelchair Sports, USA. http://www.wsusa.org.

Wheelchair Tennis. Alta Foundation. http://www.altafoundation.org/wheelchair_tennis.html.

Wheelchair Tennis. International Paralympic Committee. http://www.paralympics.com/wheelchairs/tennis_wheelchairs.htm.

Whittaker, Tom. http://www.tomwhittaker.org/.

Wikipedia. "Prosthesis." http://en.wikipedia.org/wiki/Prosthesis.

Wilbee, Brenda. "What's It All About." *Sports 'n' Spokes* (March–April, 1991): 16–19.

Williamson, Dc. "Principles of Classification in Competitive Sport for Participants with Disabilities: A Proposal." *Palaestra* (Spring, 1997): 44–48.

Winnick, Joseph P. *Adapted Physical Education and Sport* (4th ed.). Champaign, IL: Human Kinetics, 2005.

Women's Entertainment. http://www.we.tv/upload/html_area/1/1028/sandy_bio.html.

"Women's Sports Foundation." *Know Your Rights.* http://www.womenssportsfoundation.org/cgi-bin/iowa/issues/rights/article.html?record=996.

Wyeth, Duncan. Athletes with Disabilities Hall of Fame. http://www.athleticachievement.org/adhof/famers/bios/wyeth.html.

Yilla, Abu. "QR Classic Expands." *Sports 'n' Spokes* (July–August 1989): 40.

Index

INDEX

ABOUT THE AUTHORS

LINDA MASTANDREA is an accomplished athlete, attorney, advocate and author. She won 15 Gold and 5 silver medals in international wheelchair track competition, including Gold and silver medals at the 1996 Paralympics in Atlanta before retiring to pursue a career in disability law, public speaking and writing. Widely recognized as an authority on disability related topics, she has lectured to audiences worldwide on disability sport and recreation, and to nationwide audiences on topics ranging from disability sport to the Americans with Disabilities Act.

DONNA CZUBERNAT Born and raised in the Chicago suburbs, Donna is no stranger to disability issues. She has two siblings and a son with disabilities. This exposure helped Donna become an advocate who is continually researching information to share with people living with a disability. An entirely different universe of disability opened to Donna when she traveled with her sister and co-author, Linda, as she competed in wheelchair track and road racing.

A self-proclaimed late bloomer, Donna returned to school after her children were grown, focusing on the social sciences and psychology. She has worked in the legal field for 18 years, and particularly enjoys researching case law as well as the administration and management of a small law practice. Donna is currently working on a written account of her mother's 15-year struggle with Alzheimer's disease. When Donna is not writing, she can often be found studying astronomy, astro-psychology, reading, and traveling.